International Socialism

Winter 2013

Analysis

Briefings and feedback

Reviews

Pick of the quarter

Contributors

Peter Alexander is South Africa Research Chair in Social Change at the University of Johannesburg and a co-author of *Marikana: A View from the Mountain and a Case to Answer*.

Ian Birchall has just edited an issue of *Revolutionary History* devoted to solidarity action with the Algerian liberation struggle by European revolutionaries, and is currently working on a book about internationalism and the French left.

Siobhan Brown is a socialist activist based in east London.

Martin Empson is the author of the pamphlet *Marxism and Ecology: Capitalism, Socialism and the Future of the Planet*.

Denis Godard is a member of France's New Anti-capitalist Party and a member of the editorial team of the magazine *Que Faire?*

Mike Gonzalez is Emeritus Professor of Latin American Studies at Glasgow University. He has most recently edited, with Houman Barekat, *Arms and the People,* on the relations between social movements and the military, just published by Pluto.

Jane Hardy is Professor of Political Economy at the University of Hertfordshire. She is the author of *Poland's New Capitalism*.

Philip Marfleet is the co-editor, with Rabab El-Mahdi, of *Egypt: the Moment of Change*.

Camilla Royle is a socialist activist based in north London.

Panagiotis Sotiris teaches social and political philosophy at the Department of Sociology of the University of the Aegean in Mytilene. He is a member of the coordinating committee of Antarsya (Front of the Greek Anti-capitalist Left).

Ross Speer is a postgraduate student and activist at the London School of Economics.

Megan Trudell is a regular contributor to *International Socialism* and a socialist activist based in east London.

Florian Wilde is a socialist historian based in Berlin and a member of the Party Executive Committee of Germany's Die Linke.

British sounds

Alex Callinicos

The dominant fact about British politics is the slow decomposition of the Conservative-Liberal coalition government. The fundamental reason for this is the failure of chancellor of the exchequer George Osborne's deficit-cutting strategy.

In advance of his Autumn Statement on 5 December the Institute of Fiscal Studies produced an analysis arguing that the targets he had set for reducing government borrowing were in danger because the economy had stagnated: output was 0.2 percent lower in the first nine months of 2012, instead of the predicted increase of 0.7 percent. Tax receipts were also lower than projected. If growth picks up, Osborne might still achieve a balanced budget by 2017 (his main target, already pushed back two years), but government debt as a proportion of national income would rise rather than fall between 2014-15 and 2015-16 (cutting this share is a secondary target). If the economy continues to stagnate, a further round of austerity will be needed to eliminate the deficit, involving tax increases and spending cuts amounting to 1.5 percent of national income—about £23 billion in current prices.[1]

After this appraisal was largely confirmed in the Autumn Statement itself, Martin Wolf offered this damning assessment of the debacle:

1:    Emmerson and Tetlow, 2012. Thanks to Joseph Choonara and Jonny Jones for the comments on this article in draft.

One growth downgrade has followed another. We have also seen huge slippages in borrowing plans, compared with what the chancellor initially expected. Thus, in the emergency Budget of 2010, the forecast for cumulative public sector net borrowing between 2011-12 and 2015-16 was £322 billion. In the latest forecast, this increased to £539 billion, a rise of £217 billion, if one excludes various special factors.[2]

So why has the British economy stagnated? The International Monetary Fund (IMF) has caused a flutter of panic among the austerians by publishing a study that suggests austerity may cut output more than had been previously thought. It estimates that, in current conditions, where interest rates are very low and many states are simultaneously cutting spending, the fiscal multiplier, which measures the effect of changes in public expenditure and taxation on economic output, may be as high as 0.9 to 1.7 (previous estimates had placed it at around 0.5).[3] If the higher figure were correct, then for every pound cut from public spending, the economy would shrink by £1.70. This is the opposite of what Osborne predicted when he argued that austerity, by squeezing the public sector, would liberate private enterprise and generate a rapid recovery.

This study, which supports the arguments of Keynesian critics of austerity such as Paul Krugman, has come under attack, not only from defenders of government policy, but also from the Marxist economist Michael Roberts.[4] Roberts argues that the fiscal squeeze alone hasn't caused Britain's economic stagnation. A fall in corporate profitability has led to a collapse in investment as firms hang on to their profits (see Table). The investment slump in turn is responsible for a collapse in productivity, which has pushed up unit labour costs and eroded the competitiveness of British exports, on which Osborne was counting to power the recovery.[5]

Whatever the explanation, one major apologist of austerity, the outgoing governor of the Bank of England, Mervyn King, now expects the British economy to continue to stagnate. "After a period of a year of reflecting on all this, we have decided that we think the chances of a rapid recovery are a good deal less than we thought," he said in

---

2:   Wolf, 2012.

3:   IMF, 2012, pp41-43.

4:   See Krugman, 2012, pp231-238, and Roberts, 2012a. Guglielmo Carchedi offers a Marxist alternative to the Keynesian conception of the multiplier in Carchedi, 2012. Giles, 2012, criticises the IMF's use of data from an austerian perspective.

5:   Roberts, 2012b and 2012c.

mid-November.[6] The bank argues that the economy is being held back by the large number of "zombie companies" that are kept alive only by the very low interest rates that it (like other central banks) introduced in the wake of the 2008 crash. A little over three in ten companies were loss making in 2010, 30 percent more than in the mid-2000s. According to the *Financial Times*:

> The number of companies only able to pay the interest on their debts but not reduce the debt itself—a common characteristic of "zombie" companies— has risen by 10 percent to 160,000 in the past four months, according to R3, the insolvency industry trade body.

> "More and more companies are catching the zombie disease," said Lee Manning, president of R3. "It is symptomatic of a stagnant economy, with a combination of low interest rates, low liquidation rates and many businesses running at a loss".[7]

Table 1: UK gross fixed capital formation (£ billions)
Source: Roberts, 2012b

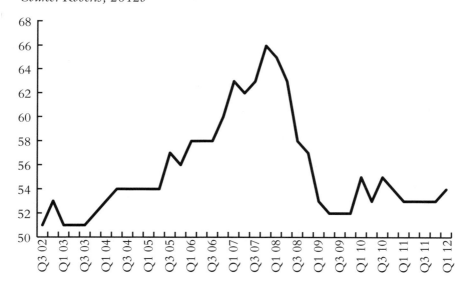

Chris Harman's portrayal of the contemporary world economy as zombie capitalism is thus being taken up by the mainstream.[8] The bank's diagnosis is interesting, because it chimes with the explanation of crises sketched by Marx in *Capital* and further developed by Harman and other contemporary Marxist political economists. The function of crises is, by destroying some of the capital accumulated in the previous period of expansion, to create the conditions for overcoming the fall in the rate of profit that is the underlying cause of these crises in the first place. Weaker capitals go bust, providing the space and cheapened machinery and labour power for stronger capitals to improve their profitability.

But, in the case of the present crisis, capitalist states, partly by bailing out the banks and partly thanks to the action of central banks in cutting interest rates and pumping money into the financial system, have prevented the necessary destruction of capital. Hence the stagnation experienced, not just by Britain, but by the advanced capitalist world more generally: the rich countries' club, the Organisation for Economic Cooperation and Development, now predicts that its members will grow by only 1.4 percent in 2013.[9]

Britain's plight, though shared by the other advanced economies, is particularly dire. As Roberts points out:

> even if employment has not deteriorated as much as in previous slumps, this recession has seen the biggest ever fall in real incomes ... Net national income per head, which is a better measure of living standards [than GDP per head], is down over 13 percent since its peak in early 2008 and is still falling—a truly horrendous reduction.[10]

That figure alone is sufficient to explain the decline of both coalition parties in the opinion polls and the matching rise in Labour's fortunes. But the coalition's woes have been compounded by a series of self-inflicted wounds that started with the March 2012 budget's cut in the 50 percent income tax rate and the imposition of the "granny tax" and the "pasty tax". These have continued with the Police Federation's successful defenestration of the government chief whip, Andrew Mitchell, and the debacle of the derisory turnout in the police and crime commissioner elections.

8:   Harman, 2009.

9:   Jones, 2012.

10:   Roberts, 2012b. The relatively low level of unemployment in Britain is discussed in Cooke, 2012.

Meanwhile scandal continues to strike at the establishment, as it has since the exposure of MPs' expenses claims during the dog days of New Labour. News International still has a power to wound David Cameron in particular, with the upcoming trials of his disgraced cronies Andy Coulson and Rebekah Brooks and the tricky problem of how to handle the Leveson report on press regulation, which divides the Tory party and unites Labour and the Liberal Democrats.

The crisis precipitated in the BBC by the revelation of Jimmy Savile's sexual abuse is maybe less directly threatening to the government, but it strengthens the picture of a thoroughly corrupt ruling class, as do revelations of the past cover-ups that protected Margaret Thatcher's parliamentary private secretary, Peter Morrison, and Liberal MP Cyril Smith.

None of this means that the coalition won't survive till its appointed end in 2015. It has changed the law so that parliament can only be dissolved with the support of a majority of the House of Commons. This gives the Lib Dems a veto over any attempt by Cameron to call an early election. Nick Clegg and his fellow ministers will want to hang on to the privileges of office for as long as possible, given that the polls suggest a Lib Dem massacre when the election does come.

But the coalition will become increasingly and more openly fractious. The turning point came in July 2012, when 91 Tory backbenchers rebelled against Clegg's proposals for House of Lords reform. When Cameron promptly gave up the effort to get the bill through, Clegg retaliated by promising to block the boundary changes to parliamentary constituencies, a measure that would increase the Tories' chances of winning future elections. The closer we come to the date of the next election, the more Tory and Lib Dem ministers will openly disagree with each other (as Cameron and Clegg did over the Leveson report). In the lead-up to the Autumn Statement, cabinet ministers were reported to be squabbling over who was to blame for the economy's stagnation.[11]

But potentially the most dangerous fracture in the government is the return of the European question, which destroyed Thatcher's and John Major's governments during the 1990s. There are two forces driving this. First, the efforts led by Germany in particular to overcome the eurozone crisis by imposing a permanent, Europe-wide regime of fiscal surveillance and (though much more incoherently) constructing an EU banking union is threatening the relatively comfortable position that British capitalism has enjoyed over the past 20 years—attracting foreign

---

11:   Parker, Pickard and O'Connor, 2012.

investment thanks to its participation in the European single market, and staying out of the dysfunctional economic and monetary union while the City of London (to the fury of rival centres such as Frankfurt and Paris) hoovers up the most lucrative eurozone financial business.

Being perched on the edge of a much more integrated eurozone would be considerably less cosy for Britain: it might, for example, lose any influence over decisions concerning the single market and find the City excluded from many of the euro-related activities it currently undertakes. Indeed Christian Noyer, governor of the Banque de France, recently attacked the City's dominance of euro trading (Britain accounts for about 40 percent of foreign exchange dealing denominated in euros), declaring: "Most of the euro business should be done inside the euro area".[12]

Threats like this have given an opening to the second main factor in the equation, the Tory right. Never reconciled to Cameron's attempt to "detoxify the [Tory] brand" by imitating Tony Blair's focus on the "centre ground", they have seized the eurozone crisis to press for Britain's departure from the European Union. In October 2012 81 Tory MPs, 43 percent of the backbench party, defied the whips and voted for a referendum on Britain's relationship to the EU.

These developments put Cameron on the spot. Many of the largest firms in Britain are now foreign-owned, investing here in order to get access to the European market. There seems to be very little business interest in leaving the EU. And Cameron needs allies elsewhere in the EU in order to try and block changes in the eurozone that would be unfavourable to British capitalism.

But the pressure from the backbenches, partly motivated by fears that the UK Independence Party is winning away more Eurosceptic voters from the Tories, is growing. (UKIP won more votes than the Lib Dems in the seven parliamentary by-elections held in 2012 and came second in Middlesbrough and Rotherham.) Cameron is condemned to ducking and diving to balance between these different forces—for example, hinting he will call some kind of referendum on Europe, but avoiding one on EU membership (which polls suggest the advocates of exit might win).

For all these problems, there is no sign of any retreat by the coalition from austerity. On the contrary, the more divided the government becomes, the more its members cling to the original rationale for their cooperation—cutting the deficit. In the Autumn Statement, Osborne announced that he would extend austerity by another year, till 2018, cut

---

12:   Noble and Barker, 2012, and Barker, 2012.

benefits and tax credits in real terms for the next three years, scrapped national bargaining for teachers, and pencilled in another £10 billion cuts in the next parliament. And many of the most vicious measures already imposed—for example, the caps on benefits and the scrapping of the Disability Living Allowance—only come into force in April. As numerous charities and NGOs have been warning, a hurricane is about to hit the poor and the vulnerable.

So how stands the resistance to austerity? The Labour Party leadership can't be counted as part of it. Ed Miliband and Ed Balls have stuck to their mantra that some cuts are necessary. Their strategy seems to be simply to wait for the government's growing unpopularity to push them up in the polls. And so far this is working. But this is of no help to anyone suffering the effects of austerity. On the ground the picture is, predictably, more mixed. Local Labour activists are often involved in campaigns against the cuts. Unite, whose general secretary Len McCluskey is one of the most high-profile critics of the coalition, is using its new community branches to recruit for the Labour Party.

There is in any case a dark edge to the electoral picture. Labour may be ahead in the polls, but UKIP's successes show that, despite the effective rout of the English Defence League by Unite against Fascism, many disaffected voters are looking towards the populist right. George Galloway's triumph in the Bradford West by-election in March 2012 conjured up the prospect that a powerful radical left pole of attraction might emerge. But his outrageous comments on the rape allegations made against Julian Assange and the subsequent resignation of Respect chair Salma Yaqoob have once again dashed the hopes invested in Galloway. This makes effective resistance now to coalition policies all the more vital in offering an alternative based on collective action.

So far the struggle against austerity in Britain has seen two peaks. The first came in November-December 2010 with the student revolt. Increasing university tuition fees to a maximum of £9,000 a year, in violation of a Lib Dem election promise, united both actual students and potential students in a series of street demonstrations whose quasi-insurrectionary atmosphere hadn't been seen in Britain for many years. What made this movement so explosive was the participation of working class college students who seized the chance to express their anger about the raw deal they get from British capitalism. This was also a crucial element in the English riots of August 2011. But as has been true of such movements in the past; they were short-lived, disappearing as quickly as they had appeared.

The second peak came with the two public sector strikes against the coalition's attack on pensions—30 June and 30 November 2011. Here the dynamic was very different. An alliance of left wing trade union officials and revolutionary socialist activists pushed for coordinated strike action by the three most militant public sector unions, the National Union of Teachers (NUT), the Public and Commercial Services Union (PCS), and the University and College Union (UCU). The result was 30 June, which built up the momentum that led much bigger unions—Unison, Unite and the GMB—to back what proved to be the largest strike day Britain has seen since 1926.[13]

Alas, the subsequent year saw this process go into reverse. Having thrown down a gauntlet to the coalition on 30 November, Dave Prentis, leader of the biggest public sector union, Unison, promptly put it back in his pocket. Heads of agreement covering Unison's two most important groups of workers in health and local government and brokered by Trade Union Congress general secretary Brendan Barber were reached on 20 December 2011. Just as the hard left unions had pulled the bigger and more right wing ones in 2011, now they started to feel the pressure to abandon plans for further action.

The turning point came in March 2012 when the NUT executive ignored their members' vote for further action and pulled out of a planned coordinated strike on 28 March (though teachers in London were called out that day). This led Mark Serwotka, PCS general secretary and the union leader most strongly identified with the strikes, to cancel plans to call his members out on 28 March. Despite valiant rearguard action by activists in the NUT, PCS and UCU, no further strike action has been called. Meanwhile McCluskey continued to use very militant rhetoric (even at one point threatening strikes in London during the Olympics), but did nothing to sustain the strike movement.

In addition to the vacillations and conservatism inherent in the trade union bureaucracy as a social layer, another factor was at play in this debacle. The chimera of union mergers as a means of strengthening the organised working class provided an important alibi for union leaders wanting to abandon strikes. There have, for example, been on-off discussions about merging Unite and PCS to form a left-led super-union. And the NUT leadership justified its failure to implement ballot and conference votes and call more action because it wants only to strike jointly with the National Association of Schoolmasters Union of Women Teachers as part of its pursuit of a merger between the two unions. But, as Martin Smith has argued in this

---

13: Kimber, 2012.

journal, the kind of mergers that led to the formation of Unison and Unite have not stemmed the decline in union membership. Only the revival of trade unions as fighting organisations that improve their members' pay and conditions can reinvigorate the British workers' movement.[14]

The entire experience reinforces the temptation by some on the left to contrast the weakness of British resistance to austerity with much bigger struggles on the continent, particularly in the light of the general strikes in Greece, Italy, Portugal and the Spanish state on 14 November 2012. Undoubtedly 14 November marked an important step forward in mounting an international response to the Europe-wide austerity drive. And it is true that the Spanish state has seen over the last decade a succession of gigantic mass movements that started in opposition to neoliberalism and war but now focus on austerity. The high pitch of social struggle in Greece is at an altogether different level from anywhere else in Europe: the week before the 14 November protests the country was shut down by a 48-hour general strike.

But even in Greece the trade union bureaucracy vacillates and manoeuvres. In France, the other European country that has witnessed large-scale social movements in the neoliberal era, the union leaders effectively killed off the 2010 struggle over pensions, leading to widespread demoralisation. The same pattern of trench warfare as worker activists seek to overcome their officials' blocking tactics, and more volatile explosions punctuating the set pieces mounted by unions is to be found across Western Europe. Britain is no exception.

The retreat from coordinated strike action has been especially demoralising for activists in the three most militant unions, NUT, PCS and UCU. But the scale of the setback should not be exaggerated. Paradoxically, as the reality of the strikes has receded, the trade union leaders have started to talk up the idea of a general strike. Unite, Unison and the GMB all voted for a motion at the TUC in September 2012 for a general strike to be considered, and the general council is accordingly consulting its member unions. The TUC march against austerity on 20 October attracted some 200,000 demonstrators: at the concluding rally Miliband was booed, while McCluskey and Serwotka were cheered when they raised the possibility of more strike action.

Of course, McCluskey in particular specialises in left wing speeches that commit him to nothing in practice. But the same mix of pressures from below, from activists who want action, and from above, from a government hell-bent on pursuing austerity, that produced 30 June and 30 November can

---

14: Smith, 2011, pp127-128.

push at least a section of the trade union bureaucracy into calling more strike action. In these circumstances, Unite the Resistance (UtR)—the coalition of left trade union officials and rank and file activists that emerged to drive the strikes through in 2011—continues to make a lot of sense.

For the Socialist Workers Party, which has played a major role in the development of UtR, the coalition performs a dual function. First, it serves as a united front between revolutionaries and that section of the left bureaucracy that wants to see strike action. Secondly, to the extent that it succeeds in building strikes, it can serve as the basis of a rank and file movement that can fight independently of any section of the trade union bureaucracy. What we saw in 2012 was a major retreat by left officials who had previously been in the lead in pushing for strike action. If that retreat were final and definitive, or if a genuine rank and file movement emerged, then the basis for UtR would no longer exist. But neither of these conditions are met. The more left wing leaders continue to wobble between rhetoric and action. And the very success of the union bureaucracy in pulling the carpet from under the strike movement indicates that rank and file workers still lack the confidence and organisation to fight independently.

Chris Harman argued during the Great Miners' Strike of 1984-5 that a united front involves revolutionary socialists working both with and against those to their right. As so often with dialectical formulations such as this, there is a tendency to slide towards one or other of the two poles— in this case, just working with the left officials, or simply working against them. These are not just intellectual errors. There are objective pulls in both directions built into the situation. The relative weakness of the rank and file creates a temptation simply to tail the left bureaucracy, while the union leaders' betrayals push activists in the direction of denunciations that aren't backed by the muscle to call independent strikes and so lead all too often to passive demoralisation.

Revolutionaries have to grasp contradictions such as this in their totality, highlighting the aspect that brings them into focus. As Lenin put it, "The whole art of politics lies in finding and taking as firm a grip as we can of the link that is least likely to be struck from our hands, the one that is most important at the given moment, the one that most of all guarantees its possessor the possession of the whole chain".[15] Here and now in Britain this means building UtR, both as a forum where activists who want to build mass strikes can get together to discuss and coordinate and as a means of putting pressure on the left officials.

15: Lenin, 1961, p502.

But it is important not to allow the call for a general strike to become a substitute for building the action that can actually be achieved now. Indeed, as we have seen, for the left trade union leaders, support for coordinated action can serve as an excuse to do nothing unless everyone acts together. Any opportunity for localised or sectional action should be seized, and not deferred in the name of a potential, perfect general strike.

The setback caused by the union leaders' abandonment of the pension strikes is unlikely to be permanent. One immediate effect of the financial crash in 2008 was the abandonment of the pay campaigns mounted by the NUT and PCS. But it didn't take these unions long to return to the battlefield. Already Osborne's decision to scrap national bargaining represents a mortal challenge to the teachers' unions that their leaders will find hard to duck. Despite interruptions, the curve of the class struggle continues to point upwards in Britain.

References

Barker, Alex, 2012, "EU Banking Reform Frustrates London", *Financial Times* (3 December), www.ft.com/cms/s/0/19246564-3d50-11e2-9e13-00144feabdc0.html

Carchedi, Guglielmo, 2012, "Could Keynes End the Slump? Introducing the Marxist Multiplier", *International Socialism 136* (autumn), www.isj.org.uk/?id=849

Cooke, Laura, 2012, "The Impact of the Crisis on the Working Class in Britain", *International Socialism 136* (autumn), www.isj.org.uk/?id=852

Emmerson, Carl, and Gemma Tetlow, "Autumn Statement 2012: More Fiscal Pain to Come?", www.ifs.org.uk/bns/bn136

Giles, Chris, 2012, "Robustness of IMF Data Scrutinised", *Financial Times* (12 October), www.ft.com/cms/s/0/85a0c6c2-1476-11e2-8cf2-00144feabdc0.html

Harman, Chris, 2009, *Zombie Capitalism: Global Crisis and the Relevance of Marx* (Bookmarks).

IMF, 2012, *World Economic Outlook* (October), www.imf.org/external/pubs/ft/weo/2012/02/pdf/text.pdf

Jones, Claire, 2012, "OECD Slashes 2013 Growth Forecast", *Financial Times* (27 November), www.ft.com/cms/s/0/92bb1a16-3874-11e2-981c-00144feabdc0.html

Jones, Claire, and Chris Giles, "Bank Turns Gloomy on Recovery", *Financial Times* (14 November), www.ft.com/cms/s/0/518c4a60-2e47-11e2-8bb3-00144feabdc0.html

Kimber, Charlie, 2012, "The Rebirth of Our Power? After the 30 November Mass Strike", *International Socialism 133* (winter), www.isj.org.uk/?id=774

Krugman, Paul, 2012, *End this Depression Now!* (W W Norton & Co).

Lenin, V I, 1961 [1902], *What Is To be Done*, in *Collected Works*, volume 5 (Progress), www.marxists.org/archive/lenin/works/1901/witbd/v.htm

Noble, Josh, and Alex Barker, 2012, "UK's Euro Trade Supremacy under Attack', *Financial Times* (2 December), www.ft.com/cms/s/0/736bd72a-3c9a-11e2-a6b2-00144feabdc0.html

Parker, George, Jim Pickard and Sarah O'Connor, "Ministers Swap Blame over Slow Growth", *Financial Times* (27 November), www.ft.com/cms/s/0/58463bf2-38b2-11e2-981c-00144feabdc0.html

Roberts, Michael, 2012a, "The Smugness Multiplier" (14 October), http://thenextrecession.wordpress.com/2012/10/14/the-smugness-multiplier/

Roberts, Michael, 2012b, "UK and US GDP and Anglo-Saxon Angst" (25 October), http://thenextrecession.wordpress.com/2012/10/25/uk-and-us-gdp-and-anglo-saxon-angst/

Roberts, Michael, 2012c, "Osborne's Mess" (5 December), http://thenextrecession.wordpress.com/2012/12/05/osbornes-mess/

Smith, Martin, 2011, "Britain's Trade Unions: The Shape of Things to Come", *International Socialism 131* (summer), www.isj.org.uk/?id=739

Stothard, Michael, and Chris Giles, 2012, "Zombie Companies Stalk UK Economy", *Financial Times* (18 November), www.ft.com/cms/s/0/d1ecf0d0-316f-11e2-b68b-00144feabdc0.html

Wolf, Martin, 2012, "Time to Use Room for Manoeuvre", *Financial Times* (5 December), www.ft.com/cms/s/0/cb107fa2-3a5c-11e2-baac-00144feabdc0.html

Why Obama won
Megan Trudell

"The people who delivered [Obama] a second term...are those who were least likely to have benefited from his first".[1] Journalist Gary Younge's comment on the re-election of Barack Obama in the United States sums up the contradiction at the heart of the election campaign. The 2012 election took place after four years of a Democratic administration that has presided over growing inequality, protecting the profits of the wealthiest and exacerbating economic pain for the majority of working Americans. Obama has failed to deliver on the hopes and aspirations for change that were so dramatically raised by his historic victory in 2008. His government's record in the domestic field and internationally has been covered extensively in this journal over the last four years and so will not be repeated in detail here, but put briefly: bank bailouts, inadequate stimulus measures and the protection and extension of privilege among the elite in the US has widened the gap between rich and poor and angered millions who have borne the brunt of spiralling unemployment, attacks on education, wage cuts and productivity drives, while a continuation of Bush era foreign policy has alienated millions around the world who had hopes of a more benign form of US imperialism.[2]

Yet Obama was re-elected—although with considerably less enthusiasm than in 2008—largely because voters felt that the Republicans would

---

1: Younge, 2012a.
2: See Callinicos, 2012; Anievas, Fabry and Knox, 2012; Trudell, 2009; and Trudell, 2011.

be worse; Obama and the Democrats were seen as being the lesser of the two evils on offer. The choice facing US voters was singularly uninspiring: On the one hand an incumbent whose policies added to, rather than alleviated, the burdens on working class Americans; on the other a businessman worth an estimated $250 million and his Tea Party backed running mate.

However, while Republican gains in the Congressional elections in 2010 came on the back of the rising Tea Party tide, Ryan's selection and Romney's tacking to the right during the campaign were part of a gamble that didn't come off. The selection of Tea Party supporters to run for the Republicans backfired on this occasion, with Todd Akin and Richard Mourdock both losing Senate races after their comments on rape and pregnancy—respectively, that women's bodies would reject pregnancies caused by "legitimate" rape, and that pregnancy after rape was "God's plan".

So what has changed in the two years since the Republicans swept the board in 2010? Much has been made of demographic changes in the US, and the fact that single women, young people, and non-white voters—part of what has come to be known as the Rising American Electorate—voted in large numbers to deliver Obama's second term. And it is certainly the case that Obama's support among single women, Hispanic voters and young people was crucial, and for obvious reasons.

The right-wing anti-abortion politics of the likes of Akin and Mourdock—and a great many other Republicans—has helped to push many women towards the Democrats, as does the fact that women tend to see issues like healthcare and reproductive choice as economic rather than social. As Jess McIntosh, a spokesperson for EMILY's List, a group committed to electing pro-choice Democratic women to office, puts it: "Birth control is only a social issue if you never have to pay for it".[3] Ironically, in the case of Indiana where Mourdock was defeated this was by Joe Donnelly, an anti-abortion Democrat—the proximity of the two evils easy to see on this occasion.

The 2 million donors to EMILY's List are overwhelmingly middle class women; nonetheless, it is an important point that for working class women as well reproductive rights are a central issue and it is not difficult to see how the continual threat posed to such rights by right wing Republican rhetoric would push many women voters towards the only apparent (electoral) alternative.

Another critical support for Obama was the vote of non-whites, especially the rising Hispanic vote. Nationally, non-white voters made

---

3:    Dailey, 2012.

up 28 percent of all voters, up from 26 percent in 2008. Obama won 80 percent of these voters, the same as four years ago. This support was a critical factor in battleground states, especially Ohio and Florida. In Ohio blacks made up 15 percent of voters, up from 11 percent in 2008. In Florida, Hispanics were 17 percent of voters, a slight increase from 14 percent in 2008. Nationally, Romney won the white vote, 59 percent to 39 percent—but the numbers of whites voting overall fell.[4] Again this is not a surprise when the aggressive anti-immigration positions of much of the Republican Party are contrasted with Obama's suggestion of allowing illegal immigrants who work to apply for citizenship.

However, beneath these apparent differences between the two parties as explanation for the result lie more fundamental shifts in the US political landscape that have less to do with demographics and more to do with the emergence during the last two years of an alternative pole of attraction to the Tea Party bandwagon. This is not, however it is articulated during an election campaign, represented by the Obama administration, but by the growth of genuine grassroots radical movements. The campaign and the result were conditioned as much by the resurgence of working class action demonstrated so powerfully in the immigrants' "day without us" demonstrations in 2009, the strike in Madison and the Occupy movement last year, and the victorious Chicago teachers' strike that took place in the midst of the election campaign.

It was poetic justice that the elitism and arrogance of the 1 percent in the US were seen as driving the Romney machine relatively early on in the campaign. In May, Romney's comments to wealthy supporters at a fundraising dinner held at the Florida home of millionaire private equity manager Marc Leder exposed his disdain for ordinary Americans:

> There are 47 percent of the people who will vote for the president no matter what. All right, there are 47 percent who are with him, who are dependent upon government, who believe that they are victims, who believe the government has a responsibility to care for them, who believe that they are entitled to healthcare, to food, to housing, to you name it... And the government should give it to them. And they will vote for this president no matter what... These are people who pay no income tax... My job is not to worry about those people. I'll never convince them they should take personal responsibility and care for their lives.

4:    Pew Research Center, 7 November 2012.

Delightfully for the 99 percent, and devastatingly for him, Romney's comments were most likely filmed by one of the people he disparaged so disgracefully—the video published on YouTube in mid-September shows white gloved waiters serving the audience, who had paid $50,000 per person to hear Romney's class vitriol.[5]

This perception that the Republicans represented the rich to a greater extent than did the Democrats benefited Obama, and owes much to the ideological impact of the demonstrations against Tea Party governor Scott Walker in Wisconsin and, crucially, the Occupy movement. The fact that the Democrats are not worthy inheritors of people's anger and rejection of the 1 percent is besides the point, Obama's victory this time around had the definite whiff of class battle about it.

In exit polls in November 81 percent of voters said that Obama "cared for people like me", against only 18 percent for Romney.[6] The accurate perception that Romney represented the very rich, the 1 percent, was a key component in the Republican defeat. Obama won three out of five voters whose family incomes are below $50,000. Among middle-income voters Romney led 52 percent to 46 percent, and 54 percent to 44 percent among voters with family incomes of $100,000 or more.[7]

The result was, however, hardly a ringing endorsement of Obama as representing the 99 percent. Turnout was lower than in 2008 and fully 40 percent of eligible voters—93 million people—did not vote at all or voted for third-party candidates. Interestingly, recent research on non-voters shows that they are generally to the left of mainstream politicians and were more likely to lean toward Obama than Romney:

> Far more non-voters than voters favour activist government. About half of non-voters (52 percent) say the government should do more to solve problems, while 40 percent say the government is doing too many things better left to businesses and individuals. The balance of opinion is reversed among likely voters: 56 percent say the government is doing too much, while 39 percent say the government should do more to solve problems. By 46 percent to 31 percent, more non-voters favour keeping the 2010 healthcare law in place than repealing the law; 23 percent do not express an opinion. Voters are more evenly divided, with 49 percent favoring the law's

5:   Corn, 2012.
6:   http://elections.msnbc.msn.com/ns/politics/2012/all/president/#exitPoll
7:   http://nbcpolitics.nbcnews.com/_news/2012/11/06/14979402-voters-back-obama-despite-economic-concerns-exit-polls-show

repeal and 43 percent saying it should remain in place; just 8 percent do not express an opinion.[8]

This is unsurprising when we consider who non-voters are. They are more likely to be poorer and younger than those who vote; more likely to have suffered directly from the consequences of the recession and to feel that nothing changes for them, whoever is elected:

> Non-voters are younger, less educated and less affluent than are likely voters. More than a third (36 percent) of non-voters are younger than 30, compared with just 13 percent of likely voters. Just 13 percent of non-voters are college graduates and about the same percentage (14 percent) have family incomes of $75,000 or more. Among likely voters, 38 percent are college graduates and a third (33 percent) have family incomes of $75,000 or more.[9]

The figures suggest that a great many Americans reject the elitism and anti working class policies of both parties, whether they do so consciously or more passively; there is a strong sense that neither party speaks for ordinary people; the difference this time around is the glimpse of a potential alternative to the Tweedledee and Tweedledum of the barren "democratic" process.

As Lance Selfa has written, Obama's victories in the two battleground states of Wisconsin and Ohio were largely a result of union households voting and campaigning against the Republicans. In the results in these states:

> It's hard not to see the impact of a broader labour mobilisation in the major battles fought over union rights against hard-right Republican governors in Ohio and Wisconsin—the massive popular uprising against Wisconsin Governor Scott Walker's attempt to strip public-sector workers of collective bargaining rights, and labour mobilisation to defeat similar legislation from Ohio Governor John Kasich in a lopsided referendum victory one year ago.[10]

Most important has been the example during the election campaign of the Chicago teachers' strike. This was a week-long dispute between the Chicago Teachers Union and Obama favourite, Mayor Rahm Emanuel, over a raft of education "reforms", including school closures and linking

---

8:    Pew Research Center, 1 November 2012.
9:    Pew Research Center, 1 November 2012.
10:   Selfa, 2012.

teachers' jobs to student results, essentially a battle over the privatisation of education and the creation of educational "apartheid" in the city. The timing of the strike was hardly to the Democrats' liking:

"Scaling back or postponing their battle with Obama's former chief of staff would have been much more palatable to CTU's parent union, the American Federation of Teachers, and to national Democratic leaders, who feared Obama would lose votes no matter which side he came down on," wrote *Labor Notes*. The teachers went ahead with the strike, and "many credit their strong support among public school parents—who supported the strike two to one—to their unsparing criticism of politicians on both sides of the aisle who stood in the way of the schools Chicago students deserved."

CTU vice-president Jesse Sharkey described union members' collective ability to put the Democrats over a barrel: "The Democrats and the Obama campaign had a problem. If they were going to demonise CTU or try and bust our union, then it makes it pretty clear how anti-union their policies are, and that it's Democrats, not the Republicans, pushing those policies this time".[11]

More of the same?
The rise of organised working class struggle represents the possibility of breaking the stultifying non-choice of the US electoral system and building a genuine radical movement. It could not be taking place at a more important time. Bitter as the consequences of economic downturn have been so far, worse is yet to come if the US ruling class has its way.

The Obama campaign made much of the fact that the economy is slowly improving. However, although the unemployment rate is lower than at the height of the recession, it is still over 12 million, where it was in January 2009 and before that not since 1982, and has increased slightly since the summer.[12] And average pay continues to fall—hourly pay was down by a penny to $23.58 in October.

If Congress pushes through austerity measures that will result from the "fiscal cliff"—the expiration of tax cuts made by the Bush government and the imposition of a 10 percent cut in government spending scheduled at the end of 2012—US workers have a significant fight on their hands. The fiscal cliff will almost certainly push the fragile US economy back into recession and the combination of tax rises for most Americans and

---

11:   Brenner, 2012.
12:   www.huffingtonpost.com/2012/11/02/october-jobs-report-unemployment-rate_n_2063675.html

swingeing cuts to Social Security, Medicare and Medicaid will be devastating for the worst off. The Bush era tax breaks for the rich that are also due to expire if allowed to do so—quite a big "if"—will certainly elicit howls of rage from the wealthy and further polarise the political landscape.

There is a very clear message from the US government that ordinary Americans will be expected to pay for the crisis, and the fiscal cliff is being used to force through cuts and austerity that are about maximising profit and stripping back workers' rights yet further. There should be no illusions about where Obama stands on this question. In October, in an interview with an Iowa newspaper, Obama made clear his commitment to austerity measures: "It will probably be messy. It won't be pleasant. But I am absolutely confident that we can get what is the equivalent of the grand bargain that essentially I've been offering to the Republicans for a very long time, which is $2.50 worth of cuts for every dollar in spending, and work to reduce the costs of our healthcare programmes".[13]

At the same time, "US companies are booking higher profits than ever. But...corporate tax receipts as a share of profits are at their lowest level in at least 40 years".[14]

Obama owes his re-election, at least in part, to the changing political culture created by the movements against his policies. Those movements can form the framework of a serious challenge to the priorities of US capitalism and can rebuild union organisation and the left. Significantly, other recent strikes include those by non-unionised workers in a day of action against Walmart nationally, and a strike in New York against McDonald's—both notorious anti-union employers.

As Jesse Sharkey summed it up: "What we saw in Occupy Wall Street, the demonstrations in Wisconsin and the teachers' strike in Chicago was a glimpse of our own power... The difficulty is that the size of the forces that support austerity may be greater than those that will fight against it but the potential of opposition to austerity is far greater than most realise".[15]

13: Obama interview with the Des Moines Register, http://foxnewsinsider.com/2012/10/24/transcript-obama-campaign-releases-transcript-of-presidents-interview-with-des-moines-register-after-insisting-that-it-be-kept-off-the-record/
14: http://online.wsj.com/article/SB10001424052970204662204577199492233215330.html
15: Younge, 2012b.

References

Anievas, Alexander, Adam Fabry and Robert Knox, 2012, "Back to 'Normality'? US Foreign Policy under Obama", *International Socialism 136* (autumn), www.isj.org.uk/?id=846

Brenner, Mark, 2012, "Election season: let's be watchdogs, not lapdogs", *Labor Notes* (2 November).

Callinicos, Alex, 2012. "Narrowing the Bounds of the Possible: the US Election", *International Socialism 136* (autumn), www.isj.org.uk/?id=843

Corn, David, 2012, "Secret Video: Romney Tells Millionaire Donors What He Really Thinks of Obama Voters", *Mother Jones* (17 September), www.motherjones.com/politics/2012/09/secret-video-romney-private-fundraiser

Pew Research Center, 2012, "Non-Voters: Who They Are and What They Think" (1 November), www.people-press.org/2012/11/01/nonvoters-who-they-are-what-they-think/

Dailey, Kate, 2012, "US Election: Women Are the New Majority", BBC website (7 November), www.bbc.co.uk/news/magazine-20231337

Pew Research Center, 2012, "Changing Face of America Helps Assure Obama Victory" (7 November), www.people-press.org/2012/11/07/changing-face-of-america-helps-assure-obama-victory/

Selfa, Lance, 2012, 'Blue votes, bluebloods and other election facts', *Socialist Worker* (US) (14 November), http://socialistworker.org/2012/11/14/blue-voters-versus-bluebloods

Trudell, Megan, 2009, "Obama's 100 Days", *International Socialism 133* (summer), www.isj.org.uk/?id=553

Trudell, Megan, 2011, "The Occupy Movement and Class Politics in the US", *International Socialism 133* (winter), www.isj.org.uk/?id=775

Younge, Gary, 2012a, "Obama's second victory is more low key, but in some ways more impressive", *Guardian* (7 November), www.guardian.co.uk/commentisfree/2012/nov/07/obama-second-victory-more-impressive

Younge, Gary, 2012b, "After Obama's re-election, liberals need to drop the blind devotion", *Guardian* (9 November), www.guardian.co.uk/world/2012/nov/09/obama-drop-blind-devotion

South Africa after Marikana

The massacre of 34 striking miners at Marikana, near Rustenburg in North West Province, on 16 August 2012 marked a watershed in the history of South Africa, ruled by the African National Congress (ANC) since the end of apartheid in 1994. Peter Alexander, who led a research team to the area immediately after the massacre, talked to International Socialism.

Peter, you are a historian of the working class movement in South Africa, so from the perspective of the history of that movement where would you place the Marikana strikes and what has developed since then?

The massacre is unique in its scale and character. In terms of the killings in a strike you have to go back to 1922 to find anything on a similar scale, and that was a much more even battle between capital and workers. [1] In terms of massacres more broadly, you have to go back to 1976 and the Soweto massacre to find anything that's bigger than what's happened in Marikana. There was a massacre of about 40 people at Boipatong in 1992, but if you assume that this particular massacre included 44 people—that is 34 people on the day and ten in the preceding week—this is even bigger than that one. So this is a massacre on a very large scale and given that it has involved a democratic government rather than an apartheid government it is very significant politically.

---

[1]: In February-March 1922 the Transvaal Chamber of Mines, with the support of the government of Jan Smuts, provoked a strike by the white miners' union that developed into a general strike and armed uprising. The Rand Revolt, as it came to be known, was crushed by the South African Defence Force using artillery and air power—see Yudelman, 1984, chapter 5, and Krikler, 2005.

You've talked about what the strike represents in terms of the actions of the state, and it's remarkable from the point of view of violence in strikes that the comparison is with the Rand Revolt of 1922, when white workers clashed with the South African state. But there's also the angle of what this means in terms of the development of the working class movement in South Africa. The organised working class today is essentially the one that emerged from the struggles of the 1970s and 1980s, and that had been defined by the unions that emerged in that period and their federation in the Congress of South African Trade Unions (Cosatu). This is a strike, or a series of strikes, that are at least partially against Cosatu and that are in the key industry in South Africa. This is a strike in the heart of the so-called minerals-energy complex.[2] It would be interesting to hear your thoughts about those sorts of questions.

I think that there are two points that are important. The first is that what emerged from the massive working class struggle of the 1970s and 1980s into the 1990s was the class compromise sealed in 1994, which legitimised capitalism in South Africa. In return the capitalists agreed to economic empowerment to develop black capitalists and agreed to support the form of democracy that was introduced at that point. At the heart of that compromise was the development of a particular labour relations regime which was emerging before 1994, but was formalised and codified in the Labour Relations Act of 1995. That involved a number of different components.

It was a tripartite arrangement at one level, in that it involved the state, for instance, in the labour courts, but it focused on centralised bargaining at an industrial level. In gold mining and coal, for instance, there are bargaining chambers which involve the workers and employers (workers through the National Union of Mineworkers mainly, but not only) and the employers of different kinds. In platinum it worked out slightly differently in that bargaining occurs at company level. Nevertheless, the key features are similar in both instances in that the system works on the basis of majoritarianism. In other words the main union in particular job categories negotiates on behalf of those categories and in this case (the case of Lonmin and other platinum companies that have faced strikes) this means in practice the National Union of Mineworkers (NUM); so it has had a monopoly of bargaining rights in platinum companies.

The second aspect is the check–off system. This means that the union gets a guaranteed flow of income. The third component is that the legislation provides for the possibility of protected strikes; that is strikes in which the employers are not allowed to sack the workers. But to have a protected

---

2:    See, for example, Ashman, Fine and Newman, 2010.

strike you have to go through a whole long set of procedures. In this particular case—Lonmin and the other strikes—workers have gone on strike without them being protected; that is they are unprotected strikes (sometimes referred to wrongly as illegal strikes), and they have challenged the majority union, NUM, and hence its capacity to continue to benefit from the check-off arrangements, and a number of other aspects we can talk about.

So that's one point in relation to a past that was institutionalised through the Labour Relations Act and which carries through into the present. The LRA in a sense froze a particular balance of forces that existed in 1994 and now what we see is a shift in the balance of forces and the old arrangements can't continue. Now they have shifted essentially because of this massive strike wave in the key industry in South Africa, and that strike wave echoes what happened in 1973 with the emergence of a new black trade union movement that was organised separately from the mainly white unions of the time. A key question is whether this will lead to the development of a new movement of the kind that developed post-1973.

Before we go on to talk about the new workers' movement that is developing, I'd like to explore the background political economy a bit more. These are strikes that are taking on the most powerful capitalist companies in South Africa and although both the mining industry and the wider South African economy have changed massively over recent decades it remains the case that mining is the place where local South African capital and transnational capital intersect to extract massive profits from the industry, much of which is then integrated into global circuits of financial capital. This is then a series of strikes that are confronting the very core of South African capital. Do you have any thoughts about how capital is responding and about the relationship between mining companies and the state, especially the ANC government?

The mining companies clearly feel threatened by the strike wave. Although Anglo-American in particular has massive interests in both, it is useful to distinguish between the platinum and gold mining industries. Platinum expanded very rapidly during the first decade of the 21st century, though profit levels subsequently fell slightly.[3] There was expansion, with new workers coming into the industry, people with heightened expectations because the industry was making such large profits, directors getting enormous salaries, and so on. There was a new younger workforce, not the same as the organised working class of the pre-1994 era. Those who have been leading the strikes, they are a younger generation, most of whom have come into the industry post-2000. So there is a younger generation in platinum

---

3:    Capps, 2012.

and, in addition, there are possibilities for getting substantial wage increases where workers push hard because the companies, even though their profit levels have gone down, nevertheless are still making very substantial profits.

Things are somewhat different in the gold industry where there has been a long-term decline and where the capacity for large pay increases is attenuated. This is a key factor. I believe that Lonmin, particularly because this is where the most significant strike had been, could have paid increases but was probably put under pressure by the government not to concede increases because of their implications for the mining industry in general, including black capitalists aligned with the ANC. We do not know this for certain but it does look as if the initiative to take a firm line with the workers at Lonmin was coming from the government and also, for the reasons that I have indicated, from the trade unions.

Let's go on to talk about the new workers' movement. Can you say something about the ways in which they are organising themselves and about the kind of tactics that they are using?
Organisationally the movement is taking two forms. Firstly there has been a recent development of a committee that brings together delegates from the different strikes. Now this is going to be a temporary arrangement because the strikes won't continue for ever, but it provides the potential for workers to get to know each other, initially across the different mines. That is very important as one of the things that has become clear at Lonmin is that to a very large degree people didn't know each other on the different shafts, even within the same mine. The strikes unite people from different work-places within particular mines, and now, in addition, we have workers from Lonmin meeting workers from Anglo-American, Impala, Goldfields' KDC mine, elsewhere in the gold mines, etc. So there is the development of a network of militants that will continue to exist and provide the possibility for new movements in the future, even when the current movement subsides.

A second aspect is the development of a relatively new union in the mining industry—the Association of Mineworkers and Construction Union (AMCU). In some respects this is a very traditional union and there-fore will be constrained in some of the ways that the NUM has been and may well begin cooperating with the mining companies in a similar fashion to the NUM. But it is not affiliated to Cosatu and has no association with the ANC and so unlike NUM, which has two pressures on it, one from the mining companies and one from the ANC, AMCU only has one. This creates space for new political developments—there are not going to be the same top-down pressures on people to comply with ANC politics.

Are there NUM members and activists who are involved in the strikes, ie is there an overlap between these new workers' organisations and the established Cosatu unions?

In the case of Lonmin there were figures presented for people who died in the massacre and 11 were NUM members and 17 AMCU out of the total of 34. So a lot of people involved in the strike were NUM members and the same is true in the other cases. They are NUM members who have become profoundly disaffected because of the way NUM operates, particularly at the local level, and one of the important things here is that NUM's senior shop stewards are paid by the companies at the level of junior managers, so they get paid about three times as much as the ordinary members. Also they do not have to work at the rock face, ie don't have to do an ordinary job. They get an office, the ability to move around and enjoy a degree of autonomy—including the ability to attend conferences and all sorts of other perks from management that don't exist for ordinary workers. So the character of NUM and its relationship to the government and the mining companies create all sorts of possibilities for careerists, and indeed for corruption, and a very large part of the current rebellion in the mines is a rebellion against the NUM leadership as well as against the mining companies.

So, presumably for those material reasons, would it be right to say that there hasn't been a significant degree of differentiation within the NUM apparatus and that there are no NUM leaders who have attempted to identify with the strike?

There are factional divisions within the NUM and the present general secretary only won his position by a very narrow margin, and some people even suggest that he didn't actually win a majority of people voting, and the main opposition to him came from an official from the Rustenburg area. So there are fractional divides. But my impression is that at the current time with these massive strikes there hasn't been any significant movement against Frans Baleni, NUM's general secretary.

About the AMCU: there was a very interesting film on YouTube of the victory rally at the end of the original Lonmin strike. While we shouldn't overstate it, there appeared to be a slightly Africanist version of traditional African nationalist politics represented by the union leader who spoke of the need to nationalise the mining industry, perhaps implicitly associating himself with Julius Malema, the ex-leader of the ANC Youth League (expelled for his opposition to the leadership of President Jacob Zuma) who has campaigned around that slogan. But there was also an emphasis on the mining industry being controlled by South Africans, and the implication was black South Africans. Would you say that that characterisation is accurate about the mood of those involved in the strikes?

I think that people involved in the strikes are happy to go along with that position. I don't know the extent to which they are driven by it or will mobilise behind it in a very active sense, but I attended a mass meeting immediately after the Marikana massacre where Malema spoke and his call for nationalisation was very well received. So there is support for nationalisation from the rank and file, and that position puts the rank and file into conflict with the NUM leaders, who have carefully distanced themselves from calls for nationalisation. It has been difficult for them because historically they have supported nationalisation—in fact in 1987 the NUM leadership backed a call for nationalisation under workers' control—so the present leadership has had to carefully separate itself from its own past in order to bring itself into alignment with the ANC leadership. To the best of my knowledge, AMCU does not have a pro-nationalisation position, so it is quite likely there will be tension between the union's leadership and its new militant membership over this.

And I suppose that we shouldn't forget that the famous Freedom Charter of 1955 calls for the nationalisation of "the monopoly industry", and if there is a monopoly industry in South Africa it is mining. So the call for nationalisation is one that must have deep resonances for anyone who is vaguely political in South Africa.

It has resonances, but there are many political people who are sceptical about the call for nationalisation, partly because it is identified with Malema and there is widespread scepticism about Malema who is seen to be an opportunist who is campaigning in his own interests, and partly because, to the extent that there are nationalised industries in South Africa, there is a widespread feeling that they are not well run. So the argument for nationalisation is not always an easy one to make.

I now want to ask you how you think the whole crisis produced by Marikana and the associated strike wave is playing out within the ruling Congress alliance, which brings together the ANC, Cosatu, and the South African Communist Party.

So far the centre has held, and one of the reasons for this is because of the South African Communist Party, which provides very important linkages between Cosatu—not just at the top level but also among a layer of shop stewards—and the government. So there are very few dissident voices within Cosatu, for instance. Even the National Union of Metalworkers (Numsa), which put together a very good statement initially, in the end went along with the consensus position on Marikana at the recent Cosatu conference.

That consensus position avoided saying that the police were responsible for the massacre. The one element of the ANC alliance that has positioned itself outside the consensus is the ANC Youth League, which immediately after the massacre backed the Marikana workers and supports nationalisation, though not under workers' control, of course.

Why do you think they have been so successful at holding the line, particularly since the massacre has such terrible echoes of the massacres that took place in the apartheid era? Isn't it surprising that there should be so few fractures opened up by this crisis?
I think there is a growing mood among rank and file workers that is sceptical at the very least about what is happening within the ANC and within particular unions, but the Cosatu conference represents a layer of older workers who have a long history of being disciplined SACP and ANC activists and they feel strongly that they should identify with the largest union in Cosatu, which is seen to be, and is presented as being, under attack. It's not clear who it is under attack from, except rank and file workers, but nevertheless it was possible at the Cosatu conference to whip up an atmosphere in which people felt it was necessary to defend their largest affiliate. The question then is, "Why does NUM take the position that it has taken?" The reason for that is associated with the ways in which the NUM leadership felt profoundly threatened by the possibility of rank and file members negotiating their own pay increases. This cuts out the union, cuts out the necessity for NUM to exist.

But it's not just material interests, is it? Although I'm sure that must be a very powerful factor binding together not just the trade union bureaucracy in Cosatu but also the broader components of the Congress alliance. There is also the role of ideology—I was very struck first of all by the speech that Blade Nzimande, the general secretary of the SACP, made at the Cosatu conference. This speech could have been made by Maurice Thorez or any one of a number of classic Stalinist leaders invoking the national democratic revolution and the need to defend it against lackeys of imperialism and so on. But what was also interesting, and which struck me very strongly, was that Numsa—which, as you said, made a much better statement initially—also made reference to colonialism of a special type which is quite an esoteric concept but is a very important part of the ideology that the SACP developed in the 1950s and 60s that sees change in South Africa as going through stages—first the national democratic revolution to get rid of colonialism of a special type (ie apartheid), then eventually socialist revolution. So presumably one thing that binds the Congress alliance together apart from material factors is this common ideology.

Yes, that's true, but the notion of colonialism of a special type can be read in different ways. There are people within the Youth League, and indeed within Numsa, who are pushing for economic democracy and they can defend that in terms of a theory of colonialism of a special type. It is quite a vague notion and that vagueness can be used by Blade Nzimande to pull people into line. But it also means that there is a certain tension, and certain possibilities, for people to mobilise despite their ideological commitments and on many other occasions Cosatu has mobilised often large numbers of people against the government, most recently over the question of labour brokers and over the tolling of roads.

It's important to bear in mind that Cosatu, partly because of its role in the Congress alliance but also because it is dominated by a trade union bureaucracy that has the same kind of material interest in class compromise that any trade union bureaucracy has, operates as a conservative force but also has a significant recent history, particularly in the public sector, of leading very big strikes. So it would be a mistake to say that Cosatu is simply rotten and that alternative unions have to be built. There is clearly an issue in the mining industry but it would be a mistake to generalise from that case.

I think there are possibilities for a degree of generalisation but I don't think that other industries are the same as mining. Nevertheless, while the mining industry has special features there are still movements towards militancy in the other unions and these can bring active members into conflict with their leaders. We saw that in 2010 with the public sector workers' strike, for instance.[4] So the mining industry is not entirely exceptional. But let me make another point about Cosatu, which is that it is necessary to look at the details of the recent history of Cosatu and the battles for leadership within it, because the present general secretary, Zwelinzima Vavi, has been a critical voice within the alliance and there were indications that he was beginning to develop an alternative vision of the future for South Africa, a vision which linked workers with the poor and was much more critical of the government.

What has happened over the past year, in my view, is that a deal was struck. Vavi's own capacity to win a majority of support to continue as general secretary of Cosatu has been undermined by the growth of the Communist Party within the leadership of a number of unions, and effectively the SACP said to him, "We will continue to back you as Cosatu general secretary as long as you toe the line, or as long as you don't speak out of line to any considerable degree." So he's been under a lot of pressure

---

4:    Ceruti, 2011.

from within Cosatu not to challenge the mainstream line on Marikana. It's fairly clear from body language, and from the things he doesn't say, that he is uncomfortable with that, but nevertheless he goes along with it.

One thing that is worth underlining is that the ambiguity and the contradictions that you are describing help to provide an explanation of why the ANC government has been able to ride this crisis. There is a quite dense network of organisations—albeit that the closer one gets to the base the weaker they seem to be—that binds very large sections of the population, particularly workers and the poor, to the government and it's possible for at least some steam to be let off and some opposition to be expressed through them. Obviously there are limits to this, and we have seen what happened with Malema, but the ability of people to be at least partially oppositional from time to time helps to keep the show on the road.

Gramsci

Yes, but I wouldn't push that argument too far. What I sense from research we've been doing in townships, as well as from the recent rebellion in the mining industry, is a shift away from looking at the alliance as the vehicle through which people can advance their interests.[5] There is a growing disillusionment and some of it is associated with what the ANC represents on the ground in particular municipalities, which is very often corruption. So increasingly people are willing to take action independently of ANC cadre.

That leads nicely to my final question, which is about the role of the independent left in South Africa. South Africa has a small anti-Stalinist left with very rich traditions going back many decades and which is now largely organised under the banner of the Democratic Left Front (DLF). From what you are saying the space in which they can operate, which has been very restricted, should be widening now.

And that is the case. As you say, the DLF has had difficulties, as has the left in general, because of the hegemony of the Communist Party within the trade unions in particular. But, as we can see, that is waning and this creates opportunities for the DLF to connect with the changing mood. It is beginning to do that through meetings organised in a number of communities where it has a presence. Its base is mainly in the communities, which means, in practice, among the poor rather than in the unions. It has benefited to some degree from people moving away from social movement type organisation towards the politics that are associated with the DLF. So that community base has largely shifted towards the DLF, which has also been able to garner some new support in areas where there have been very big community protests over the last two or three years.

5:    Alexander, 2012.

And it is now responding to the strike wave in the mines?
It is indeed. In particular it is centrally involved in the Marikana Support Committee which has been the main means of mobilising solidarity, initially for people who had been directly involved in the massacre—their families, people who had been injured, strikers and so on. But more recently it's been involved in mobilising wider support for the strike. The Marikana Support Committee has operated at a number of different levels. One has been to connect with the legal campaigns, another has been to give practical support to AMCU, which has been under attack from the state and the media, and another has been to begin to provide support for mine workers outside of Lonmin. Some of this support is just very practical stuff that people need: for instance, money for transport to get to meetings is important, and that means not only people from Marikana going out but also getting families to come from the Eastern Cape so that they can participate in the inquiry. So transport is very important but so too are all the other things that go with campaigning activity—specifically in South Africa T-shirts are what people expect if they're going to become involved in a campaigning activity.[6]

I think that's all I wanted to ask. Is there anything you wanted to add?
Two issues in particular have concerned me. One is how to characterise the trade union leadership in South Africa. It seems to me that the notion of a trade union bureaucracy is a somewhat blunt tool because there are different forms that the bureaucracy takes. The trade union bureaucracy in South Africa is different from that in Britain because of the character of its relationship with the ANC, which is different from the relationship between the Labour Party and the trade union bureaucracy in Britain. So partly because of the character of the liberation struggle the mainstream trade unions in Cosatu still regard the ANC as providing a leadership. This means that there is a top-down approach to trade unionism in South Africa, a political alignment that doesn't exist in Britain, for instance. So I was wondering about the notion of "labour lieutenants of capital"—in some ways it's too crude and not really dialectical in the way that the idea of a Janus-faced bureaucracy is. Nevertheless there are different shades that exist within the trade union leadership, and the one in South Africa at the moment seems to me to be more towards the notion of "labour lieutenants of capital".

The second issue concerns the characterisation of the nature of the regime in South Africa at the moment. One can use the idea of corporatism

---

6:   More information about the Marikana Support Committee can be found at Justice Now for Marikana Strikers, www.facebook.com/groups/275097599265710/

which certainly applied to what I referred to as the labour relations regime that emerged around 1994, and I wonder whether that might be a concept that is useful more generally now in South Africa to describe the way in which there is a close relationship between the state and capital, or at least sections of capital, and the key elements within the trade union movement. That seems to me to be what has become clearer as a consequence of Marikana and the subsequent debates.

Those are very big questions. I'd make a couple of points. Firstly it sounds a lot more corporatist than anything that we've known in Britain since Thatcher, ie for over 30 years, but it is corporatism qualified by large doses of neoliberalism and a very internationally integrated capitalist class, which is a bit different from the models of corporatism where national capital collaborates with national trade union leaders. Take Glencore, which has just taken over Xstrata, as an example—there is a strong South African element but it is based in Switzerland. Similarly, the mining houses have been allowed to move their corporate headquarters, share listings, and so on out of South Africa. These factors complicate the picture of corporatism.

On the question of the "labour lieutenants of capital", what you are saying is interesting because you are showing that the absorptive powers that the ANC alliance has had are weakening. That seems to me to be what you are describing, and the integration with capital and the state in the case of NUM has gone so far that it has provoked an irrevocable breakaway. But I would still say that there is the other side of the picture, which is that Cosatu has organised very big strikes, much bigger strikes than the British trade union leaders have organised, with the exception of 30 November 2011. I suppose that everyone thinks that their own trade union bureaucracy is particularly awful.

I agree, and if one is going to use the word corporatism then it has to be qualified in some way—it's a contested corporatism. It's contested partly through the strength of international capitalism in South Africa, which operates through the mining industry but also through the finance houses. But it's also contested from below: South Africa's working class hasn't been defeated and there is a lot of confidence among workers as well as expectations which bring them into conflict of the kind we have seen.

One of the difficulties that we need to think through is how the ruling class is likely to respond to the current developments. I had expected the trade unions, and NUM in particular, to move to the left because if they are going to retain, and to some extent rebuild, their base among mine workers they have to be seen to be delivering, and that can mean, at least rhetorically, a greater level of militancy. The analogy of Zimbabwe might be useful. There was a big rebellion among workers in 1996, led by the rank and file, who pushed the trade union leadership, particularly in the public sector, to the left, so that in 1997 there were more strike days than in 1996. So I had thought that the South African trade union leadership might respond in a similar way, and it might well still do so. On the other hand, the immediate indications are that the state may become more repressive in South Africa and I don't know how that will resolve itself. I don't believe at the moment that the state has the capacity or political possibilities for large-scale repression and perhaps the most important thing about Marikana is that the workers refused to be cowed. Amazingly, they continued their strike after 34 people had been massacred. The bravery involved in that is tremendous—for workers' leaders to pick themselves up after watching their friends being killed and then the very next day decide that the strike must continue is something which I think is unique.

References

Alexander, Peter, 2012, "Barricades, Ballots and Experimentation: Making Sense of the 2011 Local Government Election With a Social Movement Lens", in Marcelle C Dawson and Luke Sinwell (eds), *Contesting Transformation: Popular Resistance in Twenty-first Century South Africa* (Pluto).

Ashman, Sam, Ben Fine and Susan Newman, 2010, "The Crisis in South Africa: Neoliberalism, Financialisation and Uneven and Combined Development", *Socialist Register 2011: The Crisis This Time* (Merlin).

Capps, Gavin, 2012, "Victim of its own Success? The Platinum Mining Industry and the Apartheid Mineral Property System in South Africa's Political Transition," *Review of African Political Economy*, 39.

Ceruti, Claire, 2011, "The Hidden Element in the 2010 Public-Sector Strike in South Africa", *Review of African Political Economy*, 38.

Krikler, Jeremy, 2005, *The Rand Revolt: The 1922 Insurrection and Racial Killing in South Africa* (Jonathan Ball).

Yudelman, David, 1984, *The Emergence of Modern South Africa: State, Capital and the Incorporation of Organised Labour on the South African Gold Fields, 1902-1939* (David Philip).

"Never going back":
Egypt's continuing revolution
Philip Marfleet

For 35 years Egypt was a laboratory for neoliberalism—a local state in which hegemonic world powers and financial institutions played out their strategies for the global economy. It was also a stage on which the United States and its allies rehearsed policy for control of key assets in the Global South. From the mid-1970s their support for the regimes of Anwar Sadat and Hosni Mubarak were means of containing collective responses to an increasingly aggressive neoliberal agenda. When the Tahrir uprising began in January 2011 the stakes were high: could Egyptians contest *al-nizam* (the order), a state machine which bore down brazenly upon the mass of people in a local expression of global inequality and inequity? The slogans of the movement, and its aspirations, echoed worldwide—in removing Mubarak, Egyptian activists made *tahrir* (liberation) a synonym for wider resistance. Two years later Egypt's revolution is still the epicentre of opposition to capitalist "liberalism" and to the machineries of state which support its relentless search for profit. Where does the revolution stand today? What are its potentials? What is to be done?[1]

Obituaries for the revolution are produced daily in the European and

1:    Acknowledgement is due to members of the Revolutionary Socialists of Egypt, who have provided many political insights, and to Egypt's new media—especially to Hani Shukrallah and the journalists of *Ahram Online*, now Egypt's publication of record. Thanks also to Wassim Wagdy, John Rose, Anne Alexander, Alex Callinicos and Jonny Jones for comments on this article in draft.

North American press. Its detractors maintain that the Tahrir events were no more than a "reflex", at best a "revolt" which shortly exhausted participants. They maintain that a grim reality has settled over the Egyptian movement—the rise of Islamism and the certainty that atavistic religious currents will crush democratic aspirations. In an analysis of developments across the Middle East since January 2011, Agha and Malley maintain that "This is not a revolution":

> Darkness descends upon the Arab world... The peaceful demonstrations with which this began, the lofty values that inspired them, become distant memories... The only consistent programme is religious and is stirred by the past.[2]

"Amid chaos and uncertainty, the Islamists alone offer a familiar, authentic vision for the future." In the case of Egypt, "The Muslim Brotherhood prevails".[3]

When Egypt's parliamentary elections of December 2011 brought success for the Muslim Brotherhood many journalists wrote off the country's mass movement: "Arab Spring" had become "Islamist Winter".[4] They presented the Tahrir events as an interlude—an episode which merely prepared the ground for religious reaction. In conservative media and think-tanks there was palpable relief at the Brotherhood's electoral advance, seen as confirmation that Arab-Muslim societies were unable to sustain popular movements for radical change. In Israel, prime minister Benjamin Netanyahu maintained that Arab countries were "not moving forward toward progress; they are moving backwards".[5] When Mohamed Mursi, candidate of the Muslim Brotherhood, won a presidential run-off in June 2012, Islamophobes charged their pens. According to the American think-tank *Foreign Policy*, it was now a matter of "containing the Islamist revolution... It's time to retrench and protect US interests from the Islamist tidal wave".[6] In France *Le Monde* reported Marine Le Pen, leader of the neo-fascist Front National, to the effect that: "The 'Arab Spring' has changed into an Islamist Winter"; the key outcome, she said, would be a

---

2: Agha and Malley, 2012, pp71-72.
3: Agha and Malley, 2012, p72.
4: This clichéd headline seems to have originated (at least in current usage) with an article in *Foreign Affairs* in the summer of 2011: "Arab Spring, Persian Winter"—Kaye and Wehrey 2011. It appeared as "Arab Spring—Islamist Winter" in the *Washington Post* in December 2011 and has since appeared routinely, especially in the US and in Israeli media. See Byman, 2011.
5: See Mitnick, 2011.
6: Former Israeli deputy defence minister Ephraim Sneh, writing in *Foreign Policy*—Sneh, 2011.

wave of emigration from Arab countries, prompting fear among the people of Europe.[7] Here, Tahrir Square was not a reference point for global resistance; rather, events in Egypt were a further round in the imagined "clash of civilisations", demonstrating that volatile and backward Muslim cultures of North Africa threatened societies of Europe and North America.

Egypt has not experienced a religious "tidal wave" or "Islamist winter". Since January 2011 its religious activists have had a mixed experience, as electoral successes have been combined with serious retreats. The Muslim Brotherhood in particular has had a rough ride from the mass movement, which continues to insist on change and for which new authoritarian formulas, including those advanced by the Brotherhood, Salafis and other religious currents, have met with increasing impatience. The Brotherhood—far from fulfilling its own historic mission of leading Egyptian society towards an Islamic order—has suffered numerous splits and defections, losing much of the coherence developed during the Mubarak era. Egypt's Salafis, who emerged from the sidelines to achieve electoral prominence in 2011, have likewise struggled to maintain momentum. Meanwhile, some secular currents which had seemed exhausted by decades of ineffective resistance to the dictatorship have experienced a revival. Radical nationalism has been renewed and, for the first time since the 1940s, Egypt has a new left which is an organic element within the revolutionary movement. In workplaces, on campuses and in local communities the level of collective organisation is more advanced than at any time since the 1940s and there is a huge audience for ideas about self-emancipation and revolutionary change. But—a large but—Egypt's workers, the key actors in the revolutionary movement, have not advanced towards a sustained challenge to those now in power.

The Egyptian state, with all its histories of repression, is intact: the dictator has gone but the structures of repression remain. The military is still embedded at the heart of the system, controlled by an officer elite that for decades has claimed ownership of national politics. Egyptian capitalism—a hybrid formation in which private and state interests cohabit—has been destabilised but is not yet challenged by the movement from below. Those with the power to initiate further radical change are still to coordinate in ways that can meet aspirations of the mass movement—the demands for 'aysh, hurriya, 'adala igtama'eya ("Bread, Freedom, Social Justice") heard at almost every strike and demonstration. The key issue at stake is not a new rule of the ayatollahs; it is the problem of a

---

7:    *Le Monde*, 2012.

revolution in process, in which activists struggle to make the politics of the past adequate for the acute challenges they face today. Most pressing are problems presented by, on the one hand, legacies of nationalism and communism, and on the other hand by an associated religious "reformism". It is these which restrain the workers' movement, inhibit activist agendas and—in their most damaging form—provide opportunities for partisans of the old regime to reassert their influence.

Mursi and the crisis

Common to many current assessments is the notion that the Muslim Brotherhood will successfully assault Egypt's movement from below. This may be an aim of some Brotherhood leaders—but it is likely to remain an aspiration. Suppressing the movement would be a huge challenge for any government: Mubarak's successors in the Supreme Council of the Armed Forces (SCAF) failed to do so and Mursi is ill-equipped to launch his own counter-revolution. The president faces economic pressures far more serious than those which confronted Mubarak in the period before his fall. Turning to international capital to address his problems, he is ready to bear down on a population which requires him to meet basic needs and to guarantee the gains of the revolution. The Brotherhood faces its greatest political challenge since the end of the colonial era.

Mursi's problems are captured in his difficulties over the issue of bread. In Egyptian Arabic 'aysh means both "bread" and "life", and for decades subsidised loaves have been essential to the survival of most working class, peasant and poor families. Key moments in contemporary Egyptian history are associated with the availability of bread and since the fall of Mubarak there have been many edgy episodes when supplies have faltered. The cost and quality of the basic five-piastre[8] loaf are matters of daily discussion for most families and appeared at the top of a list of priorities and pledges issued by Mursi after the presidential election. Mursi says he has created a "bread file" and that he monitors supplies regularly: when he spoke at a public rally in early October 2012 he claimed that 80 percent of targets set for ending shortages had been met.[9] Government officials say they have directed "mega-bakeries", formerly used by the army and the police, to supply public needs: by this means, they claim, "any shortage anywhere can be tackled immediately".[10] There is high scepticism among

---

8:    About 0.5 British pence or 0.75 US cents.
9:    Hussein, 2012.
10:   Hussein, 2012.

the public—an online "Mursimeter" which measures the president's success in fulfilling his promises casts doubt on official claims.[11]

Even Mubarak hesitated over bread subsidies, knowing that the issue could be incendiary. In 1977 a reduction in the size of the loaf, imposed by President Sadat to meet the demands of the International Monetary Fund (IMF), produced massive nationwide protests which for several days threatened the regime. Sadat survived—but only after using the army in a risky campaign of mass repression and only after reinstating the cuts. After this "intifada of bread" Mubarak used the threat of popular protest in negotiations with the IMF and others: a tactic mobilised to resist pressures for subsidy cuts over which the Fund was increasingly forceful during the 1980s and 1990s.[12] Today Mursi also faces pressures from world financial institutions, while he is under observation by a highly mobilised and expectant population. There have been no IMF loans to Egypt since 1993; now a $4.8 billion loan, said to be among the largest lending programmes by the IMF outside the Eurozone, is accompanied by demands for sweeping subsidy cuts. Egypt's parliament (currently suspended) rejected a $3.2 billion loan on similar terms last year. The IMF is pressing hard; it views Egypt as a test case for lending in the Middle East: according to the *Wall Street Journal*, "Negotiations with Egypt will offer a laboratory for the world's emergency lender as it tries to aid the new democracies created by the so-called Arab Spring uprisings".[13] The loan is critical for Mursi: its projected 1.1 percent interest rate compares with the record (and unsustainable) 16 percent currently paid to domestic banks, to which the Egyptian government has turned for funds to meet a huge annual deficit—at some $30 billion, this is already (November 2012) $6 billion more than predicted for 2012-13.[14] When agreed, officials say, the IMF loan will release further resources from the World Bank, the African Development Bank and various Middle East states.[15] Global financial institutions approach hesitantly—Egypt is ranked as the world's tenth riskiest debtor, with a 27.3 percent chance of default over the next five years.[16]

The IMF insists that Mursi must cut state spending in general and

---

11: The Mursimeter can be viewed in Arabic at www.Mursimeter.com and in English at www.Mursimeter.com/en

12: Momani, 2005.

13: Reddy and Bradley, 2012.

14: Hyde, 2012b.

15: Wroughton, 2012.

16: Standard and Poors assessment—Hyde, 2012c.

subsidies in particular, which make up 30 percent of this year's budget.[17] In 2011 the Egyptian state subsidised each five-piastre loaf with a 19.8-piastre subsidy; in 2012 the subsidy will be 24.08 piastres, reflecting increases in the cost of wheat on the world market.[18] Last year the government doubled the price for wheat offered to local producers, marking a sharp change from Mubarak's policy of encouraging production of exotic cash crops for export. Small increases in local production are, however, described as "just a drop in the bucket":[19] Egypt urgently needs huge quantities of grain which must be found in the world market: on average over the past five years it has bought in 45 percent of annual needs from abroad.[20] With grain prices forecast to rise even more steeply, the timing could not be worse for Mursi.

The IMF wants agreement to subsidy cuts before it will deliver the loan. Other international financial organisations and governments are watching: in October 2012 the EU and the US suspended two grants worth a total of $1 billion pending agreement between the IMF and the Egyptian government. Challenged on the issue of bread by international finance on the one hand and the people on the other, the president seems initially to have made concessions to the latter. In August 2012 his officials announced that a larger ten-piastre loaf (said to be of better quality) would soon be produced: in effect, the government was ready to double the price of bread by preparing to phase out the smaller loaf. In October 2012 Ahmed Issa, the official in charge of the president's "bread file", said: "There will be no increase of bread prices which can prompt social instabilities. Subsidised bread will remain at 5 piastres".[21]

Mursi faces similar challenges in relation to fuel, where the IMF also wants big cuts in subsidies. Butane gas is used by most Egyptian families for cooking. Officially, gas cylinders are for sale at LE2.5 (Egyptian pounds) but the black market price can be 30 times as much—beyond the reach of poor families in a country in which 40 percent of the population lives on less than $2 a day.[22] There have been repeated shortages all over Egypt, with furious crowds demonstrating at distribution centres. So too in the case of petrol and diesel: long queues build up at filling stations where drivers can wait for hours for deliveries. Taxis and minibuses (integral to daily life in all Egyptian cities)

17: Hyde, 2012a.
18: Hyde, 2012a.
19: Magda Kandel, director of the Egyptian Center for Economic Studies, quoted in Detrie, 2012.
20: See figures published by the UN's Food and Agriculture Organisation—FAO, 2012.
21: Hussein, 2012.
22: Marroushi and Shahin, 2012, *Ahram Online*, 2011.

join the queues, there is traffic chaos and the issue of fuel takes on symbolic importance as an expression of general crisis. There have many protests, fights between drivers and police, and incidents in which drivers have staged collective protests including blockages and occupations of roads and railways.[23]

"Piety versus expediency"

Mursi is under enormous pressure to accede to IMF demands. Since January 2011 Egypt's currency reserves have collapsed: then they amounted to $36 billion; in September 2012 they stood at $15.04 billion: barely enough to cover three months of imports.[24] The Egyptian pound has fallen fast against hard currencies: in September 2012 it was at a seven-year low against the US dollar.[25] The IMF has called for devaluation—at the time of writing it seems that Egypt's Central Bank is allowing the pound to fall, accepting de facto a devaluation which will have further impacts, including on the government's ability to finance wheat imports. One recent assessment warns of "an economic calamity that could be triggered by a sharp fall of the Egyptian pound".[26] Loans from Qatar and Turkey have provided temporary relief but the president needs major funds to pursue his strategic aims of bringing domestic stability and of invigorating Egyptian capitalism (see below).

Many Egyptians are opposed to the whole idea of an international loan. When the SCAF-appointed government attempted to negotiate a $3.2 billion deal with the IMF last year, academics and activists in the Popular Campaign to Drop Egypt's Debt launched a high-profile media initiative opposing the loan, arguing that Egypt should abandon practices of the Mubarak era. The government should refuse to repay loans raised by the state both outside and inside Egypt, they said—the money had been misused by the former regime and the Egyptian people could not be expected to repay it. In a memo to parliament the campaign proposed that raising a further IMF loan sent an unacceptable message to the people: "We will borrow in your names so that your children and grandchildren continue paying off our debts".[27] The latter were "illegitimate" and should be abandoned in the interests of "people's welfare".[28] Many Islamists meanwhile declared that payment of interest to the IMF was *haram*—proscribed by Islamic principles in relation to usury. Before parliament was suspended

---

23: *Al Masry Al Youm*, 2012a.
24: See Reuters figures in *Ahram Online*, 2012a, also Samhouri, 2012.
25: See Haddad, 2012.
26: Samhouri, 2012.
27: Elmeshad, 2012.
28: See www.dropegyptsdebt.org/

earlier this year only six of 365 members of the Lower House (with its large Islamist majority) supported terms required for a smaller deal with the IMF: Islamist members then declared, "This loan will lead us all to hell".[29]

But Mursi insisted on pursuing the deal, which he said would serve the public interest, develop Egypt's economy and bring growth. A few months later Brotherhood leaders announced: "Our decision not to reject borrowing is based on Egypt's supreme economic interest", quoting Shari'a (the Islamic legal code) to the effect that "necessities allow the forbidden".[30] The leading Egyptian news website *Ahram Online* commented tersely on "piety versus expediency".[31] Mursi has since struggled to convince his own constituency about the loan. In October 2012 he told a public rally that repayments to the IMF would not constitute *riba*—usury. "I would never accept that Egyptians live off Riba... We would rather starve than eat off Riba", he said.[32]

Just as millions of Egyptians reject politicians and officials of the Mubarak regime as *feloul* ("remnants" of a discredited system) they oppose deals with international organisations complicit with Mubarak. The IMF was chief architect of policies that Mubarak pursued with vigour—including privatisation, de-regularisation and de-sequestration of land.[33] There is widespread hostility to further deals which imply renewal of these policies—revulsion at the idea of activities associated with Mubarak's criminality (for which he and others are in prison) being sanctioned by a new government. The prospect of a further loan also raises questions about the assets of Mubarak and others, who salted away billions of dollars in overseas bank accounts and invested in property across Europe, notably in Britain.[34] Opponents of the IMF mega-loan ask why Egypt should enter new debt relations when key states associated with the IMF, such as Britain, are still in possession of assets which belong to the Egyptian people.

The IMF loan raises a host of unpleasant associations for many Egyptians: Mubarak's criminality; unresolved allegations against *feloul*; foreign exploitation of local resources; profiteering and the role of Egyptian and foreign banks; the colonial legacy and the long history of Egyptian state debt; imperialism and its impacts on Egyptian society. When IMF chief

---

29: Alabass, 2012.
30: Alabass, 2012.
31: Alabass, 2012.
32: AFP, 2012.
33: Under the de-sequestration law of 1992, landowning families of the colonial period were given legal powers to regain lands distributed under Egypt's reforms of the Nasser era. See Bush, 2009.
34: Shenker, 2012.

Christine Lagarde visited Cairo in August 2012 she was greeted by a protest which asserted: "No to crony capitalism," "Down with capitalism," and "Reject the loans".[35] In November 2012 a coalition of 17 political organisations marched in central Cairo to protest against the IMF deal, denouncing financial "colonisation" and secret talks between the government and the IMF.[36] The Egyptian Popular Current, led by Nasserist Hamdeen Sabbahi, called for a mass email campaign in which Egyptians should protest to the IMF about its conditions for the loan. Sabahi's model message told the Fund: "Your loan is causing our poverty. Your condition to interfere in our politics [sic] is unacceptable. And the history of your institution and loans was disastrous to our economy".[37] Sabahi reflects the views of many workers, urban poor and members of the urban middle class, among whom an underlying issue at this stage of the revolution is captured by another slogan heard repeatedly across the country—"Never going back".

"Islamo-fascism"

The new mega-loan is dangerous territory for Mursi. With every evasive speech on the IMF, and on cuts and subsidies, he loses authority. An Egyptian academic and activist comments:

> The aura of religious authority which has been essential to the influence of the Ikhwan [the Brothers] has been falling away, especially since Mursi was elected. He's seen more and more as just another politician striking dubious deals. Many members of the organisation who fought in Tahrir and in other battles to get rid of Mubarak are furious about where he's going. The Brotherhood faces big problems as a party that's seen to have power but can't use it for moral purposes.[38]

Questions about the Islamist movement in general and the Brotherhood in particular are highly charged issues in Egypt and abroad. Over the past decade, as the movement re-emerged as a significant current across Arab politics—notably in Lebanon, Palestine, Tunisia and Egypt—it has prompted increasingly strident reactions. It is said to be "fascist", bent upon destruction of the mass movement, and likely to install a regime far more repressive than that of Mubarak. These assessments are widespread in Europe and

---

35: Mourad and Feteha, 2012.
36: Kalin, 2012.
37: *Ahram Online*, 2012d.
38: Interview in Cairo, September 2012.

North America but are also heard in Egypt, especially among Communists of the older generation. What is the nature of the Islamist movement—and what are the implications for the revolutionary process today?

For George W Bush, speaking in 2006 as Hezbollah engaged Israeli forces in Lebanon, the problem was one of "Islamic fascism"—an "ideology that is real and profound".[39] These comments projected worldwide terms of reference hitherto used on the political margins in Europe and North America, and more widely in Israel. A debate on their relevance, initially confined to literary magazines, received wide media coverage and disseminated the notion of Islamic political movements having a "fascist" component.[40] In Britain the conservative columnist Janet Daley applauded Bush and developed his argument: "Islamic fundamentalism is fascistic in the precise, technical sense of the word", she wrote.[41] Calling for strong endorsement of Israel (which she described as "the West's proxy") in the Lebanon conflict, Daley argued:

This enemy [Islamism] does not even bother to offer explanations for its actions that fall within the acceptable bounds of Western debate: it is overtly racist, explicitly imperialistic and unapologetically inhumane....

This is a critical moment. What we must call the "free world" will either decide that it must unite unequivocally against a force so dark that it is almost incomprehensible to democratic peoples, or else succumb to a daydream of denial that is nothing more than appeasement.[42]

Daley and others felt increasingly free to express deep hostility towards all manner of Islamist groups and parties. Their attitudes drew on long-established European traditions of prejudice vis-a-vis Islam and Muslims—centuries of Orientalism and the cultures of imperial rule. These had been renewed and sharpened by post Cold War debates about a "Clash

---

39: Greene, 2006.
40: See for example Judt, 2006, and Hitchens, 2007. Hitchens attributes the first use of the term "Islamo-fascism" to Malise Ruthven, writing in 1990. According to Daniel Pipes, the term was initially used in mainstream American politics by right wing Republican senator Rick Santorum: Pipes quotes various sources to the effect that this prompted its adoption by Bush—Pipes, 2006a. See also Pipes, 2006b, for an account of intense debates about the meanings and relevance of the term, especially among right wing politicians and commentators in North America.
41: Daley, 2006.
42: Daley, 2006.

of Civilisations", formalised by the conservative American strategist Samuel Huntington but which originated in the work of the British-American academic and partisan of Israel, Bernard Lewis. In 1990 Lewis had set out a case for the influence of both Nazism and Communism on Islamic thought in the mid-20th century, asserting that at times of crisis—and increasingly often in contemporary history—Muslim grievances expressed "an explosive mixture of rage and hatred".[43] The idea that Islamic activism/Islamism bears features of fascism and amounts to an erruption of hatred and violence has gained wider currency, especially in Europe, where it has been mobilised alongside arguments about the implausibility of multiculturalism and in support of exclusionary migration policy.[44]

When the world economic crisis began in 2008, producing new waves of resistance in the Global South, there were more systematic attempts to damn the movement. It became a target for those wishing to displace responsibility for the failures of global capital: protests, strikes and "riots" were associated with alleged cultural deficiencies of those involved, and especially with the influence of Islam.[45] Tony Judt had anticipated just such responses from both neoconservatives and "liberal" intellectuals, noting that Bush's "War on Terror", his invasion of Iraq and the 2006 conflict in Lebanon were viewed by liberals in particular as "skirmishes in a new global confrontation".[46] They were part of "a Good Fight, reassuringly comparable to their grandparents' war against fascism and their Cold War liberal parents' stance against international Communism". In a world seen once more as ideologically divided, "today's liberal intellectuals have at last discovered a sense of purpose: they are at war with 'Islamo-fascism' ".[47]

The left in Egypt has also had multiple problems with the notion of fascism. During the 1940s Communists sometimes worked with the Muslim Brotherhood in demonstrations against British occupation; when they fell out with the Brothers they dubbed the latter "fascist".[48] When Gamal Abdel Nasser and the radical nationalist Free Officers group organised a coup against the Faruq monarchy in 1952, the main Communist organisations first welcomed the initiative, then attacked Nasser and his colleagues as a "fascist dictatorship"[49] and finally embraced the Nasser regime as a progressive force

---

43: Lewis, 1990.
44: See, for example, Benhabib on the impacts in Germany—Benhabib, 2012.
45: On "IMF riots" see Marfleet, 2006.
46: Judt, 2006.
47: Judt, 2006.
48: Meijer, 2002, p118.
49: Agwani, 1969, p50.

and ally of the Soviet Union. In 1965 the Egyptian Communist Party (ECP) disbanded on the basis that the Nasser regime "alone was competent to carry out the tasks of the revolution", its leading members taking up key positions in Nasser's Arab Socialist Union (ASU).[50] This auto-liquidation was to have enormous consequences, leaving Egyptians without a coherent presence on the left and opening a large space in which Islamism—initially the radical groups of the *jihadi* tendency—soon exerted a strong influence. In 1975 remnants of the ECP formed the core of al-Tagammu' ("the rally")—the National Progressive Unionist Party—one of the "platforms" or "pulpits" (*manabir*) permitted to operate as shell parties by Sadat at a time when the Brotherhood was semi-legal.

When the Brotherhood grew as a mass organisation in the 1980s Tagammu' aligned with the state against the Islamists: with tens of thousands of members and supporters of the Brotherhood in prison, the Communists hoped for accommodation with the regime and a role in government (they were disappointed). These ECP veterans were the enfeebled left wing of what Brysk has called "low-intensity democracy"[51]—arrangements encouraged by the US and its allies in which a formal commitment to electoralism and political pluralism is accompanied by systematic repression.[52] On the fall of Mubarak, Tagammu' split—the majority entering an alliance with liberal capitalist parties, notably the Free Egyptians of billionaire Naguib Sawiris. Their main aim was to oppose the Brotherhood, accused by Tagammu' leader Rifaat Al-Said of trying to "hijack Egypt and Egyptians".[53] In the presidential run-off of 2012 Tagammu' backed the SCAF's candidate Ahmed Shafiq against Mursi, arguing that this was the only way to prevent Egypt becoming an Islamic state.[54]

Stalinist Communism was dismantled as an organised force at the global level by events in Russia and Eastern Europe during and after 1989. It continues to have a long ideological half life, however. In Egypt the remnants of the ECP maintain their historic search for a "progressive" bourgeoisie; rebuffed by Nasser, Sadat and Mubarak, they are seeking deals with the country's wealthiest business dynasty, itself networked with the military elite. Their campaigns against the Brotherhood mimic the Islamophobia

---

50: See Agwani, 1969, p86.
51: Brysk, 2002, p12.
52: On the impacts of "low intensity" regimes see Marfleet, 2006.
53: Jadaliyya, 2011.
54: *Ahram Online*, 2012c. Since the June 2012 presidential election Shafiq—Mubarak's last prime minister—has been charged with corruption. In November 2012 he was being tried *in absentia* after fleeing to the United Arab Emirates.

of Europe and North America, where those who rant at "Islamo-fascism" are often partisans of neoliberalism keen to displace the multiple failings of global capital onto the latter's victims. In the case of Egypt's domestic politics, Tagammu' displaces the failings of the Stalinist left onto Islamic activists. Having played a key role in bringing Islamism onto centre stage, its leaders now demonise both the movement and many activists who played a key role in the downfall of Mubarak and subsequent battles against the state.

Workers—uneven movement

The Muslim Brotherhood won a large parliamentary majority in elections in November and December 2011; in June 2012 its candidate was elected president. There is no compelling evidence of the classic behaviours of fascist movements experienced at such cost in Europe in the 20th century: mass offensives on the working class; systematic mobilisation of paramilitaries and vigilantes against political opponents; an obsession with national identity and the state; and the exclusion of ethnic and other minorities. One leading member of the Revolutionary Socialists (RS) says: "Mursi and the Brotherhood leaders are reactionary but not fascists—if they were we'd have been gunned off the streets by now. We have no illusions in the Brotherhood but it's really no use to present them wrongly in this way—it stops the left dealing with the real problems of Islamism".[55]

Egypt's working class movement remains remarkably vigorous. The events of January and February 2011 stimulated a huge burst of energy across Egyptian society. Strikes had played a key role in removing Mubarak and, full of confidence, workers promptly undertook the widest and most sustained industrial action since the 1940s.[56] Many strikes seemed to be successful, with concessions from private-sector and state employers on wages, bonuses, pensions, job security and a host of local issues. Some pursued broader aims: purging of local politicians and of officials responsible for key sectors of industry or commerce, of police and security officials, and of key figures in the state-controlled unions. A new Egyptian Federation of Independent Trade Unions (EFITU) was formed on 30 January 2011, with potential to develop a nationwide alternative to the official union apparatus, which for over 50 years had stifled workers'

55: Interview in Cairo, September 2012. Sections of the Islamist movement have an inclination towards public displays of hostility towards political rivals that can be expressed in what Shukrallah calls "an occasionally fascistic bent"—Shukrallah, 2012b. There is a difference, however, between such incidents and systematic assaults organised as part of a political strategy.
56: See Alexander, 2011, 2012.

struggles and played a key role in the incorporation of the old left into the state. Even the *New York Times* identified the movement as "a growing challenge for the military and the caretaker government".[57] By October 2012 EFITU claimed some 2.5 million members.[58]

Many disputes have involved large numbers of workers in their first experiences of collective action. There has been a series of national strikes, including highly visible actions affecting the public sector. In 2011 teachers closed most of the country's schools in the first such dispute since 1951;[59] a year later doctors organised the first nationwide strike across the health sector. Periods of relative calm have been followed by waves of disputes. In August and September 2012, following a period of passivity during Ramadan, there was a surge in industrial action with some 1,500 strikes across the country, more than at any time since the fall of Mubarak.[60] Many strikes have unified workers across sites: Cairo's bus drivers called action in most of the city's depots and for the first time in decades imposed highly effective picket lines. But struggles have remained uneven. Some disputes have brought tangible gains, reinforcing confidence; others have produced only promises. Many early disputes which followed the fall of Mubarak were apparently resolved by employer concessions but these agreements were not honoured or not implemented in full. And while there have been cases of solidarity and imitation, with workers learning from actions in neighbouring plants, schools or hospitals, many disputes have taken place in isolation.

There is no sign so far of local workplace democracy producing liaison across sites—of representative workers' committees or councils of action. Notwithstanding the tumultuous events since January 2011 no proto-soviet formations have emerged in which wider political agendas are developed. Nor has the movement produced a workers' party of the sort which grew rapidly in Brazil in the 1980s. An attempt to build a Workers' Party (formed early in 2011 and later known as the Democratic Workers' Party) proved unsuccessful.[61] The movement is extraordinarily energetic but lacks coordination and a political project that can advance workers' collective interests. It has not been able to deliver the promise of further radical change contained in the mass strikes against Mubarak of February 2011.

57: Shadid, 2011.

58: Charbel, 2012.

59: Ali, 2011.

60: Naguib, 2012a.

61: The party was formed to co-ordinate activities of worker militants and to establish a base for parliamentary elections. It seems to have suffered from lack of clarity as to key strategic aims.

The movement bears similarities to those which have emerged in other political upheavals over the past 50 years—in Chile in 1973, Portugal in 1974-5, Iran in 1979 or Poland in 1980-1. It is inhibited, however, by the absence of a shared political agenda among leading activists. It is not merely that the workers lack a party—a scenario common to many revolutionary upheavals—but that even networks of solidarity are undeveloped. This is associated in part with problems of resistance by the old order. For over 50 years the Egyptian Trade Union Federation (ETUF) controlled workplace organisation. It was established in 1957 under the Nasser regime as an arm of the state, working to suppress industrial struggle and to co-opt or isolate activists. Potential opposition candidates were banned from union elections and polls were routinely rigged. Over the next 60 years there were no direct elections to executive committees of any of the 23 national general unions or to the ETUF executive.[62]

The state viewed workers' collective action, comments Joel Beinin, "primarily as a security matter" and from 1954 until 2009 there were no legal strikes.[63] ETUF was integrated into the regime: its officials were part of the apparatus of state, closely connected to the National Democratic Party (NDP), which operated a vast network of patronage. Activist and radical journalist Hani Shukrallah describes ETUF as a "government-owned and run, Soviet-style dinosaur...no more than a headstone set up on the grave of basic trade union freedoms and rights".[64] In August 2011 the federation was officially dissolved but the ruling was not implemented: aiming to control labour activism, SCAF encouraged officials of the old order to continue as before. Many have retained their positions and privileges, together with access to resources which they use to discourage independent activism. This is particularly important in the state sector, where distinctions between management, unions and the security services are often blurred. Importantly, ETUF officials control local welfare schemes—*al-sanadiq al-khasr*, or "private boxes"—to which workers contribute regularly, providing funds for major expenditures such as health crises and weddings, and which are of vital importance to most families. Shaken by the uprising and by subsequent mass strikes, the old unions still have influence. It is significant that in some of the largest industrial workplaces—such as the Mehalla al-Kubra textile mill and the Helwan iron and steel plant, both historic centres of militancy—independent activists have not succeeded in supplanting ETUF-affiliated unions.

62: Beinin, 2009, p69.
63: Beinin, 2009, p69.
64: Shukrallah, 2012a.

Islamic "reformism"

Leaders of EFITU have made intensive efforts to establish new national union structures—a project which is doubly difficult when the key issue at hand is to strengthen and generalise local workplace action. They too are inhibited by the absence of a political current focused on working-class interests. The effect of Mubarak's repression, says Shukrallah, was the "eradication of politics", with activists of the left, including worker activists, confined to small circles and clandestine groups. Even the revival of the workers' movement after 2006 could not make good a historic deficit: "The dictatorship voided politics, isolating those who might have made a difference. As a result, when the revolution came there was no critical mass on the left which could relate directly to the workers' movement".[65] This is not only the outcome of repression, however: it is the result of decades of influence by political currents alien to the interests of the working class. Of these the most important is Islamism.

The Brotherhood has had a profound impact across Egyptian society, not least because of its history of anti-colonial struggle, its rhetoric of anti-imperialism and its welfare activism. The Brotherhood's roots lie in the anti-colonial movement of the late 19th century and the ideas of Jamal al-Din al-Afghani, an Iranian who was politically active in India and the Middle East, chiefly in Egypt, where he was associated with the nationalist 'Urabi uprising of 1882.[66] Afghani formalised the idea of pan-Islam as a strategy for resistance to colonialism, arguing that a notion inherent in Islamic tradition—the common identity and interest of Muslims in the *umma*, or collective of believers—was the key to addressing differences of nationality, sect, language and "race" sown by European powers as they divided Asia, Africa and the Middle East into colonial states. He maintained that Muslims should address the principles and practices of the *salaf*, the forebears or ancestors of contemporary believers, most importantly the Muslims of Prophet Mohamed's community of the 7th century CE.[67] He was strongly opposed to the colonial presence, attempting—unsuccessfully—to coordinate resistance across the Ottoman Empire.

Islamism as an engagement of religious traditions with political action was not established as an effective movement until the late 1920s when Hassan al-Banna established Al-Ikhwan Al-Muslimin (the Society of the

---

65: Interview in Cairo, September 2012.

66: For an account of Afghani's complex and unusual political career see Keddie ,1972.

67: *Salafiyya* is the term applied to both ideological and activist agendas which invoke the beliefs and practices of early Islam: in translation the term for participants is usually "salafis".

Muslim Brothers or Muslim Brotherhood). This started as a cultural association but soon took on a political agenda: in the 1930s it organised against British occupation, demanding land reform and nationalisation of the Suez Canal, and providing teams of fighters in support of the Palestinians in their struggle against both Britain and the Zionist movement.[68] The organisation grew with astonishing speed: according to Richard Mitchell within 20 years it had 2,000 branches, 500,000 members and an equal number of supporters, making it the first truly mass organisation in the Arab world.[69] The Brotherhood dominated the anti-colonial movement, creating huge problems for the British, the tame bourgeois nationalist Wafd Party and the Faruq monarchy. But it was riddled with contradictions: it moved between strident opposition to the British and the local regime, and compromise with them; it proposed active engagement of Egyptians in the anti-colonial struggle but operated with an authoritarian, highly elitist leadership; it attracted large numbers of marginalised people, including workers and poor peasants, but its core (and its leadership) was dominated by relatively affluent members of the commercial petty bourgeoisie. It was a cross-class movement that grew because of the realities of military occupation, the distorted nature of the colonial economy, the failures of secular nationalism, and the Palestine question. Its inability to challenge for state power ultimately provided Nasser and the Free Officers with their opportunity to mount a coup in July 1952.

Nasser banned the organisation and persecuted its activists. Over the next 40 years it passed through several distinct phases. Naguib comments:

> Both the pre-Nasserist history of the movement and the developments of the 1980s and 1990s show the extent to which an organisation such as the Brotherhood has represented different social groups at different moments in its development. Its history is full of shifts, contradictions, and both systemic and anti-systemic features...the Brotherhood has been in a constant state of flux as internal contradictions and changes in the social composition of the movement have forced changes in its strategy, tactics, discourse and programmes.[70]

When its leading members returned to Egypt in the early 1970s after a generation in exile in Saudi Arabia they had a much more

---

68: A key reason for the particular hostility of Israeli politicians vis-a-vis the Brotherhood and its Palestinian offshoot, Hamas.

69: Mitchell, 1969, p328.

70: Naguib, 2009, p105.

conservative agenda. Dominated by businessmen, especially those involved in Islamic banks, they played an important role in the infitah ("opening"), a programme of marketisation associated with Sadat's lurch from Moscow towards Washington and the American-Israeli camp. At the same time their younger members (many today in the leadership of the Brotherhood) reinstated work among students and youth. During the 1980s and 1990s Mubarak launched a ferocious assault on the radical jihadi current: as the latter became less effective the Brotherhood grew again as a mass organisation, especially on campuses, in the professional syndicates and through a widespread social programme based on local welfare associations, clinics and schools which provided services to poor families. It soon dominated opposition to the regime, advocating equality and social reform, criticising official corruption and Mubarak's police state, and even incorporating a "populist critique of neoliberalism in its erstwhile pro-market discourse".[71] With the left still paralysed by the absence of an independent presence the Brotherhood could be all things to all Egyptians—or at least to all Muslims (it had an equivocal stance on the rights of the large Christian minority). It recruited across the spectrum: the rich, the petty bourgeoisie, students, workers, peasants and the urban poor.

The Brotherhood's electoral programme prioritised the need for social reform guided by Islamic principles. In 2011 it entered the general election with a reformist agenda that appealed to millions of voters:

> our election programme regards achieving social justice and ensuring that distribution of revenues from economic activity achieves justice, equality and equal opportunities [as] some of the most important obligations of the state. In recognition of this responsibility, the most important goals of our election programme are addressing the issue of high prices, the elimination of poverty and unemployment, providing basic public services such as education, healthcare, transportation and other services and facilities, improving living conditions of workers and peasants, finding practical solutions to social problems like spinsterhood [sic], street children and those with special needs, supporting adoptive families, and increasing the incomes of pensioners. In all the above, we will work to bring justice to all citizens, taking into account that the recovery of what has been looted from state funds, reforming the tax system, promoting the Zakat and Waqf (national endowment and charitable trust) systems and combating corruption and deliberate waste and

---

71: Naguib, 2009, p116.

squandering of sovereign resources will provide the resources necessary to achieve the desired social justice among all citizens...[72]

This echoed social democratic programmes worldwide—with the exception of references to *zakat* and *waqf*, it might have been a reformist agenda presented by parties across Europe. The Brotherhood now had extensive networks of support in the syndicates—associations of doctors, dentists, lawyers, engineers and journalists—and through large student groups which made Islamist politics the dominant current on most campuses. At the same time they benefited from the crisis of another brand of reformism—that of the old left.

Stalinist legacy

The record of the left in Egypt since the 1960s is one of the most dismal in the history of Stalinist Communism. When the ECP dissolved in 1965 its leading figures joined Nasser's ASU, the country's sole legal party. This was in theory a mass-membership organisation with branches in villages, in every urban centre, and in workplaces and educational institutions. In fact it was a shell organisation—it had no internal life and in reality no members. Nasser himself eventually admitted: "The fact is we have no internal organisation, except on the books".[73] The union was no more than an agency of the state, run by bureaucrats and army officers, who controlled every aspect of national political life. In workplaces the ASU's formal role was to promote education: in fact it operated as part of the security services, maintaining surveillance on workers and even on local managers. The journalist Mohamed Hassanain Heikal, who was one of Nasser's closest collaborators, observed that in industry the ASU operated mainly as a spy system.[74]

In joining the ASU former Communists abandoned independent organisation for good, becoming apologists for the dictatorship. They played no meaningful role in the sustained workers' struggles of the 1970s. Young activists who formed the short-lived Workers' Communist Party attempted to make good the deficit but operated in the shadow cast by the ECP's collapse. By the 1980s the remnants of the old left were firmly established in Tagammu'. Initially the party claimed 150,000 members and an active core of 20,000; its weekly paper, *Al-Ahali*, was said to have a circulation of 130,000

72: Muslim Brotherhood, 2011.
73: Quoted in Baker, 1978, p96.
74: Heikal, quoted in Baker, 1978, p189.

copies.[75] Even if these figures were exaggerated it is clear that at a time of social turmoil the party had a large audience, which it steered unerringly towards accommodation with Mubarak. Apart from protests over Egypt's "normalisation" with Israel, Tagammu' had no distinctive profile. Its leaders saw their main task as opposing the Islamist movement and were prepared to endorse the regime's extreme violence against Muslim activists. In the mid-1990s, secretary-general Rifa'at al-Said said: "We believe that the policies of the ruling party are wrong and dangerous for the country, while Islamist groups are more wrong and more dangerous".[76] The regime used Tagammu' at will: there were frequent allegations that officials rigged elections in favour of the party in order to undermine campaigns of the Brotherhood.[77]

In 1999 al-Said made a bizarre admission, commenting that Egypt's legal political parties "represent nothing in Egyptian politics and have no standing whatsoever with the Egyptian people".[78] All such organisations, he said—including his own—were "just groupings of individuals floating on the surface of society".[79] In 2011 the party's election statement asserted commitments to all manner of political ideals: it was for democracy, freedom, the civil state, justice and equality; and against poverty, oppression, tyranny, corruption, price-fixing and unemployment.[80] Here was a different reformism: one which invoked memories of the Communist movement of the 1930s and 1940s, and a radicalism which had long since lost its meaning. It shared a key feature with Islamist reformism—each viewed the mass of people as objects of their political project, discouraging independent action and a challenge to the state. But in the truly dreadful circumstances created by Stalinist collapse, the Islamists had much greater impact—their work in the syndicates and through welfare projects, and the repression faced by thousands of their activists gave Islamism credibility as a political project.

Islamism and the left
The revolution involved a break with Islamism and the politics of the old left. In order to take to the streets and to launch mass strikes millions of people cast aside inhibitions associated with the politics of defeat. But the workers' movement is still inhibited by these traditions. How can it

---

75: Jadaliyya, 2011.
76: *Al-Ahram Weekly*, 1995.
77: Jadaliyya, 2011.
78: Comment made as part of a debate on "Twenty years of multipartyism in Egypt", in Hussein, Al-Said and Al-Sayyid, 1999, p77.
79: Quoted in Hussein, Al-Said and Al-Sayyid, 1999, p77.
80: Tagammu', 2011.

progress—in particular, how can it advance in the context of mass electoral support for the Muslim Brotherhood?

Over the past decade some political activists, especially young people, have moved sharply to the left, away from Islamism. One key reason lies in the increasing engagement alongside secular radicals of Egyptians influenced by Islamist agendas. This has been clear since the emergence of a major movement of solidarity with the Palestinian intifada of 2000, and subsequently in anti-war mobilisations, in the democracy movement, and in workers', students' and community struggles. Rabab El Mahdi refers to the "spill-over" effect of these cycles of contestation vis-a-vis the state, with each phase of struggle between 2000 and 2010 bringing increased confidence and stimulating further actions:

> [Those involved included] activists in all manner of industries and state services; parents staging sit-ins in protest at school conditions in remote villages; slum-dwellers displaced by urban clearance schemes; mothers on hunger strike against police torture of their children; scores of villages and towns marching to demand access to clean water.[81]

Throughout the 1980s and 1990s opposition to the Mubarak state had been dominated by the Brotherhood: in struggles which began in 2000 many Islamists for the first time met activists of an independent left. There was fierce debate, especially on campuses, where ideologies and practices of Islamism were being put to the test systematically. The new left slowly consolidated, attracting young people who would earlier have remained within Islamist circles. Its key strategy was, where feasible, to engage in struggle against Israel, imperialist war, the police, local employers and university bosses *alongside* Muslim activists. For the Revolutionary Socialists (RS) in particular, a group which had operated underground throughout the 1990s, the key strategic principle was to oppose the state consistently, combining in action with those who were ready to fight. RS was "with the Islamists sometimes, with the state never", always maintaining an independent politics of revolutionary Marxism.[82] This was a creative application of key principles underlying the strategy of the united front—a means of engaging directly with others in a common struggle to defend the immediate interests of the Egyptian masses against the state and more broadly against imperialism. Commenting in 2012 on their approach to the Islamists, Naguib observed:

81: El Mahdi, 2009, p100.
82: An approach set out by Chris Harman, 1994.

Our analysis pointed to the contradictions within and between the various Islamist currents, between their bourgeois leaderships and their petty-bourgeois rank and file and their large constituencies in the working class and in the poor neighbourhoods. These contradictions were always contained by ambiguous religious slogans, and despite the Islamists' repeated accommodation to the regime, in the absence of an alternative, sections of the masses looked towards them as the only serious opposition.[83]

Young members and supporters of the Brotherhood were drawn into action and into debate on questions which had not been addressed publicly from the left for decades, including highly charged issues such as the nature of religious sectarianism, anti-Zionism and anti-Semitism, women's rights and the nature of democracy. These exchanges also featured prominently in a series of large international conferences which brought together Islamists and anti-war activists on the theme of support for the people of Iraq and Palestine.[84] To have opposed Islamists on principle, ignoring Brotherhood initiatives (including campaigns to free political prisoners and in solidarity with victims of Israeli aggression) and to have abstained from debate would have been suicidal for the left—demonstrating that revolutionary Marxists had learned nothing from the tragedies of Stalinism. As a result of these engagements, the direction of travel of individual activists was from the Islamist camp towards the left—a development which reflected deep contradictions in the politics of Islamism. These soon emerged more fully as the level of struggle intensified.

The Brotherhood's predicament was clear from the start. Days before the 25 January 2011 protests one of its most prominent figures, Essam el-Erian, said the organisation would not support a public mobilisation;[85] Mohamed Mursi (now president) told activists that the Brotherhood "will not follow a bunch of kids".[86] The scale of protests on 25 January and the response of the regime soon brought thousands of its members into the front line of the struggle. The leadership promptly made a sharp turn, announcing that Friday 28 January would be "the day of the intifada".[87] It was a day of savage fighting in which many activists were killed. One member of the RS recalls:

83: Naguib, 2012b.
84: The Cairo Conference met regularly between 2003 and 2008, attracting thousands of participants, including hundreds of international delegates.
85: Fahmy, 2011.
86: Al Masry Al Youm, 2012b.
87: Mekhennet and Kulish, 2011.

The Ikhwan leaders did their organisation great damage by first telling members not to join the protests. The Ikhwan had been in opposition to Mubarak for years—but where were they when crisis finally came? Actually the leaders couldn't control ordinary Brothers and Sisters [of the Ikhwan] and they joined us anyway. They appeared in large groups, especially on 28 January—we knew they were Ikhwan—and they fought with great courage, alongside us, alongside the people. They were organised and very effective. We all united without differences of religion or organisation—but the Ikhwan was following the people.[88]

For decades Brotherhood leaders had accepted every sort of humiliation at the hands of the regime. Egypt's prisons were filled with their members, even octogenarians who had long ceased to play active roles in the movement but who Mubarak jailed for exemplary purposes. Brotherhood meetings were routinely banned or attacked and at election time polling stations in areas with popular Islamist candidates were savagely assaulted.[89] Presented with many opportunities to respond, including as part of the anti-war movement and the democracy movement, on most occasions the leadership declined—angering many members, especially among the youth. Its leaders argued that they played a long game—it was never time to take the initiative, which would come *insha'Allah* (God willing) when conditions proved fortuitous. Uncertain as to strategy, the Brotherhood retreated to an even more timid approach: in 2009 a group led by the conservative Mohamed Badei won control and began to restrict the organisation's political activities. The regime grew complacent: in the 2010 election its vote-fixing and violence proved so vulgar that even the Brotherhood withdrew, furious at the humiliation. The organisation was still licking its wounds when on 25 January 2011 the revolution began and the Brotherhood was swept into the streets.

When Mubarak fell in February 2011, leaders of the Brotherhood believed their moment was at hand—after over 80 years they were about to enter Egypt's halls of power. There were two obstacles, however: the military elite and the people. Ushering away Mubarak, military leaders had installed SCAF as the commanding authority within the state. Brotherhood leaders did not take long to refocus their efforts: consistent with decades of political practice, they oriented on those in power, setting out to court the generals. Tarek comments on the perception of secular activists that in the early months of 2011, "the Muslim Brotherhood and SCAF appeared

---

88: Interview in Cairo, April 2011.
89: Marfleet, 2009.

to be on the same page"; they enjoyed a "honeymoon", a "behind the scenes deal, agreement or accommodation, from which both sides would benefit".[90] In exchange for preferential treatment by SCAF, including an advantageous position in arrangements for elections and in writing a new constitution, the Brotherhood was ready to pacify the mass movement.

Leading members of the Brotherhood said they would not nominate a candidate for the presidency and would contest only 25 percent of parliamentary seats, implying deference to the military and its political preferences. El-Erian insisted that the Brotherhood was not a political party and was uninterested in power: "We are working with the people. Our target is the people. Not the power".[91] On the issue of the presidency, he insisted, "We are not going to have a candidate, neither men neither women. We are not going to have a candidate now, at all".[92] The Brotherhood was evasive about Egypt's peace treaty with Israel, which it had strongly opposed during the Mubarak era, and on the subject of military trials for civilians (many of its own leaders had been imprisoned by military courts). Mass demonstrations continued meanwhile, with demands for trials of Mubarak and the *feloul*, for purging of the state apparatus, and for justice for martyrs of the uprising. Strikes across industry raised all manner of economic issues and pursued *tathir*—cleansing of corrupt managers and owners of enterprises, and of hostile officials of the state-run trade unions. More and more often street actions and strikes were attacked by police in moves clearly sanctioned by SCAF; largely silent, the Brotherhood in effect endorsed the new repression, while it abstained from key national demonstrations, including a symbolically important "Second Day of Rage" in May 2011 called to pursue "completion of the objectives of the 25 January Revolution".[93] When members of the Brotherhood's youth section defied the leadership, participating in large numbers in the Day of Rage, tensions in the organisation were out in the open.

The Brotherhood now suffered a series of defections. It had long been viewed, especially outside Egypt, as a monolithic bloc in which loyalist members were inculcated into obedience on the basis of religious faith and organisational loyalty. This was consistent with a wish to depict Islamist groups and parties as homogeneous, with membership whose unquestioning loyalty to a rigid leadership paralleled fascist or Stalinist models. In an analysis for *Foreign Affairs* (the journal of the US Council for

---

90: Tarek, 2011.
91: Cairo Review, 2011, p95.
92: Cairo Review, 2011, p100.
93: Ezzat, 2001.

Foreign Relations) written after the uprising of January 2011 the Ikhwan was still said to be "the unbreakable Muslim Brotherhood", in which "members dutifully execute the aims of its national leadership at the local level", enabling leaders to mobilise followers "as they see fit".[94] This was plainly wrong. In 1996 liberal critics of the leadership left to found the Wasat Party. In 2010 dissident members established a Reform Front, which demanded a more open internal structure. When the revolution began in January 2011 many members ignored the leadership—their solidarity with workmates, fellow students, neighbours, family and friends was greater than allegiance to the old men of the Brotherhood's *maktab al-irshad* or Guidance Bureau, the key decision-making body. To paraphrase Mursi, Brotherhood members had "followed the kids". During the flowering of democratic activity which followed Mubarak's fall, rank and file members were engaged in all manner of street protests, strikes and student and community initiatives. They were profoundly affected by a rise in collective confidence across the whole society—disinclined to accept the authority of the old order and the SCAF, or the Guidance Bureau.

This was reflected in increasing dissidence among the organisation's youth. In March 2011 leading activists launched an online campaign to attract support for a new organisation, the Nahda (Renaissance) Party, emphasising the need for an economic programme adequate to the needs of the revolution, and for the rights of women and Christians. In March 2011 they and others organised a conference at which young members debated how they should address the mass movement. After months of increasing tension hundreds of young activists split from the organisation, establishing the Egyptian Current Party, which by November 2011 claimed several thousand members committed to the interests of the mass movement and to further radical change.[95] Reacting violently to the dissidents, the Brotherhood's Supreme Guide[96] Mohamed Badie said that no member of the organisation would be permitted to join any party other than its newly established Freedom and Justice Party (FJP). There were soon mass expulsions from the Brotherhood, including historic leadership figures such as Mohamed Habib and Abdel-Moneim Abu el-Futouh, who later stood in the presidential election against the Brotherhood's candidate.

94: Trager, 2011, pp119 and 115.
95: *Ahram Online*, 2011a.
96: The *murshid*—guide or teacher—usually appears in English as "Supreme Guide".

Elections, parliament and the SCAF

Lorenzo Vidino argues that these splits do not suggest fragmentation, still less collapse of the Brotherhood.[97] This is correct—but without the disciplinary pressures exerted by constant repression, and under the impact of the mass movement, the organisation has been destabilised, its component elements more clearly differentiated on the basis of class affiliation. Rank and file members have been affected by the movement from below, while the Brotherhood's bourgeois elite has developed a definite strategy which exercises increased influence over the leadership—the attempt to develop an "Islamic capitalism" on the Turkish model.

Since 2002, when it won a first electoral victory in Turkey, the Justice and Development Party (Adalet ve Kalkınma Partisi—AKP) has exerted strong influence on Islamists across the Middle East. The party promotes neoliberalism with an Islamic colouring, aiming to meet the needs of corporate capital and global financial institutions on the one hand, and religious conservatives on the other. Vali Nasr comments:

> Turkey's great progress in the last decade towards capitalist growth and increasing political pluralism has not been contingent on the benevolence of authoritarian leadership on or wads of oil money. Turkey's success has followed from liberalising, free-market reforms that have unleashed the entrepreneurial energies of the same provincial, religiously conservative rising middle class that is gaining ground all around the region.[98]

Ömer Taşpınar suggests that the key explanation for Turkey's recent growth has been the party's encouragement of "an entrepreneurial Muslim bourgeoisie".[99] The AKP's "dynamic experiment", he says, offers "seminal lessons for the Arab world".[100] Attracted by its success in apparently escaping from a form of military-bureaucratic rule in Turkey that paralleled successive Egyptian regimes, key figures in the Brotherhood have attempted to emulate the AKP. According to the Turkish press, the Brotherhood has modelled the FJP on the AKP, copying the latter's policies and even its name.[101] Formed in April 2011, the FJP aims to advance the interests of local capital by developing alliances across the Middle East and especially in Turkey. In 2012 leading FJP members formed the Egyptian Business Development

---

97: Vidino 2011, p12.
98: Nasr, 2009, pp233-4.
99: Taşpınar, 2012.
100: Taşpınar, 2012.
101: Akyol, 2011.

Association (EBDA): its launch, attended by business executives from Saudi Arabia, Turkey and the US, was described as "the coming-out party for the businessmen of the Brotherhood".[102] Hansen calls the Brotherhood's business elite the "Brothers of the 1 percent"—a network of businessmen and financiers marginalised during the Mubarak era and who now intend to claim power that matches their wealth. Many are super-rich, having prospered during the era of *infitah* and the Islamic finance boom of the 1980s and 1990s, and more recently by developing trade with Turkey. Their unofficial leader is Kairat al-Shater, formerly Deputy Guide of the Brotherhood who was imprisoned by Mubarak. When his assets were seized by the former regime in 2007 he was said to have personal wealth of at least $13 million.[103]

This is the context in which the Brotherhood entered its "honeymoon" period of collaboration with SCAF. The generals sought a means of controlling the mass movement and restricting the authority of the Brotherhood. The latter's leaders intended to seize a historic opportunity to gain power and set out to secure electoral arrangements which would give the FJP its best opportunity of electoral success. SCAF agreed to quick elections, giving the Brotherhood a huge advantage over other political currents which were still struggling to establish formal parties and national networks. The quid quo pro was a Brotherhood agreement to discourage mass action: its leaders called for calm and its most loyal activists appeared on demonstrations mainly to discourage militant action. But the "honeymoon" was also a battle for power: Robert Springborg describes a "deadly struggle" between "the cobra and the mongoose" during which each struggled for advantage against a historic enemy.[104] At the same time, the energies of the mass movement caused further problems for the Brotherhood. In October 2011 a protest by Christians and radical activists in Central Cairo was savagely attacked by police; further demonstrations resulted in battles in which scores of demonstrators were killed. The Brotherhood was compelled to send its members to the streets in half-hearted efforts to support the people. Focusing on a general election, it needed popular backing. When the polls took place in November and December it won some 40 percent of votes for the lower house: an apparent triumph and vindication for the strategies of the FJP.

Millions of Egyptians voted for the FJP as the sole credible national party, rewarding it for years of opposition to Mubarak and in the hope that

---

102: Hansen, 2012.
103: Feteha, 2012.
104: Springborg, 2012.

its promises of welfare reform would meet their pressing needs. No sooner was the election complete, however, than the organisation faced a surge of impatience and anger from the mass movement. The FJP wanted a reformed capitalism, albeit with gestures towards the masses; the people wanted bread, freedom and social justice. On the anniversary of the revolution, 25 January 2012, vast crowds filled Tahrir. To the horror of Brotherhood leaders, who attended to celebrate the uprising, the people called for more change; two days later, in a further huge protest, they attacked SCAF, widely perceived as the Brotherhood's partners in power, chanting: "Down, down with the military regime" and "We want civilian, not military [government]".[105]

The cross-class character of the Brotherhood and its internal con-tradictions were being exposed more and more clearly. In April 2012 a Brotherhood delegation arrived in Washington, aiming to convince politi-cians, strategists and businessmen that they should have a role in American plans for the Middle East. Meanwhile the FJP worked intensively with the AKP to cement regional business links. In September 2012 the Turkish government promised Egypt $2 billion in aid, including a $1 billion loan—crucial to offset the huge budget deficit and to give Mursi time to arrange the IMF loan. After decades of opposition, the Brotherhood had emerged fully as champions of the market economy, eager to develop a modified neoliberal agenda that served the specific interests of their leading members. As they approached the presidential election of June 2012, however, it became clear that other political currents were also making headway.

In a climate of increasing opposition to the Brotherhood's agenda, both liberal Islamists and secular currents made rapid progress. Abdel-Moneim Abou el-Fotouh established a coalition to back his own candidacy and Hamdeen Sabahi of the Nasserist Karama Party (hitherto a marginal political force) mobilised wide support among workers, the urban middle class and the urban poor. In the first round of elections in May Sabahi gathered over 21 percent of the vote, coming first in each and every major urban centre—a profound shock for Mursi and for the SCAF's candidate Ahmed Shafiq (placed first and second respectively). This rep-resented a clear class vote, demonstrating the wish of millions of people to advance the revolution by addressing key social and economic issues. Sabahi had been active in the anti-regime movements of 2000-2010, iden-tifying him as a principled opponent of Mubarak and offering an electoral option on the left uncontaminated by the collaborations of Tagammu'. His vote would have been larger but for a boycott campaign among some

---

105: Marfleet, 2012a.

activists, especially young people who had played a key role in Tahrir and during months of confrontations with the police. Claiming that the electoral process was flawed and could not affect national politics they adopted a policy of avoidance. This reflected some of the problems facing the new left, for after decades of ballot-rigging, fraud and deception electoral strategies developed within the revolutionary Marxist tradition had been largely forgotten. Amid fierce debates about the need for electoral engagement the second round produced a narrow victory for Mursi.[106]

The Brotherhood's vote had halved since parliamentary elections six months earlier. Then the FJP received some 10.5 million votes; in the first round of the presidential elections Mursi received just 5.7 million votes. In the run-off he won a narrow victory, despite the fact that most of the Brotherhood's competitors eventually endorsed him, fearing that success for Shafiq would be taken by SCAF as a licence for frontal attacks on the mass movement. The FJP was now under suspicion as a party with interests that lay far from those of the masses: its conduct in parliament; its dishonesty regarding a presidential candidate; its business-friendly policies; its leaders' commitment to the IMF loan; its unwillingness to address the Palestine question and the issue of Gaza...multiple problems undermined its authority, so that the vote for Mursi would have been even smaller if the stakes in the presidential run-off had not been so high.

Revolution continues

Following the election Mursi enacted a surprise move, persuading SCAF to ditch its leader Field Marshal Tantawi and his closest allies in the military leadership, and to withdraw from efforts to limit civilian government powers. This was greeted with popular enthusiasm, including among those who earlier attacked Mursi as a pawn in the hands of the generals. It demonstrated that, just as the Brotherhood is not a homogenous bloc, the military elite is also differentiated and includes factions among which some are open to Mursi's approaches. It seems likely that the president induced senior officers to concede more political space to civilian government on a guarantee of support for military privileges and—not least—of non-interference in the army's huge business ventures.[107] El-Ghobashy comments that with this move the Brotherhood has finally been admitted into the

106: Sameh Naguib summarises the position of the Revolutionary Socialists in the wake of the presidential election: "We cannot under any circumstances isolate ourselves from the political and electoral battles which are coming, as this will deny us an opportunity to raise concrete and general political demands"—Naguib 2012b.
107: On Egypt's military economy see Marshall and Stacher, 2012; Marfleet, 2012b.

corridors of power as member of a dual pact between "Egypt's two largest oligarchies, civilian and military".[108]

This is a retreat for the armed forces, one which recognises the continuing energies of the revolution: it also contains a warning, however. The Muslim Brotherhood and the army appear to have reached provisional agreement on the agenda for Year Three of the revolution: a joint effort to rescue Egyptian capitalism by pursuing a modified neoliberal agenda and increasing pressure on the movement from below. In October 2012 Mursi and the Brotherhood turned on the workers' movement. They attacked striking Cairo bus drivers for committing "an act of treason": the strike, they said, was "illegal" and "criminal".[109] Officials prepared new labour laws to inhibit collective action, no doubt anticipating strong reactions to Mursi's deal with the IMF and to austerity measures certain to affect tens of millions of people. The Brotherhood and the SCAF are wary: conscious of the strengths of the mass movement, and of the cost of intervening against it directly, they are seeking ways to isolate and weaken worker militancy. It is certain that Egyptian capital in the form of the state will eventually confront the mass movement. This will involve the military elite and private capital. The two are intimately linked—although events since January 2011 demonstrate that each is differentiated internally and that competing interests may respond variously to pressures from below. The state has its weaknesses, evident in the reluctance so far of the military command to risk a conscript army in a frontal assault on the mass movement. At the same time, the movement will not advance towards further radical social change through action on the streets alone, or mainly through electoral activity or community campaigns. Sooner or later the political will of the workplaces will be tested for evidence that Egypt's workers have developed forms of organisation that express the interests of a class for itself.

For revolutionary activists there are pressing tasks in hand: to consolidate workers' organisations and to generalise their struggles; to develop organic links between workplace militants and the new left; and to challenge reformist currents—both religious and secular—which have inhibited the workers' movement. This requires more intensive engagement with those who have been under reformist influence: more unity in action and more argument which disseminates ideas about democracy from below, workers' power and the project of self-emancipation.[110]

108: El-Ghobashy, 2012.
109: *Ahram Online*, 2012f.
110: There were signs of more effective coordination in the workers' movement in

Ibrahim El-Houdaiby is a former member of the Muslim Brotherhood—an Islamist who is also a revolutionary activist. "The state of Egypt", he writes, "is entirely prejudiced towards the interests of businessmen and senior bureaucrats at the expense of the working classes... The demands of protesters are based on genuine social grievances that touch their lives on a daily basis..." What is required, he argues, is "a true revolution" that imposes the will of the majority.[111] Sustained collective action is changing the consciousness of millions of people such as Houdaiby, who are reassessing traditions dominant in Egyptian politics for generations. The key issue at stake is the political trajectory of the new militants and the impact they can make on the wider movement.

Postscript

In late November 2012 the revolution entered a further critical phase. Events were triggered by an Israeli offensive in Gaza, during which President Mursi intervened to mediate between Israel and the Hamas government. Lauded internationally—and especially in the US—for negotiating a ceasefire, in Egypt Mursi was criticised for failing to back the Palestinians and in particular for refusing to open Egypt's border with Gaza. The most senior figure in the Brotherhood, Mohamed Badie, denounced the outcome of talks and called on Muslims to undertake jihad to liberate Palestine. "The enemy knows nothing but the language of force," he said, "Be aware of the game of grand deception with which they depict peace accords".[112] This apparent rebuke to Mursi reflected increased tensions within the Islamist movement over Palestine—and general disquiet over the president's domestic policies.

In an attempt to assert his own authority and to cement an increasingly unstable organisation, Mursi raised the stakes, issuing a declaration that presidential decisions could not be overturned by any judicial authority and that Egypt's Constituent Assembly and Shura Council (upper house of parliament) would also be immune to dissolution by a judicial body—moves described as a coup and an attempt to provide the president with "pharaonic" powers. Protests nationwide attacked Mursi and the Brotherhood. Radical activists reintroduced slogans from the "18 Days" of January and February

November 2012, when Cairo Metro workers won a quick victory after striking to demand the resignation of senior management, who they accused of corruption. The government conceded after threats from rail and bus drivers to strike in solidarity with the Metro union. See *Ahram Online* 2012f.
111: El-Houdaiby, 2012.
112: Associated Press, 2012.

2011: "The people demand the fall of the regime" and "Leave", together with "[Make] a second revolution".[113] When Mursi announced an abrupt referendum on a new constitution favourable to the Islamists some 750,000 people marched to the presidential palace near Cairo and there were protests in most cities, including the key industrial centre of Mehalla al-Kubra. With its authority at stake the Brotherhood bussed supporters from all over Upper Egypt to a rally in Cairo and detachments of its members attacked anti-Mursi demonstrators.

The majority of activists now identified Mursi and the Brotherhood as obstacles to securing basic needs and political freedoms. The key target was Mursi's constitution. The Revolutionary Socialists described it as a document offensive to the mass of people—one "which doesn't specify social and economic rights, defends the detention of journalists, reopens the door to military trials of civilians, protects the interests of the military establishment, and is dedicated to the marginalisation of Egypt's oppressed women and Christians".[114] All manner of political currents were drawn to the protests, including *feloul*. Hamdeen Sabahi of the nationalist Karama Party, together with Mohamed El Baradei of the liberal Destour Party, welcomed Mubarak-era foreign minister Amr Moussa into a National Salvation Front. The left argued that protests should not embrace supporters of the old order. In Tahrir, banners read: "No place for feloul" and "Expel the feloul".[115]

The Brotherhood seemed unable to address the realities: Khairat al-Shater insisted: "We are the people, we are the majority".[116] There was a contrast, however, between the nationwide character of anti-Mursi protests and the Cairo-centred rallies organised by the Brotherhood. Mursi's most activist allies were now among Salafis and the jihadi currents; many of his more liberal supporters, drawn to the organisation in the Mubarak era, had left with earlier defections or had fallen aside as the revolutionary movement drew them to clearer understanding of their underlying interests.

On December 8 2012 Mursi cancelled his constitutional declaration. The contentious referendum would proceed, he said, under conditions that—as this journal went press—were still unclear. He also declared a range of subsidy cuts and tax increases to conform with IMF demands: within 24 hours, however, these were cancelled under pressure from key figures in the FJP.[117] The "unbreakable" Muslim Brotherhood had failed to

113: MENA-*Egypt Independent*, 2012.
114: Revolutionary Socialists, 2012.
115: *Daily News Egypt*, 2012a.
116: *Daily News Egypt*, 2012a.
117: *Ahram Online*, 2012g.

enforce its will and now struggled to present coherent policies. The mass movement entered Year Three of the revolution intact.

References

AFP, 2012, "Mursi says IMF loan compatible with Islamic banking", *Google News* (6 October), http://bit.ly/ToxXVI

Abdel-Malik, Anouar, 1968, *Egypt, Military Society: The Army Regime, the Left, and Social Change Under Nasser* (Vintage).

Agha, Hussein, and Robert Malley, 2012, "This is a Not a Revolution", *New York Review of Books* (November 8).

Agwani, M S, 1969, *Communism in the Arab East* (Asia Publishing House).

Ahram Online, 2011a, "The Egyptian Current" (18 November), http://english.ahram.org.eg/NewsContent/33/104/26701/Elections-/Political-Parties/The-Egyptian-Current.aspx

Ahram Online, 2011b, "Airport strike spotlights Egypt's economic woes" (7 October), http://english.ahram.org.eg/NewsContent/3/12/23547/Business/Economy/Airport-strike-spotlights-Egypts-economic-woes-.aspx

Ahram Online, 2012a, "Egypt's currency reserves rose $300-400m in Oct: Newspaper", *Ahram Online* , http://english.ahram.org.eg/NewsContent/3/12/56685/Business/Economy/Egypts-currency-reserves-rose-m-in-Oct-Newspaper.aspx

Ahram Online, 2012b, "Switzerland holds $753 in frozen Mubarak assets: Swiss official" (16 October), http://english.ahram.org.eg/NewsContentPrint/3/0/55733/Business/0/Switzerland-holds-m-in-frozen-Mubarak-assets-Swiss.aspx

Ahram Online, 2012c, "Leftist Tagammu Party might support Shafiq for Egypt president" (3 June), http://english.ahram.org.eg/NewsContent/1/64/43681/Egypt/Politics-/Leftist-Tagammu-Party-might-support-Shafiq-for-Egy.aspx

Ahram Online, 2012d, "Egypt's Popular Current launches anti-IMF loan campaign" (3 November), http://english.ahram.org.eg/NewsContent/1/64/57034/Egypt/Politics-/Egypts-Popular-Current-launches-antiIMF-loan-campa.aspx

Ahram Online, 2012e, "Turkey to grant Egyptian entrepreneurs 5-year entry visas" (15 October), http://english.ahram.org.eg/NewsContent/3/12/55679/Business/Economy/Turkey-to-grant-Egyptian-entrepreneurs-year-entry-.aspx

Ahram Online, 2012f, "Cairo metro workers suspend strike following victory" (14 November), http://english.ahram.org.eg/NewsContent/1/64/58047/Egypt/Politics-/UPDATED-Metro-workers-suspend-strike-following-vic.aspx

Ahram Online, 2012g, "Egypt president Morsi halts tax hikes, calls for dialogue" (10 December), http://english.ahram.org.eg/NewsContent/3/12/60166/Business/Economy/Egypt-president-Morsi-halts-tax-hikes,-calls-for-d.aspx

Akyol, Mustafa, 2011, "Egypt's 'AKP' on its way?", *Hurriyet* (16 August), www.hurriyetdailynews.com/default.aspx?pageid=438&n=egypt8217s-8216akp8217-on-its-way-2011-08-16

Alabass, Bassem, 2012, "Piety versus expediency: Egypt Islamists change tack on IMF loan", *Ahram Online* (28 August), http://english.ahram.org.eg/NewsContent/3/0/51412/Business/0/Piety-versus-expediency-Egypt-Islamists-change-tac.aspx

Al-Ahram Weekly, 1995, "The organiser" (2-8 November).

Alexander, Anne, 2011, "The Growing Social Soul of Egypt's Democratic Revolution", *International Socialism* 131 (spring), www.isj.org.uk/?id=741

Alexander, Anne, 2012, "The Egyptian workers' movement and the 25 January Revolution", *International Socialism* 133 (winter), www.isj.org.uk/?id=778

Ali, Mostafa, 2011, "Egypt teachers strike for the first time since 1951", *Ahram Online* (19 September), http://english.ahram.org.eg/NewsContent/1/64/21568/Egypt/Politics-/Egypt-teachers-strike-for-the-first-time-since-.aspx

Al Masry Al Youm, 2012a, "Long lines, protests and fights as fuel shortage continues" (23 July), www.egyptindependent.com/news/long-lines-protests-and-fights-fuel-shortage-continues

Al Masry Al Youm, 2012b, "Day before 25 January, Morsy derided protestor organizers as 'kids', says activist" (4 November), www.egyptindependent.com/node/1219541

Associated Press, 2012, "Day after president brokered Gaza truce, Egypt's Brotherhood leader slams peace with Israel", *Washington Post* (22 November), http://wapo.st/ToykQ4

Badawy, Nada, 2012, "With loans, a flood of Turkish business", *Al Masry Al Youm* (8 October), www.egyptindependent.com/news/loans-flood-turkish-business

Baker, R W, 1978, *Egypt's Uncertain Revolution Under Nasser and Sadat* (Harvard University Press).

Beinin, Joel, 2009, "Workers' Struggles under 'Socialism' and Neoliberalism", in El-Mahdi and Marfleet, 2009.

Benhabib, Seyla, 2012, "Constructing the Self, Constructing the Other", *Jadaliyya* (31 August), www.jadaliyya.com/pages/index/7145/constructing-the-self-constructing-the-other

Brysk, Alison (ed), 2002, *Globalisation and Human Rights* (University of California Press).

Bush, Ray, 2009, "The Land and the People", in El-Mahdi and Marfleet, 2009.

Byman, Daniel, 2011, "After the hope of the Arab Spring, the chill of an Arab Winter", *Washington Post* (2 December), http://wapo.st/ToyCGJ

Cairo Review, 2011, "Rise of the Muslim Brothers" (interview with Essam el-Erian), *Cairo Review* volume 1 (spring).

Charbel, Jano, 2012, "Independent unions declare new alliance", *Al Masry Al Youm* (15 October), www.egyptindependent.com/news/independent-unions-declare-new-alliance

Daley, Janet, 2006, "'Fascistic' is the right word for Islamic fundamentalism", *Daily Telegraph* (14 August), www.telegraph.co.uk/comment/personal-view/3627116/Fascistic-is-the-right-word-for-Islamic-fundamentalism.html

Comrades from Cairo, 2012, "We Refuse Economic Bondage—Stop the Loans", *Jadaliyya* (31 October), www.jadaliyya.com/pages/index/8100/statement-by-comrades-from-cairo_we-refuse-economi

Daily News Egypt, 2012a, "El-Hamalawy: "Morsy has failed even in the simple bread and butter issues" (28 November), http://dailynewsegypt.com/2012/11/28/hossam-el-hamalawy-morsy-has-even-failed-in-the-simple-bread-and-butter-issues/

Daily News Egypt, 2012b, "Al-Shater: 'We are the people, we are the majority'" (8 December), http://dailynewsegypt.com/2012/12/08/al-shater-we-are-the-people-we-are-the-majority/

Detrie, Megan, 2012, "US drought means Egypt may look elsewhere for wheat", *Al Masry Al Youm* (27 July), www.egyptindependent.com/news/us-drought-means-egypt-may-look-elsewhere-wheat

El-Ghobashy, Mona, 2012, "Egyptian Politics Upended", *Middle East Research and Information Project* (20 August), www.merip.org/mero/mero082012

El Hennawy, Noha, 2011, "Political freedom, competition drives rifts between Muslim Brotherhood factions", *Al Masry Al Youm* (24 March), www.egyptindependent.com/node/372967

El-Houdaiby, Ibrahim, 2012, "Mubarak's class biases remain in place", *Ahram Online* (5 October), http://english.ahram.org.eg/NewsContentP/4/54854/Opinion/Mubarak%E2%80%99s-class-biases-remain-in-place--.aspx

El Mahdi, Rabab, 2009, "The Democracy Movement", in El-Mahdi and Marfleet, 2009.

El-Mahdi, Rabab, and Philip Marfleet (eds), 2009, *Egypt—the moment of change* (Zed).

Elmeshad, Mohamed, 2012, "Advocacy group rejects government's IMF-pleasing reform plan", *Al Masry Al Youm* (22 March), www.egyptindependent.com/news/advocacy-group-rejects-government%E2%80%99s-imf-pleasing-reform-plan

Elyan, Tamim, 2011, "MB says to participate 'symbolically' in Jan 25 demos", *Daily News* (23 January), www.masress.com/en/dailynews/127072

Ezzat, Dina, 2011, "Egypt's Muslim Brotherhood battles against its youth", *Ahram Online* (28 May), http://english.ahram.org.eg/News/13148.aspx

Fahmy, Heba, 2011, "Muslim Brotherhood reconsiders refusal to participate in Jan 25 demo", *Daily News* (20 January).

FAO, 2012, *GIEWS Country Briefs—Egypt*, www.fao.org/giews/countrybrief/country.jsp?code=EGY

Fetaha, Ahmet, 2012, "Muslims Inc: How rich is Khairat El-Shater?", *Ahram Online* (3 April), http://english.ahram.org.eg/News/38278.aspx

Gause, F Gregory, 2011, "Why Middle East Studies missed the Arab Spring", *Foreign Affairs* (July/August).

Greene, Richard Allen, 2006, "Bush's language angers US Muslims", *BBC News* (12 August), http://news.bbc.co.uk/1/hi/world/americas/4785065.stm

Haddad, Amira, 2012, "Egyptian Pound Falls to 7-Year Low", http://english.nuqudy.com/North_Africa/Egyptian_Pound_Fall-3091

Hansen, Suzy, 2012, "The Economic Vision of Egypt's Muslim Brotherhood Millionaires", *Business Week* (19 April).

Harman, Chris, 1994, "The Prophet and the Proletariat", *International Socialism Journal 64* (autumn), www.marxists.org/archive/harman/1994/xx/islam.htm

Hitchens, Christopher, 2007, "Defending Islamofascism: It's a valid term. Here's why", *Slate* (22 October) www.slate.com/articles/news_and_politics/fighting_words/2007/10/defending_islamofascism.html

Hussein, Mahmoud, 2012, "Egypt's bread: Mursi kneads life into subsidised staple", *Ahram Online* (8 October), http://english.ahram.org.eg/NewsContent/1/140/54982/Egypt/First--days/Egypts-bread-Mursi-kneads-life-into-subsidised-sta.aspx

Hyde, Maggie, 2012a, "A new loaf: Will Egypt tighten bread subsidies?" *Al Masry Al Youm* (17 October), www.egyptindependent.com/news/new-loaf-will-egypt-tighten-bread-subsidies

Hyde, Maggie, 2012b, "Serious govt action needed on economy, experts say", *Al Masry Al Youm* (10 October), www.egyptindependent.com/news/serious-govt-action-needed-economy-experts-say

Hussein, A, R al-Said and M al-Sayyid, 1999, "Twenty Years of Multipartyism in Egypt", in Mark Kennedy (ed), *Twenty Years of Development in Egypt* (The American University in Cairo Press).

Hyde, Maggie, 2012c, "Egypt makes top 10 list of countries not likely to pay back debt", *Al Masry Al Youm* (22 October), www.egyptindependent.com/news/egypt-makes-top-10-list-countries-not-likely-pay-back-debt

Jadaliyya, 2011, National Progressive Unionist (Tagammu) Party, www.jadaliyya.com/pages/ index/3157/national-progressive-unionist-(tagammu)-party

Judt, Tony, 2006, "Bush's Useful Idiots", *London Review of Books* (18 September).

Kalin, Stephen, 2012, "In anti-IMF march, austerity fears and economic disillusion", *Al Masry Al-Youm*, 13 November, www.egyptindependent.com/news/anti-imf-march-austerity-fears-and-economic-disillusion

Kaye, Dalia, and Frederic Wehrey, 2011, "Arab Spring, Persian Winter", *Foreign Affairs* (July/ August).

Keddie, Nikki, 1972, *Sayyid Jamal al-Din "al-Afghani": A Political Biography*, (University of California Press)

Lewis, Bernard, 1990, "The Roots of Muslim rage", *Atlantic* (September), www.theatlantic.com/ magazine/archive/1990/09/the-roots-of-muslim-rage/304643/

Le Monde, 2012, "Marine Le Pen: 'Je mets à la porte tous les intégristes étrangers'", *Le Monde* (29 September).

Marfleet, Philip, 2006, *Refugees in a Global Era* (Palgrave).

Marfleet, Phiipl, 2009, "State and Society", in El-Mahdi and Marfleet, 2009.

Marfleet, Philip, 2012a, "The Generals, the Islamists and the Egyptian Revolution", *Socialist Review* (February), www.socialistreview.org.uk/article.php?articlenumber=11901

Marfleet, Philip, 2012b, "Never 'One Hand'", in Mike Gonzalez and Houman Barekat (eds), *Arms and the People* (Pluto).

Marshall, Shana, and Joshua Stacher, 2012, "Egypt's Generals and Transnational Capital", *Middle East Research and Information Project*, 262.

Marroushi, Nadine, and Alaa Shahin, 2012, "Egyptians Hunt Cheap Fuel as Mursi Seeks to End Shortage", *Independent* (25 October), www.independent.co.uk/news/world/middle-east/egyptians-hunt-cheap-fuel-as-mursi-seeks-to-end-shortage-8225699.html

Meijer, Roel, 2002, *The Quest for Modernity: Secular Liberal and Left-Wing Political Thought in Egypt, 1945-1958* (Routledge Curzon).

Mekhennet,Souad, and Nicolas Kulish, 2011, "With Muslim Brotherhood Set to Join Egypt Protests, Religion's Role May Grow", *New York Times* (26 January).

MENA-Egypt Independent, 2012, "Update: Thousands converge on Tahrir; political leaders pledge to join sit-in", *Al-Masry Al-Youm* (30 November), www.egyptindependent.com/ news/update-thousands-converge-tahrir-political-leaders-pledge-join-sit

Mitchell, Richard, P, 1969, *The Society of the Muslim Brothers* (Oxford University Press).

Mitnick, Joshua, 2011, "Egyptian Elections Stir Disquiet in Israel", *Christian Science Monitor* (28 November), www.csmonitor.com/World/Middle-East/2011/1129/Egyptian-elections-stir-disquiet-in-Israel

Momani, Bessma, 2005, *IMF-Egyptian Debt Negotiations* (American University in Cairo Press).

Mourad, Sarah, and Ahmed Feteha, 2012, "IMF's Lagarde concludes Egypt visit amid modest protests", *Ahram Online* (22 August), http://english.ahram.org.eg/ NewsContent/3/12/51011/Business/Economy/IMFs-Lagarde-concludes-Egypt-visit-amid-modest-pro.aspx

Muslim Brotherhood, 2011, "FJP 2011 Programme on Social Justice", *Ikhwanweb*, www.ikhwanweb.com/article.php?id=29300

Naguib, Sameh, 2009, "Islamism(s) old and new", in El-Mahdi and Marfleet,2009.

Naguib, Sameh, 2012a, "Sectarianism in Egypt one year on from the Maspero massacre", *Socialist Worker* (13 October), www.socialistworker.co.uk/art.php?id=29733

Naguib, Sameh, 2012b, "Getting Egypt's Second Revolution", (18 October), http://revsoc.me 17335

Nasr, Vali, 2009, *The Rise of Islamic Capitalism* (Free Press).

Pipes, Daniel, 2006a, "At war with Islamic fascists", *Daniel Pipes Middle East Forum* (14 August), www.danielpipes.org/3848/at-war-with-islamic-fascists

Pipes, Daniel, 2006b, "More on the term Islamic fascists", *Daniel Pipes Middle East Forum* (14 August), www.danielpipes.org/blog/2006/08/more-on-the-term-islamic-fascists

Reddy, Sudeep, and Matt Bradley, 2012, "IMF's Egypt Loan Is Mideast Test Case", *Wall Street Journal* (15 October).

Revolutionary Socialists, 2012, "You shall not pass your constitution" (4 December), http://internationalsocialists.org/wordpress/2012/12/statement-of-the-revolutionary-socialists-egypt-you-shall-not-pass-your-constitution/

Samhouri, Mohammed, 2012, "Egypt's Looming Financial Crisis", *Sada* (5 June), www.carnegieendowment.org/sada/2012/06/05/egypt-s-looming-fiscal-crisis/b4jc

Shadid, Anthony, 2011, "Suez Canal workers join broad strikes in Egypt", *New York Times* (17 February).

Shenker, Jack, 2012, "Scandal of Mubarak regime millions in UK", *Guardian* (2 September), www.guardian.co.uk/world/2012/sep/02/scandal-mubarak-regime-millions-assets-uk

Shukrallah, Hani, 2012a, "Good morning revolution: A to do list", *Ahram Online* (12 February), http://english.ahram.org.eg/NewsContentP/4/5434/Opinion/Good-morning-revolution-A-to-do-list.aspx

Shukrallah, Hani, 2012b, "The Brotherhood and I", *Ahram Online* (18 October), http://english.ahram.org.eg/NewsContentP/4/55725/Opinion/The-Brotherhood-and-I.aspx

Sneh, Ephraim, 2012, "Containing the Islamist Revolution", *Foreign Policy* (28 June), www.foreignpolicy.com/articles/2012/06/28/the_islamist_revolution

Springborg, Robert, 2012, "Egypt's cobra and mongoose", *Foreign Policy* (27 February), http://mideast.foreignpolicy.com/posts/2012/02/27/egypt_s_cobra_and_mongoose

Tagammu', 2011, "The National Progressive Unionist Party [Hizb al-Tagammu']: Who are We?", *Tahrir Documents* www.tahrirdocuments.org/2011/08/the-national-progressive-union-party-hizb-al-tagammu-who-are-we/

Tarek, Sherif, 2011, "Egypt's Muslim Brotherhood and ruling military: Deal or no deal?" *Ahram Online* (28 September), http://english.ahram.org.eg/NewsContent/1/64/22042/Egypt/Politics-/Egypts-Muslim-Brotherhood-and-ruling-military-Deal.aspx

Taşpınar, Ömer, 2012, *Turkey: The New Model?* (Brookings Institution), www.brookings.edu/research/papers/2012/04/24-turkey-new-model-taspinar

Trager, Eric, 2011, "The Unbreakable Muslim Brotherhood", *Foreign Affairs* (September/October).

Vidino, Lorenzo, 2011, *Lessons Learned: Post-Mubarak developments within the Egyptian Muslim Brotherhood* (Arts and Humanities Research Council).

Wroughton, Lesley, 2012, "Key IMF Loan Talks Begin in Cairo, Reducing Budget Deficit is Focus", *Chicago Tribune* (30 October), www.reuters.com/article/2012/10/30/us-imf-egypt-idUSBRE89T09X20121030

Marikana: A View from the Mountain and a Case to Answer

Peter Alexander, Thapelo Lekowa, Botsang Mmope, Luke Sinwell and Bongani Xezwi

£7.99

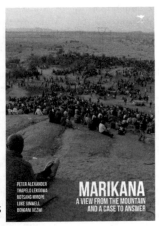

On 16 August 2012 near Marikana, South Africa, striking miners from the Lonmin company were fired on by police, resulting in 34 deaths. The heart of this book is a series of interviews with strikers, most of them recorded on "the mountain" close to where their comrades were killed.

"The book provides a bottom-up account of the Marikana story, to correct an imbalance in many official and media accounts that privilege the viewpoints of governments and business, at the expense of workers." Professor Jane Duncan, chair of Media and Information Studies at Rhodes University

"Well written, extremely scrupulous in its research and forceful in its argument." Professor John Saul, Canadian political scientist, one of the world's top experts on liberation struggle in Southern Africa

Available now direct from Bookmarks Publications; coming soon to bookshops nationwide.

BOOKMARKS
PUBLICATIONS

Bookmarks the socialist bookshop
1 Bloomsbury Street, London WC1B 3QE
020 7637 1848 www.bookmarksbookshop.co.uk
publications@bookmarks.uk.com

Latin America: the tide is turning

Mike Gonzalez

As 2012 nears its end a pattern is emerging in the political and economic picture of Latin America. It is surprising and contradictory, a dramatic example of the gulf that can open up between rhetoric and reality. After a decade of struggles characterised by their determination, their militancy but also their creativity, this is probably not where we expected to be. Those movements that successfully defied the priorities and strategies of neoliberalism, and inspired a resistance to globalisation that stretched beyond the southern hemisphere, carried into power governments and leaders who spoke their language, assumed their gestures and aspirations, and promised fervently to act on their behalf from the presidential palaces they had now come to occupy. These, after all, were the "new left governments" of Venezuela, Bolivia, Ecuador, Uruguay and Argentina, defined by their critique of globalisation and their refusal to dance to the tune of US imperialism in the way that the governments of Colombia, Peru and Mexico still did. They wore the multi-coloured and multicultural mantle of the movements and supported new constitutions that acknowledged and celebrated the diversity of the peoples of Latin America. The new parliaments were living embodiments of that diversity, in contrast to those of the previous decade, dominated largely by the white male representatives of the old ruling classes.

After a decade of impoverishment and despair, these new administrations echoed one another in their undertaking to reintroduce welfare measures that would hoist the majority out of their extreme poverty.

Education and health would be made available to all, while social programmes across the board would shield the mass of the people from the worst depredations of the global market. The funding for these programmes would come from a determined renegotiation of the terms of trade. The multinationals that had profited from the region's oil, gas and minerals in extraordinarily favourable tax regimes would now have to pay far higher taxes, and those higher returns would fund the new welfare provisions. The model here, of course, was Venezuela, where a range of social programmes had been funded by a renationalisation of the oil industry.

So what is this growing disjuncture between promise and reality? Rafael Correa, elected to the presidency of Ecuador in 2007 and recently adopted as the presidential candidate for forthcoming elections early next year, identified himself with the sustained indigenous and civic resistance of the previous two decades. It had successfully mobilised against three presidents who had failed to honour their anti-neoliberal assurances, the last of whom, Lucio Gutiérrez, had emerged as the candidate of the resistance, until he too reneged on all his undertakings. Correa's refusal to renew the agreement with the US that allowed them to maintain the air base at Manta was well received. And he confronted the more recalcitrant sectors of the bourgeoisie, based largely in Guayaquil, and pushed through a new constitution against an obstinate right in parliament. The slightly obscure circumstances of the attempted coup against him in 2010, led by opposition forces in the police, allowed him to win even greater credibility with a well-publicised act of defiance. Yet in the face of key environmental demands from the indigenous movements, based on the concept of *sawak karsay* (the good life), and in defiance of the undertaking to nationalise Ecuador's oil industry, Correa has turned against the communities fighting for control of water and land, and for regulation of oil and mining, criminalising their resistance and jailing their leaders, many of whom are currently in detention as we write (in November 2012).

The current map of the oil-bearing Amazonian provinces of the country reveals that the entire area has been divided into concessions to national and multinational companies despite massive collective resistance. Only one area remains unallocated. The Yasuni National Park is an area of extraordinary biodiversity sitting on top of an immense oil field. An international campaign moved Correa to offer foreign governments and enterprises the opportunity to finance alternative forms of production that would preserve the region from drilling. It was clever public relations, and until 2009 it seemed possible that Spain and Germany might be willing to contribute; but the sums offered never reached the required levels, and the financial crisis ensured the withdrawal of the original offers. The Hollywood billionaires, led by James Cameron, moved in—but even if the area is protected, the contamination that results from the surrounding concessions, plus the pollution in a previous period by Chevron-Texaco, has already irredeemably compromised the area. In any event, Correa has already received a $3 billion loan from a Chinese government heavily involved in mining operations in the country.

In Bolivia the TIPNIS events have exposed the profound contra-dictions unfolding there.[1] The TIPNIS National Park and Indigenous Territory in the eastern province of Beni is a protected conservation area occupied by small farmers growing a variety of crops. The decision to run a 450 kilometre highway through the park met with the organised resist-ance of local farmers and communities—the very people who had fought for and sustained the government of Evo Morales in the face of the bitter and violent hostility of the Media Luna, the vested interests controlling the prosperous eastern regions of the country. In one sense this appeared to be a battle about conservation—an issue on which Morales had taken a particularly defiant stance in echoing the centrality of the protection of Pachamama (Mother Earth) in the programmes of his government. His speech at the Copenhagen Climate Conference (ignored and silenced by its organisers), and repeated at this year's Cochabamba meeting, was a model defence of environmental conservation as an issue of social and economic justice. Later, however, Morales defended the necessity of the TIPNIS highway as an instrument of progress and development.

Yet its beneficiaries would not be the farming communities of the region; on the contrary, the development of the local economy would be the casualty of a project whose profits would be reaped by the massive, mainly Brazilian, soya producers and the multinational oil and mining companies for whom the road provided the means to carry their goods to Brazilian ports for export to the wider world. The result, of course, would be the elimination of agricultural production for local consumption in favour of the expansion of export agriculture. The protest march that left the region for a six-week march to the capital, La Paz, was met by police who attempted to repress the march with considerable violence. The minister of defence resigned in disgust at their actions. It was not the first time this had happened, but this time the marchers were rescued and sub-sequently joined by other local supporters and Morales backed down. For Alvaro García Linera, the vice-president and the ideological power behind

---

1:    See Webber, 2012.

Morales, this confrontation was a struggle against modernity, particularism set against the general good represented by Evo Morales himself.[2] In what he describes as the fifth phase of the democratic revolution, Linera declares the defeat of neoliberalism and the dissolution of state into society.

For those who made the movement that carried Morales to power, the impression is very different. The demonstrations against the increase in the price of gas late in 2011 and the protests over the limitations placed on wage increases were evidence of a contradiction in the Bolivian process that was very different from the "creative contradictions" that Linera discusses. It represented rather what Jeff Webber describes as "revolutionary containment", and defines a new period in which the mass movements in all the countries that declared themselves the representatives of a new "21st century socialism" now appear to be moving rapidly away from the revolutionary purposes of the early part of the decade.

The mass social movements of the early part of the decade were often unclear in their strategic objectives, but they shared common demands that identified the enemy. Neoliberalism, or the reorganisation of global capitalism, meant specifically for Latin America the removal of tariff barriers, which in some cases (Mexico, for example) had protected national capital. The World Trade Organisation's regulations made it illegal for nation-states to protect their own production or indeed to subsidise local producers—these represented, in the parlance of neoliberalism, "obstacles to free trade". Trade unions, and the collective agreements fought for and won by the better organised groups of workers, were clear examples of interference with the free movement of capital and its right to impose cheap labour regimes wherever it operated. Finance capital, too, could now move unimpeded—as was evident in the early 1990s in Mexico when the insurance and financial markets were simply appropriated by the big US players. Export agriculture, moved by the Monsantos and the other giants of world food production swept aside the small-scale agriculture which had sheltered for a while under the umbrella of state subsidy. One immediate result was the Zapatista rising in Chiapas, where a poor peasantry growing its own maize, the staple of the rural diet, now found itself exposed to the competition of the huge maize growing companies of the southern US that could produce their corn at a fraction of the cost of maize grown on small plots and swamp the Mexican market under the new neoliberal rules of the market.

Against the deregulation and privatisation of the region's principal resources, the movements demanded nationalisation. Against the

---

2:   See García Linera, 2011.

destruction of the public sector, such as it was, they fought for the public provision of services like health and education and appropriate subsidies to protect small producers against the land-grabbing giants. The public aversion to the impunity that allowed the torturers of the 1970s and 1980s to escape punishment demanded social justice. Faced with the arrant destruction of the physical landscape by giant oil and mining companies, the defence of Pachamama translated global environmentalist concerns into the language of indigenous tradition. And as the era was marked by resurgent indigenous resistance, the claim to cultural recognition and protection as of right occupied an increasingly central place. All of these rights would be enshrined in the new constitutions passed by delegate assemblies. The framing concept would be an anti-imperialism directed against Washington and the interests it had always protected. And the guarantee of the struggle to achieve these demands would be democratic control, the extension to society as a whole of the organisational methods that had developed within the movements in the course of their struggles.

If democratic control was a common objective of the resistance, however, there was no agreement about the meaning of nationalisation, no suggestion that the expropriation of capital or workers' control of production would be its end point. In James Petras's words, they sought a break with neoliberalism, but not with capitalism itself.[3] Thus nationalisation in Bolivia proved to fall far short of the level of state control of the oil industry that Venezuela had achieved with the nationalisation of PDVSA. Rather it was a renegotiation of contracts and royalties to provide the state with higher tax revenues. The same occurred in Ecuador. And in Venezuela, the leading edge of Latin America's "21st century socialism", the oil corporation in fact shares a range of joint operations, particularly in the Orinoco Basin, with multinationals like Haliburton and Chevron, whose names were anathema to the social movements.

Yet the language of anti-imperialism remains the lingua franca of the new Latin American governments of the left. Hugo Chavez and the other leaders have been strident in their hostility to the US, to its war in the Middle East and to its resurgent interventions in Latin American affairs.[4] The ubiquitous Chinese capital, the growing involvement of Russia and Iran, by contrast, seem not to have produced any major concerns, even

3: Petras, 2010.
4: The blatant involvement of Hillary Clinton and the US State Department in the ejection of President Zelaya of Honduras and his replacement by a pliant pro-Washington regime should be seen as a first response to the question posed by Obama during his election campaign in 2008——"Are we losing Latin America?"

though that investment has been concentrated in the extractive sectors—
oil, gas, minerals—and the export agriculture whose dominance more or
less defined the neoliberal relationship.

Far from diversifying their productive structures and reorganising
their economies to fulfil the needs of the majority of the population,
these ostensibly new governments are leading their countries back into
an unequal exchange with global capital.[The new economic projects
are clearly based on oil and mineral extraction on the one hand and an
export agriculture focusing on soya, maize for bio-ethanol, sugar and palm
oil on the other.] The multinationals that dominate these industries may
be Canadian, Chinese, Russian, European or Indian as opposed to the
US based enterprises which controlled the bulk of these activities in the
past. The finance may now come from banks in China or Russia. But the
relationship and its dynamic remain the accumulation of a surplus for the
powerful centres of global capitalism—and the new regimes have become
their collaborators.[5] The logic of mass movements of the early part of the
decade—the logic of mass democracy, people's power, workers' control,
redistribution and care for the environment—are giving way once again, it
seems, to a capitalist imperative. And if national states which surrendered
control over their individual economies to the mechanisms of the global
market have now been rebuilt under new management and with majority
support, to what extent can they be said to have won greater control?

Each of these new regimes emerged from mass struggles and came
to power claiming to represent them. Yet they are now increasingly
in conflict with their social base, and more significantly the economic
project which each is pursuing is clearly now emerging as a return to the
relationship with the world market—on renegotiated terms—in which
its resources are appropriated by global capital in exchange for goods and
services manufactured elsewhere.

Actors on a mobile stage

The *Caracazo*, the uprising in the poor barrios of Caracas and other cities
on 27 February 1989, marked the beginning of a new stage of struggle and
resistance in Latin America. It was an explicit reaction to the announcement
by the recently elected president Carlos Andrés Pérez that he was imposing
the "structural adjustment" programme demanded by the IMF. The reaction was doubly powerful because he stood for election on a promise to resist
those measures—although the bipartisan agreements (*puntofijismo*) that had

5:    See, for example, Webber, 2011, p234.

dominated Venezuelan politics since the late 1950s left little doubt as to whose interests would prevail. But the *Caracazo* was more than a spontaneous outburst of public rage. Radical groups had long been organising in the poor barrios, and they included urban cells which had worked together with the rural guerrillas through the 1960s and 1970s, as well as liberation theologians and others. Against the background of international events in 1989, the eruption on to the historical stage of the urban poor was interpreted by many as a sign that a new historical actor was emerging. The "new social movements" certainly did mobilise sections of the population that were largely excluded from the traditional organisations of the left. They did not appear from nowhere, of course, but they became more visible and more central for reasons that were both subjective and objective. Objective, insofar as working class organisation was affected by the mass unemployment that the globalisation of the 1990s would bring; subjective in that the disorientation of much of the left with the collapse of the Soviet bloc left a vacuum of political leadership that was filled by ideas that generalised from the experience of the movements rather than engaging with them in any new strategic thinking.

The same was happening elsewhere. In Argentina in 1990 the recently elected Peronist President Carlos Menem oversaw a kind of car boot sale of the whole public sector, which netted him and other cronies millions in speculative profit while providing multinationals like Spain's Telefónica with highly lucrative enterprises at bargain prices. The state sector of the economy was eliminated overnight.

In Venezuela itself, the various shock measures imposed in the aftermath of the *Caracazo* drove down the living standards of the majority of the population dramatically. By 1998, 65 percent of Venezuelans were living in extreme poverty—some 40 percent more than on the eve of the 1989 risings. The grassroots resistance did not end, however, with the repression of the *Caracazo* and the death of some 3,000 of its activists; regular and persistent mobilisations around economic and social demands continued. In February 1992, an attempted coup led by Parachute Regiment colonel Hugo Chávez lasted just 24 hours. Chávez was arrested but was allowed to appear on television to appeal to his supporters to abandon the action. The veiled promise that it was not over—only "*por ahora*" (for now)—became a watchword and, in the way of such things, it was taken up enthusiastically by graffiti artists across the country. As a result Chávez came to symbolise the continuing resistance—though the second coup attempt, in November that year, with Chávez still in prison, involved far more actual fighting.

Yet the legend of Chávez and the February coup conceals a more significant fact. His political mentors included Douglas Bravo, the unswerving leader of Venezuela's guerrilla struggle who was also extremely influential in the urban and rural movements. It had been agreed with Chávez that the February coup would be a coordinated action of the military and the civic movements; the phrase that has come to be identified with Chávez's political strategy—the "civic-military alliance"—comes directly from Bravo. The conditions were promising—an Assembly of the Barrios that year demonstrated that the resistance was widespread. Yet when February came Chávez did not issue a general call and instead restricted the movement to dissident officers. As the economic measures fell increasingly heavily on the poor, and the consensus of bourgeois parties continued to use the state to protect its narrow interests, it was particularly ironic that the package of neoliberal measures should be imposed by Teodoro Petkoff, once a guerrilla fighter.

In Mexico the EZLN—the Zapatista National Liberation Army—erupted on to the world's front pages with its attack on San Cristóbal de las Casas, the state capital of Chiapas, and other small towns, on 1 January 1994. The action was timed to coincide with the press conference at which the presidents of Mexico, Canada and the US were to announce the launch of NAFTA (the North American Free Trade Area). The contrast between the sharp suits and elegant surroundings of the presidential meeting and the barefoot indigenous fighters of Chiapas, their faces concealed by balaclavas, expressed with dramatic clarity the reality of neoliberalism. The powerful would benefit from globalisation, while the victims would be the poor of the earth, who would bear its high costs. And this was the message articulated by the charismatic Zapatista leader, the ex-Maoist Sub-Comandante Marcos, in his lengthy dispatches from the Lacandon forest. The Zapatista slogans were eagerly taken up in Europe and the US; it would take longer for them to find their echo among those in struggle in Latin America. Yet they did come to define a unifying discourse for the resistance. It was the Zapatistas, for example, who called for a meeting of the Latin American resistance at a great social forum first realised in Porto Alegre, Brazil, in 2001. The forum expressed the growing movement against globalisation—or, in its Spanish term, for an *alternative* globalisation. But it also reflected the experience of the civic resistance in several other important and complex ways

It was a key feature of globalisation that world trade was largely conducted between the major powers. Latin America's role was as a supplier of raw materials—oil, minerals—and the products of export agriculture like maize, soya, palm oil, flowers and fruit. Increasingly these industries were dominated by transnational corporations whose enormous profits were accumulated in the north, fuelling economic activity there. Starbucks coffee came largely from Latin America, yet it was consumed in the cities of Europe and

North America. The gas and oil of Venezuela, Bolivia, Mexico and Ecuador fuelled cars across the world, and were largely owned by multinational corporations based mainly (but not exclusively) in the US. Under the rules of the World Trade Organisation, for example, it was an offence—a restraint of trade—to refuse to export your resources. When Bolivia refused to sell its gas to California, the state of California sued it. It would do the same again when British Columbia refused to sell its water to it. Public sector companies were privatised in a kind of frenzy. Venezuela's national oil company PDVSA was supposedly nationalised in the mid-1990s; in fact it was a sleight of hand that allowed the company to operate wholly independently of the Venezuelan state in collusion with the oil multinationals.

In real terms, across Latin America the state withdrew from all forms of welfare provision, subsidy or control over key sectors of the economy. Instead it became an agent of multinational capital with the additional task of social repression and control. The impacts across the continent were catastrophic for the majority—while those acting on behalf of international capital enjoyed unprecedented boom years oiled by corruption and rampant speculation; the bonanza under Menem in 1990 was just one example.

The transformation of agriculture, an often violent process of expulsion and persecution, drove millions towards the exploding slums around the major cities like Sao Paulo, Rio, Mexico City and Caracas. It was a process that had begun much earlier, in a previous phase of agricultural change, but it was accelerated and intensified in the framework of neoliberal globalisation. The mass education programmes characteristic of the 1960s and 1970s in most of the continent were marketised and privatised. The closure of industries under the impact of free cross-border trade deepened unemployment as millions moved into the precarious realm of street trading and hawking and its associated drug trafficking. The *maquiladoras* or assembly plants along the Mexican US border exemplified the appalling conditions under which Latin American workers survived without the protection of the trade unions that had grown up through previous decades.

In these circumstances, the NGOs came to occupy a key role—at once practical and ideological. The withdrawal of the state from every area of social provision meant a life lived on the edge of catastrophe for millions. Its place was taken by non-governmental organisations largely financed by international agencies and major charities. The political and organisational crisis of the trade unions was a consequence of objective transformations; the working class as a collective presence faded from view, and the new urban populations, fighting for their very survival, had no collective memory to turn to. This was also true of the indigenous organisations that re-emerged with renewed impetus in the decade of the 1990s. The discrimination and persecution to which they were subject were nothing new, but reached new levels in this decade as global capital intensified its search for the oil, gas, water and minerals which often lay in the ancestral territories of indigenous communities. At the same time, the white urban elites who ran the state on behalf of their multinational masters were imbued with a racism that, in the Andean republics and in Central America, was explicit and virulent. The left, for its part, had rarely succeeded in building links between workers' struggles and the struggles of indigenous peoples or the burgeoning marginalised populations of the cities. The resurgent indigenous struggles found their reference points in ancient pre-Hispanic identities, or in cultural difference and separation, and held to them even when they were forced to migrate to vast barrios like El Alto, the wholly indigenous city high above Bolivia's capital, La Paz.

It seemed that a new political subject was now driving the resistance across the continent. The "new social movements" coalesced around single issue campaigns and struggles, which regularly brought them into confrontation with the state. They were struggles for the basic provision of services, for housing, for education and health. And although these movements had emerged in the course of the previous decade, their radicalisation and growing presence reflected a combination of factors—not simply immiseration but also the development of new ideas and understandings of what resistance meant and how it should be conducted. The weakening of the state, for example, removed the possibility of sustaining clientilistic relationships with elements within the state. The weakness of the left meant that the debates around agency were not informed by a Marxist understanding of the centrality of the working class. And the generalised presence of NGOs allowed new theories of resistance to emerge which emphasised specificity and fragmented the social struggles, creating international networks that addressed each area of repression, need and resistance separately. Hence the resurgence of ecological movements, the interventions around human rights and social justice, the movements of women and the rise of cooperatives particularly in the countryside.

This had a double and contradictory effect. On the one hand, it acknowledged the origins of many of these problems in a global reality—neoliberalism as a universal category became part of everyday political discourse. On the other hand, the specific conditions and histories in which this global reality was experienced were understood in entirely local or sectional terms. The dialectical relationship between the local and the global, and the factors—historical, social, cultural—which inhibited or enabled particular struggles to develop and link with others were

myopia

forgotten. The theorists[6] described the emergence of a new political subject with multiple and shifting identities—the plurality here was critical, since in the context of international political debates at the time the unifying category of class was abandoned. In the same way, the political struggle was redefined as cultural—a recognition of difference, the formation of identity, new social movements operating within civil society rather than in relation to the state. The authority of the Zapatista movement gave the pronouncements and declarations of Sub-Comandante Marcos an enormous weight across the movements. His concepts of "to lead by obeying" and "changing society without taking power" were both an affirmation and an expression *organic too indigenous movements* of the historic marginalisation of the Zapatista communities in particular and the indigenous communities in general. And they were expressions of courage and the depth of their political militancy that refused both incorporation and confrontation. Yet it was also significant how quickly the movement, characterised at the outset as anti-neoliberal, was redefined as a movement of indigenous liberation. The activities of the electoral left in Mexico, Cuauhtémoc Cárdenas's Democratic Revolutionary Party (PRD) in particular, served to emphasise and reinforce the suspicion of the Zapatistas towards the conventional parties of the left. The PRD's opportunism and its attempt to exploit the sympathy for the Zapatistas to its electoral advantage deepened the hostility between them. The result was an increasing exceptionalism that isolated the Zapatistas from their natural class allies. Nonetheless the anticapitalist impulse behind the Zapatistas resonated with the many fronts of resistance that were opening up in Latin America and elsewhere as the true brutality of the neoliberal project was unmasked and misery and despair deepened.

And then came Cochabamba.[7] The water wars in the Bolivian city of Cochabamba began as the 21st century began. The symbolic significance of the struggle of the trade unions, student groups, local unions and community organizations of this Bolivian city was immensely powerful. It represented not simply the first successful struggle against one of the emblematic multinational corporations of the age of globalisation—Bechtel—but also reflected some of the general features of the new social movements. The forms of organisation were horizontal and democratic, their defining locus territorial rather than social; and the organised left was by and large marginal to their activities. To the extent that there was a unifying political idea it was autonomism—a term notoriously difficult to pin down, but whose key feature was its separation

6:   See Dangl, 2010, and Petras and Veltmeyer, 2011.
7:   Lewis and Olivera, 2004.

(on anything but a symbolic level) from other struggles. The specificity of each struggle was a strength or a weakness, depending on the position from which you addressed it. For Raul Zibechi, for example, a highly respected and insightful analyst of this period, it was a virtue:

> The left and academics assure us that there is not the slightest chance of victory without structure, or that the movement's triumphs will be ephemeral and that any disarticulated and fragmented movement marches back towards its own certain defeat... [But] was it not the unification and centralisation of past movements that allowed the state and capital to neutralise them?[8]

From a Marxist point of view, however, the fragmentation of the movement was a weakness, not in Zibechi's terms because all class movements are by definition bent on centralisation to mimic the state, but rather because a struggle that lacks a common strategy cannot fight a capitalist class which acts always in the final analysis in its own collective defence. What Zibechi is arguing here, of course, is that the main danger confronting movements from below of this kind is their incorporation by the state, their bureaucratisation, or the loss of their internal democracy and collective involvement. The Latin American experience certainly gives that fear substance, as working class organisations have split and divided under pressure from reformist or populist organisations that did not posit the destruction of the bourgeois state as the starting point for revolution. But that, of course, is a function of politics, of the ideas and strategies that prevail in any given movement and their democratic content. Autonomism's suspicion of the revolutionary left generalises from Stalinism, whose victims included precisely the revolutionary left and which caused the disappearance of the concept of socialism from below and the self-emancipation of the working class from the discourse of the left.

The irony, of course, is that the Latin American mass movements between 2000 and 2005 demonstrated with dramatic clarity the potential for self-emancipation and the creativity of those in struggle. What was important about this period was not just the level of resistance but the forms of grassroots organisation, their internal democracy and their prefigurative possibilities. Here people were speaking not only of obdurate resistance, but of alternative ways of living, of a transformed relationship between human beings and the environment, of the transformation of the human heart. Yet the issue of power, state power and the structures

---

8: Zibechi, 2012, p42.

of control and domination through which *capitalist* relations of production are reproduced was not discussed—for the very reasons that Zibechi suggests. The argument was that to discuss the coordination of struggles against a common enemy was to fall into a "centralising" trap.

At the same time, the Latin American left rarely responded to the paradox of autonomism, and much of the international left, informed by a prevailing postmodernism, celebrated the movement's fragmentation and its refusal to address the question of state power as evidence of its originality and strength.

While the mass movement was facing state repression in Cochabamba's central square, Michael Hardt and Antonio Negri were preparing for publication their weighty and influential tome *Empire*, which appeared in the same iconic year 2000. The influence of their ideas was not perhaps direct in Latin America, but indirectly it echoed around the movements. As a consequence there was no critical engagement with these new formations—an engagement that would have combined solidarity in its broadest sense with debates within the revolutionary tradition about the relationship between the working class movement and other movements, and that would have drawn on analyses of reformism and the post-Stalinist crisis within the left. It was as if, as Negri himself said, these movements were starting from scratch. More directly influential perhaps was John Holloway, who generalised from the Zapatista experience in his *Change the World Without Taking Power*. If Hardt and Negri were correct in their assertion that in the period of Empire the nation-state had ceased to function—that instead capital swarmed and moved like bees[9] and the actions of the multitude shifted and changed correspondingly—then it was by definition impossible to develop any strategic thinking within it. Presumably the actions of the multitude would fragment the global order, challenging the imposed uniformities of thought that held the world's exploited in thrall. As Zibechi puts it,

Non-citizens—those stripped of their citizenship in neoliberal society—are opening up their own spaces in a process of struggle in which they develop as subjects—spaces that they create, design and control. Understanding this requires reversing one's perspective, rejecting the negative and state-centred viewpoint—that defines people by what they lack—and adopting another

---

9:    "When that happens, then, in much the same way as bees swarm when there is no longer enough honey in the hive to support an expanded population, part of it gets up and flies in search of a new home" —Holloway, 2009.

way of looking that starts with the differences they have created in order then to visualise other paths.[10]

The problem, of course, was that neither the state nor the capitalist class whose interests it organised within a given territory had disappeared nor had it given up the fight. The troops of the Mexican army surrounding the autonomous communities of Chiapas and the soldiers firing on the Cochabamba demonstrators were evidence enough of that. What was clear was that in the early 21st century the exploited and the oppressed were fighting back with an intensity and a resolution born of decades of misrule and informed by a new hope that Chiapas and Cochabamba had given them.

Models of a new world

In the year 2000 many things changed. In Ecuador the national mobilisation of indigenous peoples and trade unions brought down a government for the first time (but not the last). In Cochabamba a servant of the global market was forced reluctantly to renationalise the water company. In Chile the year began with the election of Socialist Ricardo Lagos to the presidency, but he would mount no opposition to the demands of global capital.

Outside the arena of formal politics other forces were forging a different power. In the five years that followed Cochabamba, not only would struggles over water, gas and oil impel the movement from below; they would also produce forms of democratic organisation, like the Bolivian *cabildo abierto* or open town council which ensured mass participation and grassroots control, the popular assemblies in Argentina and the *mingas* of Ecuador. The experience was reflected at the World Social Forum in Porto Alegre in its extraordinary diversity and in its understanding that the enemy was neoliberalism. But it was curious that the forum specifically excluded politics. Western social democracy, however, was heavily represented, which suggested that the prohibition was directed at the radical left. What it meant was that the question of power, of how to conquer and transform the state, was specifically forbidden as a subject of debate. The creativity of the movements was, quite rightly, celebrated—but the implication that new worlds would emerge on the terrain of politics through the sheer weight of their moral capital suggested an uncritical absorption of the Zapatista arguments and the exceptionalism of the indigenous mobilisations. And in the particular context of those first years of the 21st century, when governments were

---

10: Zibechi, 2012, p66.

falling, states seemed to be losing control, and (after 2001) the imperialist overseer was increasingly preoccupied elsewhere.

The *Argentinazo* of December 2001, like the other movements, did not come out of the blue. The militant movements of the unemployed, the *piqueteros*, had marked their presence on the political landscape with block-ades of national highways, occupations and protests. When the uprising of December (and it does seem right to call it that) occurred it borrowed from their experience, while it produced at the same time new and creative expressions of popular resistance. The weekend of 18-19 December 2001 was the mass response to the decision of the IMF to punish Argentina for its failure to properly service its debt.

Despite the proliferation of left groups, and in particular of Trotskyist organisations in Argentina, the new resistance was diverse and had no single acknowledged leadership—but its many faces reflected the character of the mobilisations already under way. The crisis produced factory closures across the country that provoked a series of occupations; the *piqueteros* added their weight. One immediate effect of the crisis was the immediate closure of banks so that there was no cash available,[11] and the capital flight of the time was stopped in its tracks. The local popular assemblies arose as responses to an immediate need. Local currencies (of which there were several, though the most widespread were the *patacones*) were essentially vouchers for barter—in the desperate conditions of those days an economy of exchange replaced the money economy, and the distribution of local resources was determined in democratic assemblies. It was true that these extraordinary developments were emergency measures—but as the crisis wore on the poli-tics of grassroots organisation began to embed itself in the movement. The state, meanwhile, was locked in a series of internal crises, as the ruling classes seemed unable to reach agreement on how to address the crisis. One presi-dent followed another, in short-lived and impotent administrations.

Yet there was no agreement on the left as to the implications of the movement. The fragmentation of the Argentine left, and the agility of the popular movement, made it unable to provide unified leadership. Different fractions claimed different struggles, and fought between themselves to assert their right of representation. It was in political terms a squandered moment, and one that reinforced the suspicion of many elements of the movement towards revolutionary politics. There is no doubt that the anti-politics of Holloway and others flourished in that environment and made a virtue both

---

11: The film *Nine Queens* (directed by Feliksas Bielinski, 2002), about a botched bank robbery that coincides with the financial crisis in Argentina, is well worth watching.

of spontaneity and of the lack of debate around the strategic objectives of the movement. The argument offered, and repeated endlessly in the autonomist perspectives, was that the left was entirely oriented on the state. The new movements, by contrast, were seeking autonomous spaces in which to build—and the subject of this new politics was the movement itself. As Diane Raby put it brutally, "The insistence on direct, unmediated popular protagonists is admirable but becomes a futile distraction if it is elevated to the status of dogma",[12] because "there is no alternative to the search for an alternative".[13] And that alternative must inescapably involve the question of state power—not because the revolutionary project is about an alternative leadership bent on taking over the state, but because the construction of a new form of society, a new popular democracy, depends upon it being in a position to confront its enemies, whose principal instrument of class rule is the state. Chile 1973 was not so far in the distance that its lessons should be forgotten!

A meeting at the crossroads

Between 2002 and 2005 the movements advanced apparently inexorably, establishing their political presence throughout Latin America. The political reforms enshrined in Venezuela's new 1999 Constitution included the right to revoke public servants and the recognition of indigenous rights, and flagged the intention to nationalise oil. But it was neither the Constitution nor the election of Chávez in itself that changed the political landscape. Throughout 2001 the right wing in the state machine mobilised and manoeuvred against his government. The prize, from their point of view, was the oil industry—the golden goose that had guaranteed the wealth of the minority of the population who worked in the oil corporation or associated departments of state, and the commercial enterprises that serviced this wealthy untaxed layer with their luxury goods. They had not suffered any perceptible decline in their living standards through the late 1990s, while the majority were suffering the assaults of structural adjustment. Now they prepared to use their economic power, and their continuing control of the state, to undermine Chávez by any means possible. The right wing strikes of 2001 were a practice run for the events of the following year.

Then in April 2002 elements of the army and the bureaucracy together with the corrupt leadership of the Venezuelan Trade Union Federation and the Employers Federation mounted a coup and announced the arrest of Chávez. The short-lived attempt to reclaim the power the bourgeoisie

---

12: Raby, 2006, p3.
13: Raby, 2006, p5.

had controlled for forty years lasted 48 hours. The RTE documentary *The Revolution Will Not Be Televised* memorably captured the reasons why,[14] as the poor cascaded down from the barrios on the hills and gathered in their tens of thousands around the presidential palace, demanding the return of the president. This was the first act of the Bolivarian Revolution, when the mass movement acted directly to defeat the coup. The mobilisation was organised from below—Chávez himself did not have at his disposal a political organisation capable of mobilising people in this way, and his reliance on the army was severely weakened when his fellow officers divided equally in their allegiances. At this moment the masses became the subject of history, just as they had in Ecuador from 1999 onwards, in Bolivia from 2000 and repeatedly in the years that followed, and briefly in Argentina in 2001-2. The final act of this drama was played out from early December 2002 and for the three months that followed. On 3 December the right wing in the oil corporation dealt their final hand, calling out 18,000 employees on an indefinite strike. They paralysed the computers that controlled the complex business of the production and distribution of oil, they threatened and attacked workers attempting to go into work and they even cut the cables under the floor of the corporation's offices. They were clearly willing to destroy the source of most of Venezuela's export earnings (and incidentally of their own inflated incomes) in order to bring Chávez down. This too failed, as the mass of workers and community organisations mobilised across the country to defend the installations and keep the industry moving. It came very close to the edge, but the strike failed because the mass movement seized the historical initiative.

The subsequent creation of the *misiones*, the social programmes funded by Venezuela's oil income, seemed to open the possibility of a transfer of power to the grassroots. The state remained dominated by the old order, which blocked and delayed every Chávez initiative. The response was to set these welfare and social projects in motion directly through the parallel organisations that at this early stage were largely controlled and run from below. The implementation of the health programme involved 20,000 Cuban doctors, their presence paid for with oil. The subsidised state supermarkets, Mercal, raised the general level of nutrition, a key indicator in the poverty statistics. In 2004-5 poverty levels fell significantly for the first time, and health data showed consistent improvement—unsurprisingly since most of Venezuela's poor simply had previously had no access to healthcare. The virtual disappearance of a Venezuelan medical profession used to very high incomes in the private sector spoke volumes.

14: *The Revolution Will Not be Televised* (directed by Kim Bartley and Donnacha Ó Briain, 2003).

At this stage the *misiones* came close to becoming a kind of parallel state. As Gregory Wilpert makes clear,[15] the consequence would be either the transformation of the Venezuelan state itself or the incorporation of its activists into the existing state. It was the latter process that prevailed, as the system of patronage, corruption and the trading of favours that had character-ised *puntofijismo* persisted and began to corrupt the Chavista state itself. The critical thing at this point was the significance of the Bolivarian Constitution.

As Wilpert puts it, "What makes the difference between a constitu-tion that is actually implemented and one that is merely a formality is the country's political culture".[16] This could equally be applied to the consti-tutions of Bolivia and Ecuador. A constitution without legal instruments to enforce its provisions is little more than a declaration of faith. Yet at this critical moment the movements still seemed to be leading the process of change as their demands were taken up in the electoral processes in which, between 2005 and 2006, new leaders presented their presidential candidacies under the new constitutional arrangements. The high point in the period of mass mobilisation—what Linera himself (without conscious irony) describes as a revolutionary moment—was a curious encounter at the Porto Alegre World Social Forum in January 2005. The forum had been backed by Lula, Brazil's president elected at the end of 2002 in a euphoric moment that very rapidly turned into confusion and dismay. He was the candidate of the Workers Party (PT), formed in 1980 in the wake of a major strike wave in heavy industry in which Lula was a leading union official. The 2002 election campaign made great play of Lula's humble origins, presenting him as a candidate above party. It was a conscious appeal to the mass movement led in Brazil by the Landless Workers Movement (MST), identifying Lula with the new social movements and understating his membership of the Workers Party itself and his past in the trade unions.

In reality, Lula was an extremely popular career politician and the Workers Party a major political force in Brazil which already controlled many state and municipal governments. The MST's hesitations about Lula stemmed from the tensions that had often arisen between the MST, which mobilised the poorest and most marginalised sections in direct actions like occupations, and the PT at various levels of government. Nevertheless, when Lula arrived at the Porto Alegre conference in January 2003 he was received with joy by the local population which turned out in numbers to cheer him. In a matter of days, however, Lula's agenda became clear,

---

15: Wilpert, 2007, p147.
16: Wilpert, 2007, p42.

as he flew directly from Porto Alegre to Davos where he met (and was photographed) with George Soros and other luminaries of global capitalism at the World Economic Forum. His reception in Porto Alegre two years later was very different. He was heckled persistently when he came to speak at the city's basketball stadium, which had largely been filled with government employees to avoid just such a hostile response. Within a short time of assuming the presidency Lula had attacked public sector workers' actions over pensions, MST activists had been arrested and dissidents within the PT had been expelled. The promise of a basic welfare food programme, Fome Zero, was fulfilled, but it was the commitment to winning for Brazil a place at the top table of world capitalism that drove Lula's government. Brazilian capital very rapidly came to occupy a dominant role in Latin America, and Lula's decision to send Brazilian troops to Haiti to support the US occupation was widely seen as a declaration of Lula's real allegiances. Brazilian capital asserted itself aggressively in Paraguay and Bolivia, using its economic power to pressure and control the smaller economies of Latin America.

At the end of the same week Hugo Chávez came to Porto Alegre, where he spoke in the same stadium to rapturous applause. It was there that he announced Venezuela's commitment to 21st century socialism. It was a pivotal moment. But the enthusiastic adoption by the emerging leaders of the Latin American "new left" did not clarify what Chávez understood by socialism, and what his message was to his own supporters in Venezuela and outside. It seemed clearest at the level of foreign policy, where Chávez's witty and adamant anti-imperialism was echoed by other leaders. Hostility to the United States and the pursuit of national independence were the central message, combined with the promise to build a strong local state able to recover control over national resources and negotiate from strength with external forces. Chávez's lyrical passages about the creation of a political culture of solidarity and community were received with equal enthusiasm. But the form that it would take, and how solidarity with a radical state would differ from a horizontal form of collective organisation was not addressed. And the economic strategies of the new vision of the state remained equally unclear in reality, if not at the level of discourse.

So 21st century socialism grew out of a fierce critique of neoliberalism, yet it was not anti-capitalist in the sense of proposing a new socio-economic formation not based on the market. It proposed instead a fairer market in which a bloc of Latin American nations could negotiate their conditions of existence within it from a stronger position. Even its most radical wing, the Chávez government in Venezuela, did not advocate expropriation of big capital, nor any assault on the private ownership of the means of production in general. In the wake of the coup and the bosses' strike of 2002, for example, "patriotic" capitalists like Cisneros and Ruperti emerged stronger than ever—and their interests have remained untouched ever since. While government lands were redistributed to small farmers through the *misiones*, few large private landholdings were taken over—other than by peasant organisations seizing the land directly, and usually suffering repression as a result. The industries that were taken over—the aluminium plant Alcasa, for example, or some milk processing factories—were usually nationalised under threat of closure and compensation was paid at market prices.

In what sense, then, were these governments socialist—in a 21st century sense? If the rejection of 20th century socialism (for which read Stalinism) was of its undemocratic, centralised and bureaucratic character, then to what extent could 21st century socialism claim to be offering an alternative form of social organisation? The much vaunted cooperatives established in Venezuela and Bolivia, for example, were fundamentally small businesses. Working class demands were met with hostility by the state with the familiar accusation that organised workers were putting their own interests above those of "society as a whole". Chávez's attacks on trade unionists, for example during the metro strike of 2010, surprised his own supporters and the organised refusal to negotiate with the newly formed rank and file trade union federation (the UNT) reinforced their suspicion.[17]

It increasingly appeared that 21st century socialism was far from being the logical development of the experience of grassroots democracy, workers' control of industry or the socialisation of the economy. Supporters of the Bolivarian Revolution abroad were understandably excited by Chávez's announcement in 2005. Against the background of worldwide hostility to imperialist war, and a global condemnation of neoliberalism, and the experience of a Latin American resistance that had produced a new, combative historical subject, 21st century socialism promised to open enormous new possibilities.

In retrospect, however, it seems clear now that the direction that was signposted by 21st century socialism was very different, despite the frequent allusions to Trotsky, Gramsci and Rosa Luxemburg, from Marx's conception of socialism as the "self-emancipation of the working class": "The coincidence of the changing of circumstances and of human activity or self-change can be conceived and rationally understood only as *revolutionary practice*".[18]

17: See Stobart, 2010. In May 2012 a new labour law was passed. Its operation remains to be properly tested
18: Marx, 1845.

The election of Evo Morales as the candidate of the MAS to the Bolivian presidency in 2005 clearly marked a new stage. For those in the movement the rise of their most prominent mass leader felt like a victory—and it was. He was the representative of the great mass risings of 2003 and again in 2005, not simply electorally, but in terms of his background and his role as leader of the Coca Farmers organisation. The subsequent elections to a Constituent Assembly, however, sowed confusion and doubt. Delegates, it was announced, would represent political parties only—the movements themselves would not be directly represented except insofar as their spokespeople were members of a registered organisation, in reality of the Movimiento al Socialismo, the MAS. And insofar as the MAS did not have a majority in the Senate, the Law of Convocation of the Assembly could be passed only with the cooperation of the right. This was very different from the gathering envisaged by Oscar Olivera, speaking on behalf of the Coordinator of Mass Organisations:

> The Constituent Assembly should be understood as a great sovereign meeting of citizen representatives elected by their neighbourhood organisations, their urban and rural associations, their unions, their communes. These citizen representatives would bring with them ideas and projects concerning how to organise the political life of the country... Let us be clear: Neither the executive branch nor the legislative branch, nor even the political parties, can convoke the Constituent Assembly.[19]

In Venezuela this vision of the "*Constituyente*" was advanced in the wake of the events of 2002-3 by Roland Denis, another leading figure in the autonomist wing of the movement,[20] echoing in turn the Zapatista concept of "*la otra política*"—the other politics that was grassroots and non-electoral. A year later, after his re-election with an increased majority, Chávez announced (and note that it was *announced* on television in his customary unpredictable way) the creation of a new national organisation, the United Socialist Party of Venezuela (PSUV). Its birth, fully grown, with small organisational and political committees already formed, caused a deep political crisis among the parties of the left—and produced, or at least brought to the surface, profound internal divisions. The juggling of terminologies confused matters further. This, according to the Comandante, was "*poder popular*", people's power. Yet its central political expression was nominated, not elected, and its political

---

19: Quoted in Webber, 2011, p85.
20: Denis, 2001.

manifesto written by a committee of four. Nevertheless, and as testimony to the enormous popularity and authority of Chávez, the call to join convinced nearly 6 million Venezuelans.

The promise that there would be internal debate, and the reality that the country's working population were now members, convinced most of the left to join. The internal debate, however, proved very limited and restricted to the lower echelons. The practice of nomination to the upper levels of the party persisted. But what kind of party was it, and what vision of 21st century socialism did it express? In the first instance, it was a conduit from the presidency to a mass movement with very little room for independent action. It served for the implementation of policies and positions most of which appeared to come from Chávez's private thoughts direct to the world beyond, and to be framed in a Bolivarian ideology whose socialist elements were at best very vague.

It was certainly nationalist and anti-imperialist, but what was its transformative content? There was no reference to redistribution beyond the allocation of oil revenues to social programmes, directed from the state by an emerging powerful political class that people began calling the "Bolibourgeoisie". They were accumulating huge personal wealth and influence, and deploying that influence in much the same way as the previous occupants of the state. There was no doubt that the best elements of the mass movement, the most consistent and committed workers, and the most sincere advocates of people's power were in their vast majority within the PSUV. But their actions were contained and limited by a highly centralised and increasingly bureaucratic organisation whose principal role seemed to be electoral, as elections followed referenda followed elections. There was little space here for public debate and still less for critical responses to a shifting reality. There was little about it that was democratic.

In Ecuador, Correa's confrontation with the old oligarchy in Guayaquil and the landowning classes gave brief hope that his commitment to 21st century socialism was more than skin deep. But the beneficiary proved to be another section of the bourgeoisie, based in Quito, rather than the mass movement. While Correa is welcomed into the ample salons of 21st century socialism, he has reimposed, or reaffirmed the place of Ecuador in the global economy.

As Jeffrey Webber shows in great detail, Bolivia's 21st century socialist government is equally enthusiastic in confirming Bolivia's place as an extractive economy in which decisions and directions are determined by the most powerful players in world capitalism. Their nationality is secondary—the language of exploitation may have changed from English to Portuguese or Chinese or Russian—but the relationship is the same. The armed confrontations and accumulating lists of dead activists in Peru, Bolivia, Ecuador and Paraguay, for example, are the evidence of a renewed appropriation of land, this time in areas neglected up till now because they were inaccessible or home to large indigenous communities. The ruthlessness of these invasions is all the more dramatic when they are supported by the military and the police. Whatever we call the coming period, be it "post-neoliberalism" (Dávalos) or "neoliberalism reconstituted" (Webber), it bears no resemblance to a socialism whose watchword is self-emancipation. Pablo Dávalos's withering critique of the Correa era leaves very little doubt:

> Post-neoliberalism offers two basic dynamics—accumulation by dispossession and the institutional transformation of State and market—within a single political process. It is worth pointing out that these dynamics have a different vision of the state which is why it can be seen as a form of opposition to neoliberalism and the Washington Consensus. But this is just an optical illusion: the centrality of the state is fundamental for guaranteeing the juridical security of corporations and investors involved in extractive industries. That is why accumulation by dispossession involves violence and pillage.[21]

García Linera, in Bolivia, was equally clear that Bolivia is entering a phase of the creation of an Andean capitalism. The adjective may feel reassuring, but the key is the noun—capitalism—whose compelling and remorseless laws of accumulation have already claimed victims from TIPNIS and shown their true colours to the indigenous protesters marching against higher gas prices and frozen wages.

The gulf between rhetoric and reality grows ever wider. The Orinoco Basin's immense reserves of oil are represented as the guarantee of Venezuela's "socialist" future. Yet they are all being developed by joint enterprises with multinational companies, which do not enter agreements for the general good. China, Russia and Iran's involvement is hardly disinterested—they lend at high interest in China's case, they profit from arms sales in Russia's, and they find a market for their cars and lorries in Iran's (or at least they will do when the troubled and inefficient manufacturing plant finally moves into production).

The 21st century socialist model appears to have certain characteristics in common: A newly strengthened state, a charismatic and authoritative leader, and a political apparatus whose role is the transmission of decisions

---

21: Davalos, 2011.

and the implementation of government decisions. If there is a model for this characteristic political apparatus, it would seem to be the Cuban Communist Party—despite its high level of centralisation and complete lack of internal democracy.[22] Yet private capital is protected in these new regimes and responds when it is called upon to exhibit its patriotism by investing, for profit, in local enterprises with state support. Though the Latin American right is active, vocal and shrill in its denunciations of the new governments in the region, there has been no assault on its class interests, no expropriations, no increased tax obligations upon it. And the silence or confusion of the mass movements that fought neoliberalism with such courage cannot be seen as consent.

The new arrangements for the global trade in raw materials, gas and oil have implied higher royalties, and the world price of these commodities has provided a surplus that has enabled each of these new states to fund welfare and social programmes which have lifted the living standards of the majority above the poverty line. But it has not been achieved through redistribution of wealth or through the creation of social redistributive economies. The Venezuelan Missions, like the Fome Zero programme in Brazil and their equivalents elsewhere in Latin America, create a new dependence on the state and undermine the sense that advances are achieved by independent mass action. And in the medium term the leaders of these movements are incorporated into the state—abandoning their leadership roles and their accountability to the movements to become, in reality, intermediaries acting on behalf of the state. The effect has been to demobilise and disarm the mass movements that placed such hope in the new era.

The practice of the social movements inspired a vision of a different world—responsible to the whole of society, respectful of the environment, democratic in its actions and its purposes, that would consign exploitation and oppression to the annals of history. The once invisible face of indigenous America is now to be seen in many of the region's parliaments. But that is not people's power. The warning shots have already been fired. The removal of Fernando Lugo in Paraguay, by a coalition of national and international agricultural interests, was one. The barely discussed midnight kidnapping of President Zelaya in Honduras with the open approval of Washington was another.

The recent agreements between Hugo Chávez and President Santos of Colombia are a case in point. Santos, after all, was the minister of defence under Uribe, whose support of the paramilitaries financed by

---

22: Gonzalez, 2012.

the drug barons was never in doubt. And Santos has not changed his spots; he has made it clear that during the current negotiations with the guerrillas of the Farc (Revolutionary Armed Forces of Colombia), brokered by Venezuela, military operations in Colombia will continue. Their purpose now, though they will be described as counter-terrorism, will be to deepen the expulsion of the small farmers currently occupying the lands required by the agricultural corporations to expand their cultivation of export crops. In Chile the presidency is occupied by Chile's wealthiest capitalist. The recent nationalisation of a Spanish oil company by the government of Cristina Kirchner in Argentina is almost certainly a prelude to its resale to the Brazilian giant Petrobras. Against this background Latin American integration looks increasingly like the strengthening of a new capitalist bloc.

How then can Roland Denis's "third republic" be reconstituted?[23] The truth is that the movement has never disarmed—but it has been incorporated and manipulated by a discourse of popular power that has veiled the continuity of a capitalism now claiming once again its rights over Latin America's natural resources. Its water, its oil, its gas, its copper, its lithium are the prize that global capital is competing for—the sole change being that today there are more bidders in this grand auction for Latin America's future. The silence of the left in the face of the attacks on the mass movements—on the Yuxpa peoples and trade union activists in Venezuela, on workers' protests in Bolivia and on the indigenous communities of Ecuador—is a dereliction.

The social movements live this reality daily. And yet there is an air of confusion, of uncertainty about them. That will not be resolved only by action. It is a moment in which politics should prevail. What future do the movements envisage—and is it really possible to imagine that future without taking power from that still small minority class that controls the means of production and distribution? How is it possible that García Linera can approvingly quote Hardt and Negri in the name of "Andean capitalism"?[24] Clearly 21st century socialism has failed those who fought for it. Perhaps this is the moment to return to Marx's understanding of socialist revolution—the transfer of power from one class to another, the definitive appropriation of the future by the majority who have been denied it thus far. And it will not be won by the acts of powerful individuals or by negotiating with capital on a world scale, but by building an internationalism based on common struggles and on the authentic

23: See Denis, 2011.
24: Garcia Linera, 2011.

democracy of a new, self-emancipated, historical subject, a working class whose struggle embraces all those who capital exploits and oppresses.

It is striking that the constitutional changes that have been carried out in the region should be seen as the end point of historical processes, when in fact they have consolidated and ratified political and economic liberalism and closed down the liberation projects of the people. It is even more alarming how…the radical, critical iconoclastic left that challenges the discourse of power has now lowered its critical banners and tries to justify the unjustifiable.[25]

We can join forces against imperialism without falling silent when governments of the left cease to represent those in whose name they govern. Any socialism of the 21st century can only be produced from below, by a working class movement prepared to conquer its own liberation.

25: Dávalos, quoted in Uzcategui, 2010, p240.

References

Dangl, Benjamin, 2010, *Dancing with Dynamite: Social Movements and States in Latin America* (AK Press).

Dávalos, 2011, "Alianza País réquiem por un sueño", http://alainet.org/active/54769&lang=es

Denis, Roland, 2001, *Los Fabricantes de la Rebelión* (Ed Primera Linea).

Denis, Roland, 2011, *Las Tres Repúblicas* (Ed La Espada Rota).

Garcia Linera, Alvaro, 2011, *Las Tensiones Creativas de la Revolución*, (Office of the Vice President), www.alames.org/documentos/tensiones.pdf

Gonzalez, Mike, 2012, "A Political Monolith", *Review 31*, http://review31.co.uk/article/view/50

Holloway, John, 2009, "The Reform of the State", http://libcom.org/library/reform-state-john-holloway

Lewis, Tom, and Oscar Olivera, 2004, *Cochabamba: Water Wars in Bolivia* (South End Press).

Marx, Karl, 1845, *Theses on Feuerbach*, www.marxists.org/archive/marx/works/1845/theses/original.htm

Petras, James, 2010, "Latin America's 21st Century Socialism in Historical Perspective", http://petras.lahaine.org/?p=1823

Petras, James, and Henry Veltmeyer, 2011, *Social Movements in Latin America: Neoliberalism and Popular Resistance* (Palgrave Macmillan).

Raby, Diane, 2006, *Democracy and Revolution* (Pluto).

Stobart, Luke, 2010, "Venezuela at the Crossroads: Voices from Within the Venezuelan Revolution", *International Socialism* 126 (spring), www.isj.org.uk/?id=635

Uzcátegui, Rafael, 2010, *Venezuela:la revolución como espectáculo* (Editorial Libertario).

Webber, Jeffrey, 2011, *From Rebellion to Reform in Bolivia* (Haymarket).

Webber, Jeffrey, 2012, "Revolution Against Progress: the TIPNIS Struggle and Class Contradictions in Bolivia", *International Socialism* 133 (winter), www.isj.org.uk/?id=780

Wilpert, Gregory, 2007, "Venezuela's New Constitution", http://venezuelanalysis.com/analysis/70

Zibechi, Raul, 2012, *Territories in Resistance* (AK Press).

bookmarks

the socialist bookshop 020 7637 1848
1 bloomsbury street london wc1b 3qe
www.bookmarksbookshop.co.uk

read.learn.fight

Britain's leading bookshop for radical books

From climate change to anti-war, from black struggle
to histories of uprisings in every part of the world.

Visit our shop or buy online to support bookselling
independent of the big chains. We can provide
any title currently in print and give advice on a
wide range of topics from multicultural children's
books to Marxism, economics and philosophy.

Bookmarks provides stalls at trade union conferences
and campaign meetings. Let us know if you would like
us to supply books for your organisation or event.

New divisions of labour in the global economy

Jane Hardy

It has become a rarely challenged commonsense assumption that, as part of the globalisation process, there is an inexorable haemorrhaging of jobs from the "Global North" to the "Global South". China and other countries in Asia are cited as prime examples of new centres of accumulation, which are a magnet to foreign investment and employment at the expense of workers' jobs in more advanced capitalist economies. Transnational corporations are treated as juggernauts that can set down or uproot without impediment within a short time frame.

Offshoring production has featured in high-profile political debates.[1] It was a major issue in the 2012 presidential election when Barack Obama criticised Mitt Romney for investing in companies that sent jobs abroad when he worked for the private equity firm Bain Capital. Guy Standing claims in his book *The Precariat* that new divisions of labour within the firm and the shift of some activities overseas contribute to the division between "core" and "peripheral" workers and the increasing precarity of the latter.[2] The American Federation of Labor and Congress of Industrial

---

1: The terms "outsourcing" and "offshoring" are used rather loosely and interchangeably in this article. Outsourcing is the process of contracting part of a firm's operation or value chain to a third party and therefore relates to ownership. Offshoring is a spatial concept to do with firms relocating part of their production to another country: this could be outsourced to a third party or kept in-house when a subsidiary is opened.

2: Standing, 2011.

Organizations (AFL-CIO)[3] peddle a particularly apocalyptic version of offshoring where China is "viewed as the most important source of downward pressure from trade with less developed countries, because it pays very low wages and because it is responsible for nearly 40 percent of US non-oil imports from less developed economies".[4]

John Smith claims that outsourcing has transformed the global working class and is a way that profits are extracted by transnational corporations from imperialist countries through the super-exploitation of workers in the Global South. He argues that:

> The vast wave of outsourcing of production processes to low-wage countries...was a strategic response to the twin crises of declining profitability and overproduction that resurfaced in the 1970s in the form of stagflation and synchronised global recession, a course that was conditioned by the imperialists' reluctance to reverse the expensive concessions that have helped convert the workers of the "Global North" into passive bystanders, or even accomplices, to their subjugation of the rest of the world.[5]

From contradictory perspectives, workers in core capitalist economies are simultaneously victims of unfair competition (AFL-CIO) and bystanders/accomplices in the super-exploitation of workers in the Global South (Smith), while workers in the Global South are simultaneously perpetrators of unfair competition (AFL-CIO) and super-exploited in a race to the bottom (Smith). The arguments of both the AFL-CIO and John Smith are divisive, pitting the interests of workers in the core capitalist economies and developing countries against one another—in both accounts workers are powerless in the face of mobile capital.

The dynamic nature of capitalism is constantly changing the global division of labour, and there are undoubtedly significant shifts in the geography of production and accumulation.[6] However, accounts that treat capital as super-mobile, the haemorrhaging of jobs as inexorable and workers (both in the core capitalist economies and in the developing world) as passive victims of capital need to be challenged. This article is organised around three central arguments. The first proposition is that the mobility of capital (in aggregate) is exaggerated, and in particular that

3: www.aflcio.org/Issues/Jobs-and-Economy/Manufacturing/Outsourcing-Trade-and-Currency.
4: Scott, 2008, p1.
5: Smith, 2012, p40.
6: Early significant works were Fröbel, Heinrichs and Kreye, 1981 and Huws, 1986.

the state continues to play a critical role in the process of accumulation. The second argument is that contradictions in the process of accumulation make the movement of capital and jobs neither inevitable nor irreversible. Third, it is suggested that the empirical foundations on which some of the more apocalyptic claims are based are shaky and wherever capital settles it is met with resistance from workers. I start off by looking at the way in which stagnating profits and competition are an organisational headache for the owners and managers of capital.

Annihilating space with time: a challenge for capital

Throughout the history of capitalism, the drive to accumulate, compete and reduce turnover time has led to a reduction of the time and costs of production. In the 19th century the steamships, canals, railways and the telegraph revolutionised communication and the movement of raw materials and goods. In the 20th century the advent of the jet aircraft, computers and satellites dramatically reduced geographical barriers, while containerisation increased the efficiency of moving goods.[7] Marx understood the drive for new markets when he talked about the relentless expansion of the system:[8]

> While capital must on the one side strive to tear down every spatial barrier... to exchange and conquer the whole earth for its market, it strives on the other side to annihilate this space with time, ie reduce to a minimum the time spent in motion from one place to another. The more developed the capital, the more it does strive simultaneously for an ever greater expansion of the market and for ever greater annihilation of space by time.[9]

From its inception capitalism has brought previously inaccessible destinations into the network of exchange through improvements in transport and technology, opening up new places of accumulation and new markets. This has been reinforced by the liberalisation of trade and investment as powerful capitalist economies have broken down barriers through their domination of international institutions such as the International Monetary Fund (IMF) and the World Trade Organisation (WTO). This intensifies competition between capitalists for favourable sites for both the relocation of production and the domination of markets.

Marx predicted that competition would lead to concentration as

---

7:   Nayyar, 2006.
8:   For an accessible account of Marxist economics, see Choonara, 2009.
9:   Marx, 1973, p539.

weaker capitals disappeared or were taken over by stronger capitals—a process intensified by periodic crisis. This is clearly evident in the gargantuan transnational corporations that have emerged in energy, finance, food and automotives. In the face of intense competition these firms (and smaller ones) are constantly engaged in organisational innovation to reconfigure their arrangements with other units of capital for producing goods and services in an attempt to steal advantage from their competitors. They are confronted with endless configurations of contractual arrangements with suppliers and competitors within a variety of geographical locations. This menu of arrangements includes segmenting tasks and moving functions or entire departments and sub-units to different locations. The result is intricate and increasingly extended chains of fragmented activities that make up the circuit of capital from extraction to realisation of surplus value.[10]

Where powerful firms dominate these complex value chains their purpose is to extract and appropriate a greater chunk of surplus value from weaker capitals which are their suppliers.[11] In the business jargon, firms concentrate on their "core competences" and spin-off or outsource tranches of their production process to other firms. The flexibility that they can gain from exerting pressure on suppliers enables them to reduce their turnover time to the minimum.[12] The more smoothly all parts of the production process can be synchronised with just-in-time methods and state of the art logistics, the faster the production and realisation of surplus value and the higher the rate of profit.

Huge supermarkets in the United Kingdom dominate food production and through competition, force processors and producers of food to drive down their costs. Sophisticated sourcing methods combine scouring the globe for food with the hyper-exploitation of (often migrant) workers in the domestic economy. Firms that produce branded clothing and footwear, and companies such as IKEA, are constantly reshaping their value chains to extract a disproportionate share of surplus value from their suppliers, who have much less power and who in turn are forced to squeeze their workers.

But these examples refer to specific transnational corporations and particular sections of capital. All too often these high profile and limited

---

10: Others, from both Marxist and non-Marxist perspectives, have looked at how unevenness is constructed through the intricacies of global value chains. See Coe, Dicken, and Martin, 2008, Rainnie, Herod, and McGrath-Champ, 2011.

11: Starosta, 2010.

12: Turnover time is given by the sum of production and circulation time—Marx, 1978, pp235-236.

examples are generalised into an argument about the mobility of capital as whole, with scant attention paid to the specific nature of different capitals.

The limits to capital mobility

In the absence of countervailing forces that make production "sticky" in one place, "the individual search for excess profits would keep the [space] economy of capitalist production in a state that resembles an incoherent and frenetic game of musical chairs".[13] Therefore, it is important to understand the limits to and constraints on the mobility of capital.

First, only some sections of capital are mobile. For example, the whole swathe of activities associated with constructing and maintaining the physical and human infrastructure of capitalism is fixed. Whether provided by the public sector or commodified, education, care for the elderly and the majority of health provision are immobile. The capital associated with the physical infrastructure—airports, transport, energy, construction and telecommunications—are also fixed in one place.

Second, those sections of capital that are more mobile still face constraints on their ability to move production. The longer the turnover time, the less the geographical and temporal mobility of capital. Therefore, industries employing large quantities of fixed capital cannot relocate easily. In the case of automobiles, the constant costs such as building new plants and investing in machinery are high. In contrast, the clothing and shoe sector has low barriers to entry and low constant capital costs, which make it accessible to virtually any developing country.

But despite the hyper-mobility of the clothing industry, production has not relocated exclusively to low-wage sites. Since the liberalisation of the clothing industry in 2005,[14] China's share of world exports in clothing has risen from 18 percent to 34 percent,[15] but Europe's share has also increased from 28 percent to 31 percent in the same period. Networks of production in Europe have been restructured. Either suppliers are being drawn from low-wage European economies or firms are increasing their use of technology and automation.[16] The labour process and extraction of surplus value are one (important) point in wider circuits of capital, but proximity to markets and flexibility are important in reducing turnover time.

13:   Harvey, 2006, p393.

14:   The Multi Fibre Arrangement (MFA) governed the world trade in textiles and garments from 1974 through to 2004. It imposed quotas on the amount that developing countries could export to developed countries. It expired on 1 January 2005.

15:   WTO, 2011.

16:   Pickles and Smith, 2011.

Clothing and electronics are high-profile sectors where capital is mobile, but there are few examples of sectors that have exhibited such a propensity to move between countries in a short time period. Automotive firms, for example, have relocated, but over a much longer period of time. Rather than seeking *absolute* low wages, they have built regional networks in adjacent *relatively* lower wage economies, for example American firms in Mexico, and German and Italian ones in Central and Eastern Europe. Japanese auto firms have exhibited a similar pattern in South East Asia with the outsourcing of components to lower cost countries such as South Korea and Taiwan initially, and more recently lower wage cost locations in Indonesia, Malaysia and the Philippines.[17]

In her study of restructuring the US auto industry Nicole Aschoff looks at the way that US firms have reorganised their operations almost continually since the 1980s.[18] She explains how, rather than the single trajectory of production moving to low-wage sites in the US South or Mexico, auto industry restructuring has resulted in an "auto alley" stretching from the Great Lakes to the Gulf of Mexico. She concludes that:

> the restructuring of the auto industry over the past three decades is not a simple globalisation story of investment leaving for low-wage sites. Instead, it has been a story of constant restructuring with growth and decline occurring simultaneously in time and space.[19]

The same pattern is true of auto production in the European Union. The sites of production for Peugeot and GM show the core capitalist economies as the most important locations, followed by Spain with Central and Eastern Europe playing a peripheral role (see Table 1). Where auto firms have moved into the markets of developing countries, this is to access rapidly expanding demand rather than low costs. According to Nicole Aschoff the so-called BRIC economies (Brazil, Russia, India and China) accounted for one third of global car sales in 2009.[20] And in the same year China was GM's largest market. So while new growth is concentrated in a handful of developing countries, the majority of sales and production takes place in North America, Western Europe and Japan.

17: Moody, 1997.
18: Aschoff, 2012, p143.
19: Aschoff, 2012.
20: Ascoff, 2012.

Table 1: Peugeot and GM: countries of production
Source: Reed, 2012

Peugot		GM	
Country	Units of production (000s)	Country	Units of production (000s)
France	1,324	France	442
Spain	452	Spain	366
Slovakia	178	Slovakia	208
Portugal	50	Portugal	174

From the perspective of different sections of capital, shares of world exports provide a crude indication of divisions of labour. Table 2 shows that China has made significant gains in capturing a share of world exports in iron and steel, clothing and integrated circuits and electronic components, but has had little penetration in medium technology (automotives) or high technology (pharmaceuticals), which remain in the core capitalist economies and Europe in particular.[21]

Third, and the most serious issue to address, are notions that shifts in capital are frictionless in a global economy where firms are free from the shackles of national states and can roam the globe in search of profits without impediment. Nigel Harris argues that since 1980 the world has been dominated by the transition to a single "economic globalisation", which:

> increasingly imposes on the world a new pattern of territorial specialisation, organised by global markets, not as hitherto believed, by nation states... The free flow of the factors of production has created a single world economy.[22]

21: See Hardy and Budd, 2012 for a discussion of the technological unevenness of China's production and its dependence on Western technology.
22: Harris, 2012, p138.

Table 2: Share in world exports for selected goods and countries
Source: Author's selected compilation from the WTO, 2010.

	Iron & steel		Integrated circuits & electronic components		Automotive products		Clothing		Pharmaceut-icals	
	2000	2009	2000	2009	2000	2009	2000	2009	2000	2009
Europe	47.0	38.5	19.1	13.5	49.8	49.7	28.5	30.7	65.0	67.0
Japan	10.4	10.0	13.8	10.3	15.3	13.7	n/a	n/a	2.5	1.0
China	3.1	9.4	1.7	11.4	0.3	2.6	18.3	34.0	1.6	2.0
US	4.4	4.1	20.4	10.7	11.7	9.1	4.4	1.3	12.1	10.3

Accounts of highly mobile capital roaming the global economy unimpeded in search of lower wage costs ignore (or at best underplay) the role of states and their constant attempts to intervene and influence capital accumulation within their boundaries.

The state and the "frenetic game of changing destinations"
The territorial organisation of the state forms the fixed geographical environment in which investment processes operate that lead to interstate rivalry to provide the social, institutional and infrastructural conditions most propitious for capital.

The state secures the conditions for the accumulation of capital and for extracting (and realising) surplus value. It provides the physical infrastructure for capital (transport, energy) and the institutional architecture that governs the relationship between capitals (their size and potential for competition) and capital and labour (labour and employment law). In addition, states embrace a wide range of institutions concerned with the reproduction and enhancement of labour within their territory. Universities, for example, have been overtly marshalled to improve the competitive conditions for capital through their production of skilled workers and the focus on managerial and scientific know-how.

There is a whole machinery of regional development agencies that compete intensively to provide the best package of land, subsidies and institutional support. This is also manifest in the building of technology parks, which usually amount to little more than wishful thinking on the part of local ruling classes and their acolytes and rarely translate into attracting the high technology production to which they aspire.

But the state does not simply passively provide the conditions for capital—rather it actively seeks to attract capital in locational tournaments that pit country against country and regions and localities against other regions and localities, both within nation-states and in other nation-states. [23] For example, in the film industry subsidy wars abound. On a global level there is competition between North America, Europe, New Zealand/Australia and parts of the developing world. For example, the filming of the *Lord of the Rings* trilogy in New Zealand generated huge tax breaks for New Line Cinema—estimated by the OECD to be in the $300 to $400 million range.[24] In 2010 Warner Brothers and New Line threatened to pull out of filming in New Zealand until the government promised more subsidies and legislation that undermined union-negotiated contracts.[25] Even within countries there is intense competition. In the US film industry in 2008 40 states spent $1.4 billion on tax credits, write-offs and grants. Interstate competition for location shooting is especially intense, and as of 2009 only six states did not provide movie production incentives (MPIs).[26]

It is instructive that in the United States, where the rhetoric of the free market and a restricted role for the state is so strong, the reality could not be more different. Generous government incentives try to win capital to particular states, as the following quote shows:

The latest [2008] cheap manufacturing site for European companies is not in Asia or Eastern Europe but the US... The reason is less the value of the dollar...but rather the large number of incentives that some US states are offering companies to set up factories in their region... A senior executive of Fiat...said "with the amount of money US states are willing to throw at

23: Dicken, 2011.
24: Van Biesebroeck, 2008.
25: 3News, 2010.
26: Good Jobs First, 2010a.

you...you would be stupid to turn them down at the moment"... Thyssen Krupp...is receiving more than $811 to build a steel mill in Alabama... The chairman of a large Swiss group said: "States are more willing to pay for new roads, re-train workers and offer huge tax breaks—that is a competitive package that not many parts of the world can match when you look at how productive US workers are and where the dollar is".[27]

Despite their size, global success and profits, producers of semi-conductors have hijacked and siphoned off significant public subsidies. For example, in Tennessee in 2008 Hemlock semiconductor group was offered $114 million in development and training grants, plus $74 million in local subsidies and 50 percent property abatement worth an estimated $40 million.[28] Similarly in biotechnology, viewed as the magic bullet of economic development, there is huge interstate competition for what were regarded as state of the art jobs. This includes not only subsidies to individual companies but also government funds to build research parks or to create public pools of venture capital.[29] In the car industry in the early 1990s global foreign car firms received massive state subsidies to locate in the southern states of the US. In 2008 VW, which had abandoned US manufacturing in 1988, announced plans to spend up to $1 billion on assembly operations in Chattanooga, Tennnessee. The state and local package was in excess of $400 million.[30]

There is a similar story of government support in individual European states and in the European Union as a whole. For example, in November 2012 the European Union launched a plan to bolster the "struggling" car industry. The strategy dubbed *Car 2020* includes a raft of proposals including promoting investment in new technology and green vehicles, streamlining regulations, supporting skills and training and helping make carmakers compete globally including through "balanced trade agreements".[31]

Beyond subsidies to attract and retain investment the representatives and owners of capital lobby states (and regional groups of states such as the EU) to organise the terms of trade in their interests. Marx's analogy of hostile brothers is a good description of how governments tussle over the rules of global competition. Governments protect their industries with, often, spurious claims that other countries are competing unfairly. The use of tariffs and quotas has declined as a result of tortuous rounds

---

27: Dicken, 2011, pp227–228.
28: Good Jobs First, 2010b.
29: Good Jobs First, 2005.
30: Good Jobs First, 2010c.
31: Fontanella-Khan and Reed, 2012.

of negotiations through the WTO, and _anti-dumping_ has emerged as the dominant form of trade protectionism. These anti-dumping duties allow a country to impose temporary duties on a good exported by a foreign producer that is accused of selling the good at a price below that charged in the foreign producer's home market. These laws were drafted initially by the US and European ruling classes to protect themselves from "low price competition". They were the first to take advantage of these laws and were the most active users of them, but more recently the dynamic has shifted. Over the last decade India and China have been aggressive users of anti-dumping laws as offensive weapons against their trading partners.

Table 3: Users and targets of anti-dumping, 1995–2011
Source: Wu, 2012

Top three users of anti-dumping investigations		Top three targets of anti-dumping investigation	
India	656	China	853
US	458	Korea	284
EU	437	US	234

Another arena for battle is exchange rates. The aftermath of the economic crisis 2010 saw a round of currency wars—the main combatants were the US and China, with some emerging markets (Brazil in particular) joining in. There were accusations and counter-accusations that competitive devaluation had been used to boost exports and steal an unfair advantage.[32]

This is not a world in which the location and relocation of capital takes place on the basis of the careful calculations of the owners or managers of capital about how to maximise profits in some unfettered global market for trade and investment. National and local states constantly intervene to protect the capital in their territories and to enhance the structures for attracting new capital, and use the full range of legal weapons at their disposal to gain advantage over their competitors.

But there are also contradictions within the process of accumulation and expansion, which means that the movement of capital or employment to other countries is not inevitable, inexorable or irreversible.

32: Beattie, 2012; Beattie and Ross, 2012. *Real terms capital is still 'sticky'*

The temporary "spatial fix" of relocation

Although capitalist production is subject to the law of value—external to the individual firm—capitalists have latitude to make individual decisions. In other words, capitalists have to manage large and geographically spread organisations in a context of increasingly intense competition. Transnational corporations search the globe for the best fit of skills, wages and regulatory frameworks before they commit to a location.[33] But managers make decisions without knowing what their competitors are doing with uncertainty hanging over the outcomes of their decisions. Firms try to assess the costs of competing destinations and then recalibrate their strategy as relative wages and other costs change. Managers are not the rational agents with perfect knowledge that are central to neoclassical economics. Richard Hyman points out that strategic decisions made by capitalists are an attempt to resolve a series of contradictions inherent in capitalist production:

> Marx's whole analysis was an insistence on the tendential contradiction between forces and relations of production, between the production and realisation of surplus value. Monopolisation or state intervention alter the form of such contradictions but do not transcend them. For individual capitals—as for capital in general—there is no "one best way" of managing these contradictions, only different routes to partial failure. It is on this basis that managerial strategy can best be conceptualised: as the programmatic choice among alternatives none of which can prove satisfactory.[34]

Moving to new locations to produce (cost driven) or realise (market driven) surplus value in order to resolve the contradictions of capital is what David Harvey refers to as a "spatial" fix.[35] But moving to new locations, rejigging contractual arrangements with other capital and/or adopting new technology are only temporary fixes for individual capitals and the system as a whole. Competition drives other capitalists in the same sector to follow a similar strategy—in other words, if one capitalist expands output and shifts production then other capitalists are compelled to follow a similar strategy to defend their competitive position.

By relocating across national boundaries firms may be able to employ workers who they can hire for a lower wage or who they can compel to work longer and harder. This is one of the countervailing influences on

---

33: Harvey, 2006.
34: Hyman, 1987, p30.
35: Harvey, 2006.

the falling rate of profit identified by Marx.[36] However, the higher the rate of profit achieved in a particular sector, the more rapidly that exceptional rate of profit will be eroded by the entry of new capital into that sector (assuming that there are no barriers to entry). Competition on the labour market and the attendant rise in confidence of workers collectively or individually will push up wages and erode the differential. However, the fact that labour has less freedom to move across national boundaries than capital means that differences in the rate of exploitation may be sustained for long periods of time—depending on the strength and combativity of workers.

There is a complex interplay between the rate of exploitation and the level of investment per worker which means that the impact on profits cannot be simply read off the strategies of firms and sectors. However, the influx of investment to China on the basis of low costs does provide a clear example of the erosion of the success of a particular model of social relations.

China's eroding low-wage advantage

According to the CEO of Collective Brands, a US footwear company shifting some of its production from China to Indonesia, the "utopia for one stop sourcing for quality and low price has been China...but utopias never last".[37] The advantages that can be gained from a particular locality can only be temporary, and the opportunities for excess profits from location are eliminated by the mobility of capital. The advantages and excess profits to be extracted from China's regime of low-wage, labour-intensive production are being eroded. The meteoric rise of China's economy with average growth rates of 10 percent for the last 30 years was based on an endless supply of cheap migrant workers from inland China to the Special Economic Zones (SEZs) in the coastal regions. But there is no longer an endless stream of pliant migrant workers happy to accept monotonous and exhausting work. Labour markets have tightened with more vacancies than workers looking for work.[38] This has meant expectations of better working conditions, the possibility of trading jobs, a higher turnover of workers and upward pressure on wages. All of these reduce the level of profit that firms can make in a particular locality.

Some labour-intensive businesses are moving from the coastal regions to inland China. Nike used to make most of its trainers in China, but many of its big suppliers have moved elsewhere, and in 2010 Vietnam became the

---

36: See Harman, 2007, and Choonara, 2009.
37: Brown, 2011.
38: Hardy and Budd, 2012; Hille and Jacob, 2012.

company's biggest global production base.[39] Hourly manufacturing wages average $1.80 in Thailand, 49 cents in Vietnam, 38 cents in Indonesia and 35 cents in Cambodia, and there has already been a significant transfer of work in apparel, footwear and sporting goods to South and South East Asia.

In 2011, citing many examples of companies moving their production back to the United States, the Boston Consulting Group (BCG) argued that the differential is closing between the opportunities offered in China and in the southern states of the United States. They concluded that China's overwhelming cost advantage over the United States is shrinking and that higher US productivity, a weaker dollar and other factors will close the cost gap between the United States and China. According to BCG:

> Rising labour rates have been a fact of life in Chinese factories for years. Average wages leapt by 150 percent from 1999 through 2006...a period when China emerged as the workshop of the world for a range of industries. Those increases started from a low base, but now the tipping point is in sight. For one thing wage growth has accelerated much faster than productivity growth. From 2000 through 2005, pay and benefits for the average Chinese factory worker rose by 10 percent annually. From 2005 through 2010, wage hikes averaged 19 percent per year, while the fully loaded costs of US production workers only rose by only 4 percent... Minimum wages rose by more than 20 percent in 20 Chinese regions and up to 30 percent in Sichuan province.[40]

BCG specifically compares China with the southern states of Alabama, Mississippi and South Carolina, which have anti-union laws and lower wages. Further, the cost of industrial land is higher in China, ranging from $11.15 on the coast to $21 in Shenzhen (opposite Hong Kong) with a national average of $10.22 per square foot.[41] Compare this with industrial land in Alabama, which ranges from $1.10 to $7.43 per square foot; in Tennessee and North Carolina the price ranges from $1.30 to $4.65. In this case capital returns, but on new terms, with poorer terms of employment and lower wages.[42]

Any differential is further eroded by the appreciation of the renminbi against the dollar, and the "costs and headaches"[43] of extended supply chains, as well as inventory expenses, quality control, unanticipated travel needs and the threat of disruption due to port closures and natural disasters. For US

39: Markillie, 2012.
40: Sirkin, Zinser and Hohner, 2011, p7.
41: Sirkin, Zinser and Hohner, 2011, p7.
42: Sirkin, Zinser and Hohner, 2011, p7.
43: Sirkin, Zinser and Hohner, 2011, p11.

corporations, the possibility of intellectual property theft and trade disputes resulting in punitive duties reduce differentials even further.

This is not to suggest that all US production will leave China or that firms will cease to locate there—for some sections of capital it will continue to be advantageous for production and to access the vast market.[44] But the implications of this are that there is not an inexorable and irreversible flood of jobs from high to low wage economies in China and South East Asia. The laws of competition erode any initial advantage and this results in a new round of relocations either back to the home economy or, in the case of some capitals, to other cheaper destinations.

Substituting technology for workers

As some sections of capital reach the limits of operating in low-cost locations they may look to another strategy for staving off, limiting or temporarily resolving the aggregate crisis of accumulation by adopting more or newer technology.

The example of Foxconn illustrates the limits of low-wage production predicated on a particular set of social relations. Foxconn is a Taiwanese firm that has a gargantuan manufacturing operation in China as a subcontractor for large transnational corporations such as Apple and HP. It employs 1 million workers, many of who live in dormitories in factory towns. The monthly pay (Rmb1,800/$285) is higher than the minimum wage, but the work is repetitive and mind-numbingly tedious:

> Most spend their days seated beside a conveyor belt, wearing white gowns, face masks and hair nets so that stray hairs and specks of dust won't interfere as they perform simple but precise tasks, again and again. Each worker focuses on a single action, like putting stickers on the front of an iPhone or packing a finished product into a box...it takes five days and 325 steps to assemble an iPad.[45]

This led to a spate of suicides in 2010, and in September 2012 there was a riot involving 2,000 workers. Based on a division of labour that involves a series of repetitive tasks, there is little room for any sort of enlightened work practice as this would undermine the basis of the model. Terry Gou (CEO of Foxconn) said: "As human beings are also animals,

---

44: Markillie, 2012.
45: Larson, 2012.

to manage 1 million animals gives me a headache".[46] Aside from the disgraceful reference to workers as animals, this remark reveals the limits of mass production. Foxconn has diversified its strategies. It plans to shift some of its production to Brazil, Mexico and Eastern Europe. Also, although Foxconn continues to build new plants and hire thousands of extra workers to make smartphones, it also plans to install a million robots inside of three years to supplement its workforce in China.

But the calculus of how to extract maximum surplus value can change, and an alternative strategy is to return some or all production to the higher labour cost home country and invest in new technology. At the Phillips Electronics factory on the coast of China electric shavers are assembled by hundreds of workers by hand. However:

> At a sister factory...in the Dutch countryside, 128 robot arms do the same thing with yoga-like flexibility... One robot arm endlessly firms three perfect bends in two connector wires and slips them into holes too small for the eye to see. The arms work so fast that they must be enclosed in glass cages to prevent the people supervising them from being injured. And they do it all without a coffee break—three shifts a day, 365 days a year. All told, the factory here has several dozen workers per shift, about a tenth as many as the plant in the Chinese city Zhuhai.[47]

It is not suggested that all foreign firms will switch their production from China or that workers will be replaced by robots. Automating assembly lines would require the rejigging of entire manufacturing processes. Smaller firms cannot afford to invest in robotics. However, the point is that the technological capacity of capitalism changes incessantly and there will be developments in technology that will change how things are produced in incremental or revolutionary ways and which will alter the balance sheet of profits. How far and how quickly new technologies will be adopted is not predictable, and it will be uneven between firms. However, there will be a pressure on them to adopt these new technologies in order to keep pace with their rivals. The falling costs and growing sophistication of robots mean that individual firms may be able to steal an advantage over their competitors, but for the system as a whole it leads to falling profits.[48]

46: Markoff, 2012.
47: Markoff, 2012.
48: See Harman, 2007, and Choonara, 2009.

Shaky empirical foundations

The whole process of measuring offshoring and outsourcing is riddled with problems and imperfect statistics. I begin by looking at foreign direct investment (FDI) as a proxy for the extent to which capital is being internationalised. Table 4 shows that between 2006 and 2011 there was a shift towards China capturing an increasing share of global flows of FDI, but the majority of flows were concentrated in the core capitalist economies of the United States and Europe. Despite the hype about the BRICS (Brazil, Russia, India, China and South Africa), it is worth noting that Brazil, Russia and India accounted for only 10 percent of global FDI between them.

Table 4: Flows of foreign direct investment by selected region and country, 2006, 2009 and 2011, as a percentage of the world total
Source: Adapted by the author from UNCTAD, 2012, pp169-176

	Inflows			Outflows		
	2006	2009	2011	2006	2009	2011
Europe	39.9	33.3	27.8	48.0	38.9	38.4
US	13.2	11.9	14.8	15.8	22.7	23.4
Japan	−0.4	0.9	−0.1	3.5	6.4	6.7
China	5.0	7.9	8.1	1.5	4.8	3.8
Hong Kong	3.0	4.4	5.5	3.2	5.4	4.8
Brazil	1.3	2.1	4.4	2.0	−0.8	−0.06
Russia	2.0	3.0	3.5	1.6	3.7	3.9
India	1.4	3.0	2.1	1.0	1.3	0.8

However, FDI is a broad and imperfect measure. Subcontracting arrangements are not captured in these statistics and therefore they underestimate the linkages that exist between capital and fail to capture the complexity of value chains. The iPad, for example, is exported from Foxconn in China, but has components from the United States and several countries in South East Asia embedded in it and therefore without detailed information it is very hard to track value added.[49] Published information from companies is likely to be inaccurate, not least because of manipulations involving transfer pricing.[50] Finally, because the figures are aggregates for individual nation states, they do not give important information about the regional dynamics of changes in production, which masks the emergence of large centres of accumulation within national economies.

Notwithstanding all these problems, an analysis of UNCTAD data does raise important questions about the usefulness of dividing the global economy into the "Global North" and "Global South". It should be noted that swathes of the global economy receive very little foreign investment.[51] In 2011 the developing world (as defined by UNCTAD) received 45 percent of foreign investment flows, but this was highly unevenly distributed. Within the foreign investment going to developing countries, 30 percent of the total went to China and 62 percent went to Asia more broadly, while Latin America received 32 percent. The entire continent of Africa captured only 6.2 percent of the flows to developing countries, which translates as a mere 2.8 percent of the global total.

Therefore, beneath these broad observations a great deal of unevenness persists—the post-Communist economies of the European Union, for example, still lag significantly behind in their levels of foreign direct investment, despite some countries having pockets of success in the automotive sector.[52] In economic terms, to conflate China with the Global South overstates the extent to which many regions, or in the case of Africa entire continents, are locked into global flows of capital.

From the early 1990s outflows of jobs in business services have been high profile. Call centres generated widespread media coverage as well-known UK companies moved to India. Initially simplified and routinised tasks in production such as call centres or back-office functions were off-shored to so-called emerging markets such as India and the Philippines. However, since 2004 there has been an acceleration in offshoring more skilled tasks such as research and development, sophisticated software development, design, mathematics-based finance and actuarial functions that require post-graduate or higher level skills.

But the hyperbole about the scale of offshoring back-office jobs, call

---

49: Johns, 2006, concerns a study of value chains in the video games industry.
50: Simply put, when companies arrange their accounts to show that profits are made in countries with the lowest level of tax.
51: The following statistics are based on the author's calculations from UNCTAD, 2012.
52: Hardy, 2009.

centres and BPO (Business Process Outsourcing) has to be put into perspective. Offshoring has been hugely and intensively promoted by consultants for whom this is very lucrative business.[53] McKinsey, for example, promised "dramatic price reductions" because of mouth-watering low wages. "The enticement to companies of a worker who earns $2 an hour in India as against ten times that amount for a worker in the United States is obvious".[54] From being a win-win game, McKinsey is now generating more business by arguing that it might not be the panacea that was first suggested.[55]

There are no accurate statistics for the offshoring of business services because this is an amalgam of a range of activities that does not correspond to any existing classification scheme. Further problems exist with the lack of consistent data, which arises from non-reporting and double counting (due to re-export).[56] The scale of offshoring business services has been hyped, in some places at least. For example, Central and Eastern European economies have been promoted as new destinations for business services. However, this employment creation was estimated to amount to a total of 18,000 jobs in Hungary, the Czech Republic and Slovakia (combined) across the whole business sector in 2010.[57] This looks small compared with 70,000 call centre workers employed in the Greater Manchester area alone.[58]

There has also been little attention paid to "backshoring" as bosses rediscover lower wage costs on their own doorstep. In the United States they have "discovered" the phenomenon of "rural sourcing"—simply put, the idea that they can get away with paying less in small towns than in big cities. "Companies that make use of this rural outsourcing phenomenon can pay 25 percent to 50 percent less than they'd pay outsourcers in metropolitan areas".[59] Or in the case of the United Kingdom, "northsourcing" refers to jobs from overseas coming back to Britain or moving from what is regarded as the expensive south east. Overall the north west of the United Kingdom has 700 call centres (up from 521 in 2004) and employs 183,000 people (a 50 percent increase from 2004). So rather than all jobs "going to India"—new jobs have been created in or have returned to the United Kingdom.

There are few studies of backshoring, but one report on the activities of German companies found that 570 out of 1,484 companies surveyed had

53: Farrell, Agrawal and Remes, 2003.
54: Farrell, Agrawal and Remes, 2003, p1.
55: Goel, Moussavi and Srivatsan, 2008.
56: Sass and Fifekova, 2011.
57: Hardy, Fifekova, and Sass, 2011.
58: Bounds, 2012.
59: Carlson, 2010.

backshored part or all of their foreign production.[60] Therefore, for every third relocating company there is currently one backshoring company. The main reasons given were problems with quality, flexibility and delivery capability—all functions crucial to the annihilation of "time through space". Reinforcing earlier arguments, unexpected or increasing labour costs followed as the third motive, when promising calculations for relocating no longer appeared advantageous.

Where have the jobs gone?

The outward flow of jobs from outsourcing in the US has to be understood in the context of the labour market. A report from a US think tank points to an increase of 27.3 million jobs between 1990 and 2008.[61] This expanding labour force was absorbed almost exclusively by the service sector, with the biggest growth in government and healthcare (10.4 million). The government is the largest single employer, with a 20 percent increase in employment from 1990 to 2008, over half of which was in education.

According to the report there has been some loss of employment with the out-migration of functions in global value chains; however, this reduction has been to do with labour-saving technology rather than outsourcing.[62] In electronics, jobs have fallen by 650,000 over two decades, but value added has increased by 363 percent, by far the largest increase among all industries. In the US auto industry from 1990 to 2007, 172,000 jobs were lost as domestic industry declined, but the value added per job increased by 85 percent from 1990 to 2008. From mid-2009 to mid-2010, however, the auto industry gained more than 50,000 jobs, increased profits for the first time since 2005 and increased exports abroad as the US government bailed out and restructured General Motors and Chrysler.

The report goes on to point out: "Yet the economy did not have an unemployment problem, at least until the crisis of 2008".[63] Massive cuts in the public sector, as well as job losses in the private sector since the economic crisis have increased unemployment. To put this in perspective, 650,000 jobs have been lost in the electronics industry *in the last two decades* partly due to outsourcing, but also as a result of overproduction and the

---

60: Kinkel, 2012. I have included some general observations whereas the article compares trends before (2004 and 2006) and after (2007 to 2009) the crisis.

61: Spence and Hlatshwayo, 2011. This is a useful and robust analysis drawing on historical time series data analysis from the Bureau of Labor Statistics and Bureau of Economic Analysis between 1990 and 2008.

62: Spence and Hlatshwayo, 2008.

63: Spence and Hlatshwayo, 2008, p31.

increased use of technology. Compare this with the 627,000 jobs lost *in the last three years* in the public sector from June 2009 to June 2012.[64]

Where there is capital there is conflict

Kevin Doogan points out that talking up offshoring by some who profess to have left wing sympathies is self-limiting and pessimistic.[65] These arguments coalesce around a view that workers in a single labour market are forced into competition with one another by perfectly mobile capital, and that the new organisational arrangements of capital, such as offshoring and outsourcing, bring competitive pressures on organised and unorganised workers and weaken their bargaining power in a race to the bottom. States use the spectre of this competition as a stick with which to beat workers and tell them that the wages, pensions and working conditions (and other market-distorting benefits) are barriers to competition.

Beverly Silver, in her book *Forces of Labor*, provides an excellent antidote to these defeatist views.[66] She argues that volume one of Marx's *Capital* can be read as "a history of the dialectic between workers' resistance to exploitation at the point of production and the efforts of capital to overcome that resistance by constantly revolutionising production and social relations".[67] These revolutions in the organisation of production and social relations may undermine some elements of the working class, in the short term at least, but new sites of accumulation will emerge along with new conflicts and forms of struggle. The cheap labour economic miracles of the 1970s and 1980s—ranging from Spain and Brazil to South Africa and South Korea—each created new working classes that produced militant labour movements in the expanding mass production industries. Not only were these labour movements successful in improving wages and working conditions, but they played a key role in the struggle for democracy in these countries.

Silver traces the high point of struggles as they followed the relocations and the growth of the auto sector—from the United States and Canada in the 1930s, to the United Kingdom in the 1950s, to France and Italy in the 1960s, to Germany and Spain in the 1970s and to Argentina, Brazil and South Africa in the 1980s and 1990s. More recently, as a chunk of European auto production has moved to the lower wage economies of Central and Eastern Europe, car factories have become sites of union revival

---

64: *New York Times*, 2012; Bivens, 2012.
65: Doogan, 2009.
66: Silver, 2003.
67: Silver, 2003, p19.

in Poland.[68] Therefore, wherever capital flows, so-called spatial fixes have recreated similar working classes and class conflict. Far from the image of "Third World workers being on a hopeless treadmill without international protection",[69] the geographical relocation of production has strengthened and recreated new working classes and new struggles.

Conclusion

The internal dynamics of capitalism and the law of value are constantly shaping and reshaping the spatial distribution of production. From the perspective of capital, locations offer different opportunities for extracting and realising surplus value. The organisational challenges to the owners and managers of firms are immense in terms of their relationships with other capitals (competitors, collaborators and suppliers). But only some sections of capital are mobile, and then only to a limited degree. States intervene constantly to alter the conditions for accumulation in their territories, by reducing costs or trying to influence the rules of the game.

While an individual firm can steal an advantage on its competitors by moving to low-cost locations this can only be a temporary fix. Undoubtedly, China has become the workshop of the world in the last decade for a range of goods, reflected in its status as the largest global exporter. But its low-cost, low-productivity, mass production model has limits, particularly as it meets increasing passive and active resistance of workers. There has been a shift towards the production of certain goods in China, often as part of the long and complex chains of transnational corporations, but it is unlikely that this will continue with the same velocity, and in some cases is reversible.

There are no rigorous statistics to support an apocalyptic view of offshoring. Models that are peddled as "scientific" are not so; they have more to do with attempting to browbeat workers with threats of job loss and plant closure as well as creating lucrative contracts for consultants. Moreover, blaming other groups of workers for unfair competition deflects attention from a system that cannot provide jobs for everyone.

The obscene levels of unemployment in Europe—especially for young people—have nothing to do with the outsourcing or offshoring of jobs. Rather this is related to the long-term stagnation of capitalism, and more immediately the fallout from the 2007-8 crisis and the draconian austerity measures, which have slashed the living standards of workers. When workers accuse those in other countries of "taking their jobs", they

68: Hardy, 2009.
69: Greider, 1999, p5, cited in Silver, 2003, p168.

are lining up with their own ruling class. It is only when workers understand their common cause across national boundaries that there can be a real defence of jobs and employment and the beginnings of a force that can challenge an anarchic system that regularly destroys the livelihoods and welfare of working class people.

References

3News, 2010, New Zealand (28 October), www.3news.co.nz/How-The-Hobbit-came-to-stay-in-NZ/tabid/418/articleID/183575/Default.aspx

Aschoff, Nicola, M, 2012, "A Tale of Two Crises: Labor, Capital and Restructuring in the US Auto Industry", in Leo Panitch, Greg Albo and Vivek Chibber (eds), *Socialist Register: the Crisis and the Left* (The Merlin Press).

Beattie, Alan, 2012, "Tricks of the Trade Law", *Financial Times* (29 October).

Beattie, Alan and Alice Ross, 2012, "A Fragile Armistice", *Financial Times* (4 October).

Bivens, Josh, 2012, "Public Sector Job Losses: An Unprecedented Drag on the Recovery", Economic Policy Institute (5 April), www.epi.org/publication/public-sector-job-losses-unprecedented-drag

Bounds, Andrew, 2012, "Call Centres Come in from the Suburbs as the Trend for 'Northshoring Rises'", *Financial Times* (16 July).

Brown, Kevin, 2011, "Rising Chinese Wages Pose Relocation Risk", *Financial Times* (15 February).

Carlson, Caron, 2010, "Popularity of 'Rural Sourcing' Grows", FierceCio (10 July), www.fiercecio.com/story/popularity-rural-sourcing-grows/2010-07-10

Choonara, Joseph, 2009, *Unravelling Capitalism: A Guide to Marxist Political Economy* (Bookmarks).

Coe, Neil, Peter Dicken and Martin Hess, 2008, "Global Production Networks: Realizing the Potential", *Journal of Economic Geography*, volume 8, number 3.

Dicken, Peter, 2011, *Global Shift: Mapping the Changing Contours of the Global Economy* (Sage).

Doogan, Kevin, 2009, *New Capitalism: The Transformation of Work* (Polity).

Farrell, Diana, Vivek Agrawal and Jaana Remes, 2003, "Offshoring and Beyond: Cheap Labor is the Beginning, Not the End", *The McKinsey Quarterly*, volume 4 (December), www.mckinseyquarterly.com/Offshoring_and_beyond_1367

Fonantella-Khan, James, and John Reed, 2012, "Guarded Welcome for EU Drive to Help Struggling Car Industry", *Financial Times* (9 November).

Fröbel, Folker, Jürgen Heinrichs and Otto Kreye, 1981, *The New International Division of Labour* (Cambridge University Press).

Goel, Ajay, Nazgol Moussavi and Vats Srivatsan, 2008, "Time to Rethink Offshoring?", *McKinsey Quarterly* (September), www.mckinseyquarterly.com/Time_to_rethink_offshoring_2190

Good Jobs First, 2005, "Report on Biotechnology Subsidies", www.goodjobsfirst.org/corporate-subsidy-watch/biotechnology

Good Jobs First, 2010a, "Case Study: Film Production", www.goodjobsfirst.org/corporate-subsidy-watch/film-production

Good Jobs First, 2010b, "Report on Subsidies to Semiconductor Industry", www.goodjobsfirst.org/corporate-subsidy-watch/semiconductors

Good Jobs First, 2010c, "Report on Subsidies to Foreign Auto Plants", www.goodjobsfirst.
    org/corporate-subsidy-watch/foreign-auto-plants

Greider, William, 1999, "The Battle Beyond Seattle", *The Nation* (27 December).

Hardy, Jane, and Adrian Budd, 2012, "China's Capitalism and the Crisis", *International
    Socialism 133* (winter), www.isj.org.uk/?id=777

Hardy, Jane, 2009, *Poland's New Capitalism* (Pluto).

Hardy, Jane, Martina Fifekova and Magdolna Sass, 2011, "Impacts of Horizontal and Vertical
    Foreign Investment in Business Services: The Experience of Hungary, Slovakia and the
    Czech Republic", *European Urban and Regional Studies*, volume 18, number 4.

Harman, Chris, 2007, "The rate of profit and the world today", *International Socialism 115*
    (summer), www.isj.org.uk/?id=340

Harris, Nigel, 2012, "Characterising the Period", *International Socialism 135* (summer),
    www.isj.org.uk/?id=826

Harvey, David, 2006 [1982], *The Limits to Capital* (Verso).

Hille, Kathrin, and Rahul Jacob, 2012, "China: Beyond the Conveyor Belt", *Financial Times*
    (15 October).

Huws, Ursula, 2006, "Fixed, Footloose or Fractured: Work, Identity and the Spatial
    Division of Labor in the Twenty-First Century City", *Monthly Review*, volume 57, number
    10 (March), http://monthlyreview.org/2006/03/01/fixed-footloose-or-fractured-work-
    identity-and-the-spatial-division-of-labor-in-the-twenty-first-century-city

Hyman, Richard, 1987, "Strategy or Structure? Capital, Labour and Control", *Work,
    Employment and Society*, volume 1, number 1.

Johns, Jennifer, 2006, "Video Games Production Networks: Value Capture, Power Relations
    and Embeddedness", *Journal of Economic Geography*, volume 6, number 4.

Kinkel, Steffen, 2012, "Trends in Production Location and Backshoring Activities:
    Changing Patterns in the Course of the Global Economic Crisis", *International Journal of
    Operations and Production Management*, volume 32, number 6.

Larson, Christina, 2012, "Migrant Workers in China Face Competition from Robots",
    Technology Review, www.technologyreview.com/news/428433/migrant-workers-in-china-
    face-competition-from-robots

Markillie, Paul, 2012, "The Boomerang Effect", *The Economist* (21 April), www.economist.com/
    node/21552898

Markoff, John, 2012, "Skilled Work, Without the Worker", *New York Times* (18 August),
    www.nytimes.com/2012/08/19/business/new-wave-of-adept-robots-is-changing-global-
    industry.html?pagewanted=all

Marx, Karl, 1973, *Grundrisse* (Penguin), www.marxists.org/archive/marx/works/1857/grundrisse/

Marx, Karl, 1978, *Capital*, volume 2 (Penguin), www.marxists.org/archive/marx/
    works/1885-c2/index.htm

Moody, Kim, 1997, *Workers in a Lean World: Unions in the International Economy* (Verso).

Nayyar, Deepak, 2006, "Globalisation, History and Development", *Cambridge Journal of
    Economics*, volume 30, number 1.

New York Times, 2012,"The road to more jobs" (11 July), www.nytimes.com/2012/07/12/
    opinion/the-road-to-more-jobs.html

Pickles, John, and Adrian Smith, 2011, "Delocalisation and Persistence in the European
    Clothing Industry: the Reconfiguration of Trade and Production Networks", *Regional
    Studies*, volume 45, number 2.

Rainnie, Al, Andrew Herod and Susan McGrath-Champ, 2011, "Global Production
    Networks and Labour", *Competition & Change*, volume 15, number 2.

Reed, John, 2012, "Carmakers Hope New Road is Way to Survival", *Financial Times* (25 October).

Sass, Magdolna, and Martina Fifekova, 2011, "Offshoring and Outsourcing Business Services to Central and Eastern Europe: Some Empirical and Conceptual Considerations", *European Planning Studies*, volume 19, number 9.

Scott, Robert, 2008, "The China Trade Toll: Widespread Wage Suppression, 2 Million Jobs Lost in the US", *Economic Policy Institute* (July), www.epi.org/publication/bp219.

Silver, Beverly, 2003, *Forces of Labour: Workers' Movements and Globalisation since 1870* (Cambridge University Press).

Sirkin, Harold, Michael Zinser and Douglas Hohner, 2011, "Made in America Again: Why Manufacturing Will Return to the US", Boston Consulting Group, www.bcg.com/documents/file84471.pdf

Smith, John, 2012, "Outsourcing, Financialisation and the Crisis", *International Journal of Management Concepts and Philosophy*, volume 6, numbers 1/2.

Spence, Michael, and Sandile Hlatshwayo, 2011, *The Evolving Structure of the American Economy and the Employment Challenge*, Working Paper from the Maurice R Greenberg Center for Geoeconomic Studies, Council of Foreign Relations.

Standing, Guy, 2011, *The Precariat: the New Dangerous Class* (Bloomsbury).

Starosta, Guido, 2010, "Global Commodity Chains and the Marxian Law of Value", *Antipode*, volume 42, number 2.

UNCTAD, 2012, *World Investment Report* (United Nations).

Van Biesebroeck, Johannes, 2008, "Policy Watch: Governments at the Bidding Table", Working Paper, University of Toronto and NBER, www.iscr.org.nz/f390,10883/jvb_110208_GOV_AT_THE_BIDDING_TABLE.pdf

WTO, 2011, *International Trade Statistics, 2010*, www.wto.org/english/res_e/statis_e/its2011_e/its11_toc_e.htm

Wu, Mark, 2012, "Anti-dumping in Asia's Emerging Giants", *Harvard Law Journal*, volume 53, number 1.

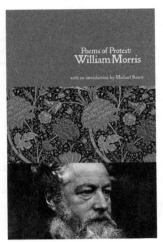

The dynamics of revolution

Alex Callinicos

A review of Neil Davidson, **How Revolutionary Were the Bourgeois Revolutions?** *(Haymarket, 2012),* £*22.99*

This is a book in the grand style. This is true physically—getting on for 700 pages of text, 70 of notes and nearly another 70 of bibliography, and beautifully produced (an achievement at a time when the book as a material object is meant to be obsolescent: both author and publisher are to be congratulated). But it is a grand work also in intellectual and historical scope. In addressing the question set by his title, Neil Davidson effortlessly displays analytical intelligence and erudition rare among historians of any persuasion. And the reader put off by the sheer size of the book will be reassured by Neil's easy, fluent style, plentifully interlarded with humour. If there were any doubts about Neil's calibre as a Marxist historian after his two books on Scottish history (which looms large in this work as well—no one could come away from it without knowing it was written by a Scot), and his numerous articles, these have now been removed.

Revolutions for capital

So what is the problem that Neil is addressing? Though, as he shows, the idea of bourgeois revolution takes shape during the English Revolution of the 17th century and particularly in the 18th century Enlightenment in Scotland and France, it receives definitive formulation by Marx and Engels during the years surrounding the revolutions of 1848. Thus, writing in December 1848, Marx contemptuously contrasted the timid Prussian bourgeoisie of his day with its more revolutionary predecessors:

The *March revolution in Prussia* should not be confused either with the *English* revolution of 1648 or with the *French* one of 1789.

In 1648 the bourgeoisie was allied with the modern aristocracy against the monarchy, the feudal aristocracy and the established church.

In 1789 the bourgeoisie was allied with the people against the monarchy, the aristocracy and the established church.

The revolution of 1789 (at least in Europe) had as its prototype only the revolution of 1648; that for the revolution of 1648 only the revolt of the Netherlands against Spain. Both revolutions were a century ahead of their prototypes not only in time but also in content.

In both revolutions the bourgeoisie was the class that really headed the movement. The *proletariat* and the *non-bourgeois strata of the middle class* had either not yet any interests separate from those of the bourgeoisie or they did not yet constitute independent classes or class sub-divisions... The revolutions of 1648 and 1789 were not *English* and *French* revolutions; they were revolutions of a *European* type. They did not represent the victory of a *particular* class of society over the *old political order*; they *proclaimed the political order of the new European society*. The bourgeoisie was victorious in these revolutions, but the *victory of the bourgeoisie* was at that time the *victory of a new social order*, the victory of bourgeois ownership over feudal ownership, of nationality over provincialism, of competition over the guild, of division of the land over primogeniture, of the rule of the landowner over the domination of the owner by the land, of enlightenment over superstition, of the family over the family name, of industry over heroic idleness, of bourgeois law over mediaeval privileges.[1]

The bourgeois revolutions were thus the political transformations that established the domination of capitalism. Marx formulated this concept to make sense of his own time, but also as part of the process of developing his theory of history, which in the immediately preceding years crystal-lised in *The German Ideology* and *The Poverty of Philosophy*. Neil rightly says: "The Marxist theory of history *required* a concept of bourgeois revolution," but, strangely, he doesn't stop to explain why.[2] In my view, there are two

---

1:    Marx, 1977, pp160-161.
2:    Davidson, 2012, p117.

reasons. First, the idea of bourgeois revolution was theoretically needed to conceptualise the relationship between the long drawn out economic transition from the feudal to the capitalist mode of production and the much more dramatic and concentrated political transformations that created the modern state system. Secondly, since these transformations were continuing in Marx's and Engels's own time, the concept was also politically needed to differentiate what they regarded to be still bourgeois revolts against the aristocratic old regime that continued to dominate 19th century Europe from the socialist revolutions that the emerging capitalist system was beginning to make possible. Neil quotes an excellent passage where Georg Lukács makes this second point:

> One of Marx's greatest theoretical achievements was to distinguish clearly between bourgeois and proletarian revolution. This distinction was of the utmost practical and tactical importance in view of the immature self-delusions of his contemporaries, for it offered the only methodological instrument for recognising the genuinely proletarian revolutionary elements within the general revolutionary movements of the time.[3]

So the concept of bourgeois revolution was needed as both a theoretical and a political tool. Yet, beginning with 1848, the bourgeoisie ceased to play the heroic role Marx had attributed to its English and French predecessors.[4] This reality provoked rich and complex debates, thoroughly reviewed by Neil, among Russian Marxists at the beginning of the 20th century. The most important single result was Trotsky's theory of permanent revolution: he argued that the uneven and combined development of the world capitalist economy tends to create in "backward" societies islands of advanced industrial capitalism from which militant workers' movements can emerge. Fear of their workers and dependence on foreign capital make the bourgeoisie of these countries even more cautious in confronting the old regime. But the fusion of advanced and backward also means that struggles for democratic demands, which don't in principle threaten the existence of capitalism, can merge under workers' leadership with the

---

3:   Lukács, 1970, pp47-48; Davidson, 2012, p240.

4:   Neil argues that the passage from "The Bourgeoisie and the Counter-Revolution" quoted above is sometimes translated in a way that presents Marx as "holding a more positive view of the bourgeoisie that he in fact did": Davidson, 2012, p717 n205. But the translation I have used suffers less from this defect: in any case, the whole construction of the passage is to compare the Prussian bourgeoisie unfavourably with the English and French, which implies that the latter showed greater revolutionary vigour.

struggle for socialism and the bourgeois revolution "grow over" into proletarian revolution, as indeed happened in Russia in 1917.

The consolidation of Stalinist "orthodoxy" in the 1920s and 1930s was based, of course, on the rejection of Trotsky's theory, which he first generalised beyond Russia in the course of the debates within the Communist International over the Chinese Revolution of 1925-7.[5] The Stalinist alternative involved insisting on a sharp separation between what now tended to be thought of as "bourgeois-democratic" revolutions and socialist revolutions: these represented distinct stages of the struggle, and during the first the working class should ally itself to the "progressive" bourgeoisie. This was a version of what the Mensheviks had advocated within the Russian revolutionary movement before 1917 (Lenin and the Bolsheviks had a more complex position that, while rejecting Trotsky's theory, insisted the proletariat could lead the peasantry and petty bourgeoisie in a bourgeois revolution from below that would set the stage for a more or less rapid shift to the struggle for workers' power). The conception of bourgeois revolution implied by the Stalinist strategy drew on themes that had already emerged in the "orthodox Marxism" of the Second International before 1914, where history also tended to be understood as evolving through clear distinct stages. Elaborated in some cases by high-calibre left wing historians such as Georges Lefebvre and Christopher Hill, this view is summarised by Neil thus:

> From the 16th century, a class of urban capitalists began to develop within European feudalism, gradually laying the economic foundations of a new form of society. Despite their growing economic weight, these capitalists were consigned to a position of social inferiority by a rural class of feudal landowners and excluded from political power by the absolutist states... In order to release capitalism from its feudal restrictions, the absolutist states needed to be overthrown; but since the capitalist class was still only a minority of the population...it had to lead a coalition of classes to accomplish the revolution.[6]

After the Second World War this conception of bourgeois revolution came under sustained intellectual attack from what came to be known as "revisionism". Mainstream historians such as Alfred Cobban, François Furet,

---

5:   See my discussions of the development of the theory of permanent revolution in Callinicos, 1982, pp98-102, and Callinicos, 1990, pp6-11. Geras, 1975, is a superb account of the Marxist debates before 1917 about the nature of the Russian Revolution.
6:   Davidson, 2012, pp264-265; see also pp254-256.

and Conrad Russell launched themselves at the "social interpretation" of the English and French Revolutions. The effect was, in the academic world, thoroughly to discredit the very idea of bourgeois revolution. As Neil puts it:

> By the end of the 20th century then, the pre-existing orthodoxy had been replaced by a new consensus that can be summarised as follows: prior to the so-called bourgeois revolutions, the bourgeoisie was not "rising" and may even have been indistinguishable from the feudal lords; during the so-called bourgeois revolutions [the bourgeoisie] was not in the vanguard of the movement and may even have been on the opposite side; after them, the bourgeoisie was not in power and may even have been further removed from control of the state than it had previously been; above all, these revolutions had nothing at all to do with either the emergence or the consolidation of capitalism… Instead, revisionists claimed, these revolutions—if indeed they could be called revolutions—were just what they appeared to be, and what participants said they were: expressions of inter-elite competition for office, differences over religious belief and observance, or movements in defence of regional autonomy.[7]

That the orthodox conception of the bourgeois revolution should come under attack is not particularly surprising, both because of the analytical and empirical problems it involved, and also in the light of the Cold War context in which the revisionist assault was mounted. What is a bit more unexpected is the way in which a Marxist current has in the last couple of decades joined in on the attack. This is the school of Political Marxists who take inspiration from Bob Brenner's interpretation of the transition from feudalism to capitalism. Ellen Meiksins Wood, in many respects the intellectual leader of Political Marxism, has defended an extremely narrow conception of capitalism which in effect requires that it originate in the kind of agrarian capitalism that emerged in 17th and 18th century England.[8] Following Brenner's cue, Political Marxists have also taken aim at the idea of bourgeois revolution. George Comninel, in what may be the worst book by a contemporary Marxist, elaborates the standard revisionist interpretation of the French Revolution as a conflict within the ruling class with the claim (supported by a travesty of Marx's theory of

---

7:    Davidson, 2012, p366.
8:    For example, Wood, 2002. Brenner's key essays on the transition are published, along with critical responses, in Aston and Philpin, 1985. Harman, 1989, is a powerful critique of Brenner; my own view of the debate will be found in Callinicos, 2009, chapter 3.

history) that capitalism did not exist in 18th century France.[9] Wood offers a more general critique:

> The concept of bourgeois revolution is confusing for several reasons. Was a revolution necessary to bring about capitalism, or simply to facilitate the development of an already existing capitalism? Was it a cause or an effect of capitalism? Although much has been claimed for the bourgeois revolution as the critical moment in the transition to capitalism, no conception of bourgeois revolution exists in which the revolution explains the emergence of capitalism.[10]

Rethinking bourgeois revolution

Wood's argument is unimpressive, conflating as it does two different registers—the epochal transitions from one mode of production to another and the political transformations that secured the dominance of the new economic system. Marx never invoked the concept of bourgeois revolution to explain the *emergence* of capitalism: he uses a much wider canvass to account for this complex process in part 8 of *Capital*, volume I. But this doesn't mean that all was well with the orthodox theory of bourgeois revolution. Conceptually, it suffered from an ambiguity between *agency* and *outcome*: is what makes a revolution bourgeois that it is led by representatives of the bourgeoisie or that it promotes the development of capitalism? Proponents of the orthodox theory essentially replied: both. But from the 1960s onwards a number of writers—for example, Trotsky's biographer Isaac Deutscher, the intellectual historian Gareth Stedman Jones (before he became a post-Marxist), Christopher Hill in his later work, and the historians of modern Germany David Blackbourn and Geoff Eley—initiated a rethinking of the theory that insisted it was the outcome of a revolution that determined whether or not it could be called bourgeois. Perry Anderson expressed this reversal of perspective most sharply: "these transformations [the bourgeois revolutions] could never have been the linear project of a single class subject. Here the exception was the rule—every one was a bastard birth".[11]

9:   Comninel, 1987, criticised in Callinicos, 1989, pp141-151 and 161-164. See Brenner, 1989, for his take on bourgeois revolution. Neil's book originated in his Deutscher Prize Lecture; because the prize was awarded jointly to him and a Political Marxist, Benno Teschke, the lecture was organised as a debate: see Davidson, 2005, and Teschke, 2005. Shamefully, the balance was tilted against Neil by Comninel being added as a third speaker.

10:   Wood, 2002, pp118-119, quoted in Davidson, 2012, p420.

11:   Anderson, 1992, p113. This important essay, though written in 1976, was only published

Neil is kind enough to say that an article of mine published in this journal in 1989 represents "the strongest and most comprehensive" statement of this approach, dubbed "consequentialism" by the Political Marxist Benno Teschke. [12] So I hope I will be forgiven for quoting myself:

> Bourgeois revolutions must be understood, not as revolutions consciously made by capitalists, but as revolutions which promote capitalism. The emphasis must shift from the class which makes a bourgeois revolution to the effects of such a revolution—to the class which benefits from it. More specifically, a bourgeois revolution is a political transformation—a change in state power, which is the precondition for large-scale capital accumulation and the establishment of the bourgeoisie as the dominant class. This definition requires, then, a political change with certain effects. It says nothing about the social forces which carry through the transformation. [13]

On the basis of this re-conceptualisation, I distinguished three types of bourgeois revolution. First, the "classical" bourgeois revolutions—above all England 1640 and France 1789—where authentically bourgeois forces, however intermingled with the old regime, did lead broad coalitions of small producers of town and country in movements to smash the absolutist state and replace it with political forms much more congenial to the development of capitalism. [14] Secondly, the bourgeois revolutions "from above" that, against the background of a world economy being reshaped by industrial capitalism, transformed the 19th century state system. In Germany, Italy and Japan sections of the rural landed class presided over

in 1992, so I was unable to discuss it in my 1989 article, summarised below. Surprisingly, Neil pays little attention to it.

12: Davidson, 2012, p481; Teschke, 2005, p6.

13: Callinicos, 1989, p124. This article, written as part of a special issue to mark the bicentenary of the French Revolution, was a subject of some controversy on the *International Socialism* editorial board—partly because of its great length, partly because of the relative sympathy it expressed for Brenner's interpretation of the transition. It was edited, efficiently but robustly, by Lindsey German, which may help explain the somewhat jerky quality of the prose. But, for reasons that Neil discusses, the actual conception of bourgeois revolution I put forward was not controversial. It had been much more economically stated by Duncan Hallas a year or so earlier—Hallas, 1988.

14: I didn't discuss the 16th century Dutch revolt in any depth, in part because I mistakenly believed that the early-modern northern Netherlands were not a capitalist society: but see now Brandon, 2007. Ironically, Brenner himself has uncovered the vanguard role of a specific group of capitalists, the so-called "new merchants" in the English Revolution: see Brenner, 1993, and Callinicos, 1994. As Anderson comments, "here, if ever, were indeed revolutionary bourgeois"—Anderson, 2005, p251.

processes of gradual transformation of the existing state (involving in the first two cases interstate wars of unification, in the third civil war) into a form promoting capital accumulation: Gramsci dubbed this process "passive revolution", which limited popular participation or excluded it altogether.[15] The American Civil War represented a slightly different version of the same type, where the Northern-dominated federal government under Abraham Lincoln used methods of total war and increasingly relied on the slaves' rejection of their masters to break the secession of the South and forge a centralised state that mightily accelerated the development of industrial capitalism in the US. Third, the very different case analysed by Tony Cliff of "deflected permanent revolution": in the 20th century colonial and semi-colonial world, sections of the intelligentsia filled the vacuum left by the failure of the working class to constitute itself as a revolutionary political subject and broke the foreign hold in order to constitute a new state capitalist order—for example, China 1949, Egypt 1952, Cuba 1959.[16]

In essence, Neil's book is a restatement, extension, but also interrogation of this "consequentialist" conception of bourgeois revolution. Painting on a much larger canvas than any previous study, he is able to explore a much wider range of issues in much greater depth. There are many treasures in this book. Thus Neil is splendidly sarcastic about the revisionists' shift in social sympathies:

> It transpired that it was not only, as Edward Thompson thought, "the poor stockinger, the Luddite cropper, the 'obsolete' handloom weaver, the 'utopian' artisan, and even the deluded follower of Joanna Southcott" who needed to be rescued from "the enormous condescension of posterity". So too did the rich tax farmer, the conspiratorial Royal exile, the former mistress of the Queen's bedchamber, the misunderstood grain speculator, the former San Dominican slave-owner, and many more besides.[17]

Neil also offers many insights such as the following on why, among the leaderships of the 19th century revolutions from above, the Lincoln administration was alone in risking radical measures reminiscent of Cromwell and Robespierre:

15: See more generally on passive revolution Callinicos, 2010.
16: Cliff, 1963. Neil muddies the waters somewhat by asking how cases of deflected permanent revolution fit into the distinction between bourgeois revolutions from above and below—Davidson, 2012, p478. The answer is that they don't—they represent a different type of bourgeois revolution from either of the other two.
17: Davidson, 2012, pp361-362.

The fact that revolutionary violence could be directed outward to a now effectively external enemy, through the mechanism of disciplined state power, meant that a far greater degree of radicalism could be attempted than if the struggle had been a purely internal one conducted, as it were, by civilians. In other words, the Northern bourgeoisie were ultimately prepared to embrace the logic of total war rather than face defeat, even if this meant the emancipation of the slaves and harnessing the freedmen against their former masters as part of the Union's military apparatus.[18]

So *How Revolutionary Were the Bourgeois Revolutions?* represents a formidable addition to the intellectual armoury of historical materialism. But—yes, there is a but—the book suffers from serious weaknesses. These can be placed in three categories. The first is that there are quite a lot of minor factual errors and somewhat more serious conceptual anomalies.[19]

18: Davidson, 2012, pp615-616. As Neil also notes, "the peculiarities of American development meant that it was here...that the bourgeoisie made its last stand as a revolutionary class." Davidson, 2012, p168.

19: Examples of minor factual errors: the Yellow Shirt movement against Thaksin Shinawatra was in Thailand, not Indonesia (Davidson, 2012, pxvi); Neil presumably meant that Arab astronomical (rather than astrological) practices revived during the Renaissance (p12); Charles I was James II's father, not his uncle (p104); Bismarck was appointed minister president, not state chancellor, of Prussia in 1862 (p162); was the Chinese peasantry really "a section of the rural bourgeoisie"? (p256); it was James Klugmann who reflected on Communist Party cultural policy in the 1930s, not Jack Klugman once of Quincy fame (p266); as Neil correctly acknowledges later in the book, Hayek did not believe capitalism corresponds to human nature (p334); Conrad Russell no longer sits in the House of Lords, or indeed anywhere else, because he is dead (365); slaves and peasants don't produce surplus value (p496); does "Egypt 2011-?" belong in a list of "failed socialist revolutions'? (p499); the author of *The Imaginary Institution of Society* was Cornelius, not Carlos, Castoriadis (p521); British Upper Canada was not "Ottawa", but large parts of what is now the province of Ontario (p617); on numerous occasions, perhaps symptomatically of Neil's Scottish grounding, Jacobinism is rendered as 'Jacobitism'.

The most serious theoretical mistake not pertinent to the overall argument: Neil claims that Marx uses the expression "formal subsumption of labour" to characterise cases where, "during the transition to capitalism, small independent producers...could carry on production in their traditional manner, but on behalf of the usurer or merchant, even though the latter pair may play no direct role in organising the labour process"—Davidson, 2012, p576. In fact Marx argues that the formal subsumption of labour under capital presupposes the capital-wage-labour relationship, rather than preceding it. Here:

"the *worker* confronts the capitalist, who possesses money, as the proprietor of his own person and therefore of his own labour capacity, and as the seller of the temporary use of the latter...*the objective conditions of his labour* (raw material, instruments of labour and therefore also means of subsistence during labour) belong, completely or at least in part, not to him but to the buyer and consumer of his labour, therefore themselves confront him as capital. The

These are, perhaps, to be expected in a work of this scope. Secondly, there are a series of problems that arise from the form of the book and that are expressed in its length. Neil describes the book as "essentially an exercise in the history of ideas". [20] Thus he traces the genealogy of the idea of bourgeois revolution, and then its development, rejection and reformulation. Consequently, the truth (so to speak) emerges towards the end of the book with the development of "consequentialism" and Neil's own overview in the concluding Part Four, "The Specificity of the Bourgeois Revolution". The reader is therefore left to glean the unifying argument from the unfolding intellectual history. This is, of course, how things are supposed to work in the Hegelian dialectic: "absolute knowing" only emerges at the end of *The Phenomenology of Spirit*. But for someone relatively new to the terrain, the journey would be arduous. It is a pity that Neil didn't start off the book with a clear statement of his overall argument to serve as a guide. (Hegel tended to disparage such expedients as cheating, but his prefaces and introductions often contain the best statements of his philosophy.)

The book's form as an intellectual history also means that there is no compact narrative or analysis of the bourgeois revolutions themselves. Discussions of particular problems or episodes there are aplenty, but they are dispersed through the book. Sometimes this leads to repetition: thus Neil makes the point I quoted about the American Civil War twice.[21] But it can also mean that important questions are sometimes not pursued. So Neil says more or less in passing that "the [American]

---

more completely these *conditions of labour* confront him as the property of another, the more completely is *the relation of capital and wage labour* present *formally*, hence the more complete the formal subsumption of labour under capital."

"As yet there is no difference in the *mode of production* itself. The labour process continues exactly as it did before—from the technological point of view—only as a labour process now *subordinated* to capital"—Marx, 1994, p95.

The real subsumption of labour involves, not the introduction of wage labour, but the continual technological transformation of this hitherto unchanged labour process that we see in successive industrial revolutions. Marx considers the kind of case Neil discusses as an example of transitional "forms in which the capital-relation does not yet exist formally, i.e. under which labour is already exploited by capital before the latter has developed into the form of productive capital and labour itself has taken on the form of wage labour"—Marx, 1994, p117. In a potentially related mistake, Neil offers Political Marxists a huge hostage to fortune when he endorses Marcel van der Linden's proposal to submerge wage workers in the much broader category of "subaltern workers" (pp415-416; compare van der Linden, 2008).

20: Davidson, 2012, pxviii.
21: Thus see Davidson, 2012, p169.

War of Independence involved a *political* revolution against British rule that neither achieved nor consolidated any change in social relations".[22] This contrasts with the view of the Political Marxist Charlie Post who (as Neil points out), in contradiction to the teaching of Ellen Wood, argues that "the American Revolution and Civil War can, at best, be viewed as bourgeois revolutions because they helped to secure the political and juridical conditions for the development of capitalism in the US".[23] Post's argument is part of a rich and in many ways persuasive interpretation of American history; Neil may nevertheless be right, but, since he offers no developed analysis of the Revolution of 1776, we are left with no way of judging this.

The focus of his argument is further blurred by an ambiguity in the book's title: *How Revolutionary Were the Bourgeois Revolutions?* This invites us to reflect on the nature of revolution in general, as well as that of bourgeois revolutions. To some extent this is unavoidable. As Lukács stresses, the distinction between bourgeois and socialist revolutions is politically crucial. To quote myself again:

> Bourgeois revolutions are characterised by a disjunction of agency and outcome. A variety of different social and political forces—independent gentry, Jacobin lawyers, *Junker* and *samurai* bureaucrats, even "Marxist-Leninists"—can carry through political transformations which radically improve the prospects for capitalist development. No such disjunction characterises socialist revolutions. "All previous historical movements were movements of minorities," writes Marx… "The proletarian movement is the self conscious, independent movement of the immense majority." [24]

But Neil's exploration of the general topic of revolution extends much more broadly than this. The very first chapter concerns the early modern transformation of the concept of revolution from a cyclical movement to a progressive transformation. More general reflections recur throughout the book. Thus Neil devotes a long and crucial chapter on classical Marxism between 1924 and 1940 to three figures: "Trotsky the exile,

---

22: Davidson, 2012, p59.
23: Post, 2011, p426. In the following sentence Post absurdly says that the American Revolution was led by "a non-capitalist merchant class". What exactly is a non-capitalist merchant—one who isn't interested in profit? Has such a being ever existed? Marx, of course, argued that "trading capital…is older than the capitalist mode of production, and is in fact the oldest historical mode in which capital has an independent existence"—Marx, 1981, p442.
24: Callinicos, 1989, p160.

Gramsci the prisoner, Benjamin the wanderer".[25] The inclusion of Trotsky and Gramsci needs little justification, since these are the years when they respectively generalised the theory of permanent revolution and developed the idea of passive revolution. But—although Neil provides some excellent reasons for placing Walter Benjamin in the camp of classical Marxism, rather than, as is usual, treating him as a Western Marxist—his rather brief and uneven reflections on Benjamin's thinking about progress and tradition don't seem to add anything to the discussion of bourgeois revolution.

Digression is, however, deep in the very weft of the book. Sometimes this seems to function almost like *Tristram Shandy*, where one association sparks off another. So a discussion of the absolutist state, which Neil argues (rightly in my view) is the form of feudal state that tends to prevail in the transition to capitalism, leads to quite an extensive discussion of the tributary mode of production, where peasants are exploited by a state independent of the landowning class: there's a connection between the two topics, but dealing with one doesn't demand discussing the other.[26] Beyond a certain point it is probably churlish to complain about this and other, apparently less motivated digressions. Neil likes to explore issues in a leisurely fashion, pursuing arguments by introducing complications and seizing what sometimes seem like rather random opportunities for broader reflections. He writes so well and intelligently that the journey is an enjoyable one (in Abe Lincoln's words, "people who like this sort of thing will find this the sort of thing they like," as I do). But the result is a book of extended ruminations, not a focused theoretical or historical analysis.

This is not, of course, to say that Neil offers no arguments. Indeed, the third area of weakness concerns where he seeks to extend the "consequentialist" conception of bourgeois revolution. The problem is partly the tendency sometimes to overcomplicate as noted above. Thus he raises two rather pettifogging objections to my version of this conception. The first is that I argue that a bourgeois revolution, like revolutions more generally are (in the words of Perry Anderson), is "an episode of convulsive political transformation, compressed in time and concentrated in target, that has a

---

25: Davidson, 2012, p275.

26: Davidson, 2012, pp539-551. Incidentally, Neil generally appears to agree with Jairus Banaji and me that the tributary mode is a distinct precapitalist economic system different from feudalism: see Banaji, 2010, pp15-40, and Callinicos, 2009, pp116-124. But there is an anomalous passage where he says that in "the great tributary empires...the state acted as a collective feudal overlord"—Davidson, 2012, p422. This seems closer to the views of Chris Harman and Chris Wickham, for whom tributary social formations are a sub-type of the feudal mode: see Harman, 2004, and Wickham, 2005.

determinate beginning—when the old state apparatus is still intact—and a finite end when that apparatus is decisively broken and a new one erected in its stead".[27] Neil objects that in the case of passive revolutions (including that in his native Scotland in the mid-18th century) "the establishment of unified states was the result of more or less prolonged periods in which revolution equalled the cumulative effect of conventional military operations supported by juridical enactments—a 'process', in other words".[28] This is true enough, but hardly to the point. The context in which I quoted from Anderson was one where I was concerned to insist on the necessity to secure the domination of capitalism through a transformation of the state irreducible to the more long drawn out and gradual socio-economic processes through which capitalist production relations spread. And, sure, passive revolutions are processes, not instantaneous events. But then so too are all revolutions, as we have had occasion to remind ourselves since January 2011. Certainly the process of passive revolutions takes a different form from those of both "classical" bourgeois revolutions and socialist revolutions: it is indeed the point of the distinctions I drew to establish this.

Secondly, there is the "greater...problem...that the vast majority of nation states in the world—now amounting to nearly 200—have not experienced 'convulsions' even of those associated with the revolutions from above".[29] Indeed not, but I don't recall suggesting that they would have to. One of the great strengths of the "consequentialist" rethinking of the idea of bourgeois revolution is that it situates these upheavals in the context of the development of global capitalism. As I put it, "one of the most important general propositions about bourgeois revolutions is their cumulative impact. Each revolution alters the terms for its successors".[30] Competitive pressure from the powerful capitalist state forged by the English Revolution helped to create the crisis of Bourbon absolutism that precipitated the French Revolution. The onset of industrial capitalism that these transformations made possible in turn encouraged the subversions of the old regime from within represented particularly by German unification and the Meiji restoration in Japan. But, beyond a certain point, the global domination of capitalism created so powerful a constraining context

27: Anderson, 1984, p112, quoted in Callinicos, 1989, p126.
28: Davidson, 2012, p482. On Scotland, see Davidson, 2010a.
29: Davidson, 2012, p482.
30: Callinicos, 1989, p141; see also Callinicos, 2009, pp123-136, which incorporates and greatly develops this part of the argument of my 1989 article. Teschke is therefore quite wrong to pontificate about "the absence of the international in Marxist attempts to retain the notion of 'bourgeois revolution'"—2005, p9.

for other states that they underwent a gradual process of adapting their economic, political and social structures to those of the leading bourgeois states. Neil himself writes:

> by the middle decades of the 19th century and the formation of the capitalist world economy, bourgeois revolution was no longer essential for either the initiation or the consolidation of capitalist development, provided it was formally independent of external control. Under these conditions a prolonged process of adaptive reform, perhaps punctuated by a succession of political revolutions, could achieve the same result that had previously required a social revolution.[31]

Farewell to permanent revolution?

Indeed so: but this is a supplementation to, rather than, as he suggests, the resolution of a "difficulty" in the consequentialist approach. Much more problematic is Neil's critique of the theory of permanent revolution, first developed in the pages of this journal—a critique that, while acknowledging the theory's historical importance (he calls it "one of the boldest innovations in historical materialism since the death of Marx himself"), asserts that it is now obsolete.[32] His argument involves two basic moves. The first is the distinction between political and social revolutions. This is implicit, as Neil shows, in Marx's and Engels's writings, and is stated clearly by Trotsky: "History has known...not only social revolutions, which substituted the bourgeois for the feudal regime, but also political revolutions which, without destroying the economic foundations of society, swept out an old ruling upper crust (1830 and 1848 in France, February 1917 in Russia, etc)".[33]

31: Davidson, 2012, p609. Neil here endorses a very similar argument by Joseph Choonara—Choonara, 2011, p181. Neil, picking up on a comparison drawn by Rosa Luxemburg, seems also to suggest that colonial conquests of "tribal societies" can be seen as cases of bourgeois revolution—Davidson, 2012, pp607-608. But, since these didn't necessarily involve the transformation of the state, it seems better to follow Marx in treating them as, at most, examples of primitive accumulation—the creation of the conditions of capital accumulation through the dispossession of the direct producers. This view is indeed shared by Luxemburg, who portrays imperialism as involving a continuous process of primitive accumulation as the "natural economies" of the precapitalist periphery are forcibly subordinated to capital and destroyed—Luxemburg, 1971, chapters 26-32.
32: Davidson, 2012, p223. See Davidson, 2010b, which develops many of the themes explored more extensively in this book, and, in reply, Choonara, 2011.
33: Trotsky, 1972, p288.

Political revolutions thus represent changes in state power that remain within the boundaries of the existing mode of production. Social revolution, however, facilitates a change in mode of production. As Hal Draper suggests, the concept "is most clearly used for a political revolution that expresses a social-revolutionising drive towards the transference of state power to a new class. It is a 'political revolution with a social soul', in Marx's earlier (1844) formulation".[34] I found Neil's most extended discussion of political and social revolution very hard to follow. He rightly objects to a third category introduced by Draper of "societal revolution" because it is used to refer to the "transition from one mode of production to another", which, as I have already argued, it is necessary to keep distinct from political transformations with "a social-revolutionising drive" such as bourgeois revolutions. But then he goes on to write: "Only three epochal processes fall into the category of social revolution. At one extreme is the transition from slavery to feudalism. At another extreme is the socialist revolution…which, if achieved, will begin the transition from capitalism to socialism. Between those two extremes lie the bourgeois revolutions".[35] There are two puzzles here. First, a page after differentiating social revolutions from transitions between modes of production, he includes in his list…a transition between modes of production. Neil's discussion of the end of classical antiquity focuses on the change in mode of production without any consideration of the political transformations meticulously studied by Chris Wickham in *Framing the Early Middle Ages*. Secondly, why so few social revolutions? When Neil writes that the transition from slavery to feudalism is "the first direct passage in history from one exploitative mode of production to another" one is inclined to ask: what about the shift from tributary palace bureaucracies to city states based on heavy citizen infantry and increasingly reliant on slavery in Greece during the early centuries of the first millennium BC, or the formation of the Chinese empire a few centuries later?[36] No doubt others could add more to this list of candidates.

Confusing though it is, Neil's discussion of social and political revolutions is a necessary prelude to the second stage of his argument, namely to restrict the scope of the theory of permanent revolution. Trotskyists, he suggests, seeking the "consolations of familiarity", are inclined to discover the dynamic

---

34: Draper, 1978, p19.
35: Davidson, 2012, pp493, 494-495.
36: Davidson, 2012, p497. Neil also, at least in his presentation, confuses what logicians call type and token. Even if for the purposes of argument we accept there have only been three *kinds* of social revolution, there may have been more than one instance of each kind. There have, for example, been many cases of the general category of bourgeois revolution.

of permanent revolution at work in cases where all that is normally on the agenda is a political revolution, ie some more or less forced reorganisation of capitalist state power.[37] Neil shows that Trotsky, when generalising his theory, applied it to two distinct but overlapping cases. First, the Russian original, where, despite the powerful processes of capitalist development at work, the state remained feudal-absolutist, and, as well as situations like it, those where "colonial regimes that had constrained local capitalist development to meet the economic requirements of the metropolitan power": here bourgeois revolution was still on the agenda.[38] Secondly, cases (for example, interwar Spain) where the state had become capitalist, but, as a result of uneven and combined development, major democratic demands remained unfulfilled, creating the potential for a "growing over" of struggles around these demands into socialist revolution. Neil thinks that this extension of the concept to cases where bourgeois revolution is no longer on the agenda was a mistake and should not be followed.[39]

Orthodox Trotskyists have sometimes tried to collapse the two cases together by arguing that the process of permanent revolution is incomplete until the "tasks" of the bourgeois revolution—usually listed as national independence, agrarian reform and democracy—are completely fulfilled. I argued 30 years ago that this kind of defensive manoeuvre, which relies on a normative model of the bourgeois revolution typically based on France, should be rejected: "Surely it is more sensible, rather than to invoke the metaphysical conception of a 'complete and genuine solution', to judge a bourgeois revolution by the degree to which it succeeds in establishing an autonomous centre of capital accumulation, even if it fails to democratise the political order or to eliminate feudal social relations?"[40] The alternative—to deny that India and Brazil, for example, are today capitalist states because of the numerous flaws in their social and political structures—would seem as ridiculous as the hype that now portrays them as superpowers. But what leverage then has permanent revolution in a world where bourgeois revolutions have been more or less relegated to the past? (Neil argues their era ended in 1974, when the Ethiopian Revolution overthrew the last absolutist regime: strangely he ignores the case of the Palestinians, denied a state and elementary rights of movement and residence by Israeli settler colonialism.)[41]

37: Davidson, 2012, p622.
38: Davidson, 2012, p620.
39: Davidson, 2012, pp284-308, in some respects the theoretical core of the book.
40: Callinicos, 1982, p110, criticising Löwy, 1981. See also Neil's discussion of somewhat similar criticisms of orthodox Trotskyism by Perry Anderson: Davidson, 2012, p454.
41: Davidson, 2012, p621.

Neil uses a number of arguments for the conclusion that "permanent revolution, and consequently deflected permanent revolution, are now historical concepts".[42] None are very persuasive. Thus he says that the theory of permanent revolution is not needed as the basis of a critique of Stalinist stages strategy because (a) "no Stalinist organisation…ever genuinely intended the revolution to pass through a 'democratic' stage of any sort" and (b) since 1989-91 and the collapse of bureaucratic state capitalism, "the basis for the entire strategy of stages has been removed".[43] This represents a remarkable approach to the critique of ideology, relying as it does on the idea that we can ignore theories if we think their exponents are fibbing and what they propose isn't feasible. One wonders why Marx bothered with *Theories of Surplus Value*, since he thought none of the political economists' social schemes could be realised and denounced many of them as scoundrels. Stages strategy was *never* practicable (that was the point of Trotsky's critique), but that doesn't mean that as an ideology it can't still exercise a hold because of the social needs it serves. Thus one of the interesting things about South African politics after the Marikana massacre is the divisions the massacre has opened up within the ruling Congress alliance, where both sides invoke the "national democratic revolution", whether to defend or criticise the ANC government.[44]

Neil also accuses Trotsky of "stretching the concept of permanent revolution until it was virtually synonymous with that of socialist revolution as such".[45] The philosopher of science Imre Lakatos has shown that "concept-stretching"—extending a concept to cover cases it wasn't originally intended for—can be a source of scientific innovation.[46] Sometimes the result of concept-stretching can be incoherence: I've tried to show that this happened to the idea of passive revolution even in Gramsci's hands.[47] But I don't think the

---

42: Davidson, 2012, p627. Given the changed structure of global capitalism, Neil is probably right that fully-fledged cases of deflected permanent revolution are now unlikely. That does not mean that I completely agree with what he says on this topic but, to spare the afflicted reader, I shall not say anything further about this here.

43: Davidson, 2012, p623.

44: Thus compare the excellent statement by the National Union of Metalworkers of South Africa (http://bit.ly/Uef2Ou) with an appalling speech by Blade Nzimande, general secretary of the South African Communist Party (www.sacp.org.za/main.php?ID=3750). Neil's entirely justified loathing of Stalinism leads him sometimes to be a bit cavalier with the nuances of Communist Party ideology and strategy: thus he telescopes the positions taken by the Spanish CP during the first half of the 1930s, omitting the impact of Popular Front policy—Davidson, 2012, pp259-260.

45: Davidson, 2012, p307.

46: Lakatos, 1976.

47: Callinicos, 2010.

same is true of Trotsky's extension of his theory. What it does is to address a range of situations where the process of uneven and combined development builds into the structure of the local capitalism restrictions on democracy that become a major social fracture and a source of mass struggles. A not quite historical example would be apartheid South Africa, where the state had been capitalist since the "revolution from above" following the British conquest of the Afrikaner republics at the beginning of the 20th century, but the particular forms of capital accumulation centred on mining were embedded in structures of systematic racial oppression (the migrant labour system, influx control, the exclusion of Africans from citizenship).[48] The result was that the cycle of struggles centred on the black urban working class that began with the Durban strikes of 1973 and the Soweto rising of 1976 had the potential to develop in a socialist direction. Another example is contemporary Egypt, a state—unquestionably capitalist since the 1952 revolution—presided over by an autocratic military regime that in recent decades, in close alliance with US imperialism, launched a neoliberal restructuring that threatened many of the socio-economic reforms introduced under Nasser. The revolution unleashed in January 2011 started with political demands centred on the Mubarak dictatorship but has constantly spilled over into social and economic issues.

To detect the presence of the dynamic of permanent revolution in cases such as these is not merely to assert the universal truth that socialist revolution represents the solution to every society's problems. It is to recognise the peculiar fluidity of political and social struggles that uneven and combined development induces in some but not all situations. One index of the presence of this dynamic is the centrality of democratic demands. Recent British mass movements—against the war in Iraq, student fees and austerity—have all raised democratic demands, often against police repression and state surveillance, but these have not been at their centre. Compare Egypt, where the focus of the Revolution moved from removing the remnants of the Mubarak regime to a struggle against the Supreme Council of the Armed Forces. Democratic demands here have a unifying character absent in the British case.

Neil complains that the "new meaning of permanent revolution... misrepresents the nature of contemporary revolutions by assuming that socialism is their normal or expected outcome".[49] But this is an assertion unsupported by evidence. My own response to the outbreak of the Arab

---

48: On the formation of the South African state see especially Yudelman, 1984, Keegan, 1986, and Krikler, 1993.
49: Davidson, 2012, p626. How "new" is this meaning, given that it was formulated by Trotsky during the interwar years?

revolutions placed them within the perspective of permanent revolution, but stressed that what had happened so far were political revolutions and that there was nothing inevitable about their developing into social revolutions.[50] As my old friend Colin Sparks liked to stress back in the 1970s, the theory of permanent revolution is a theory of *alternatives*: it outlines possibilities, not necessities. There seems no reason to abandon the theory understood in this way. Neil's unwillingness to see the potential for permanent revolution that may be present in political upheavals in capitalist states sometimes leads to some strange choices: thus he virtually ignores the Mexican Revolution of 1910-20, one of the greatest upheavals of the 20th century and the subject of a major study by the Trotskyist historian Adolfo Gilly, apparently on the grounds that the Mexican state was already capitalist, and devotes more space to colonial Canada's mid-19th century reorganisations.[51] More generally this failure and the associated insistence on sharply distinguishing political from social revolutions mean that he misses what Draper calls "the modern tendency for political revolution, however narrowly initiated, to waken the elements of social revolution from dormancy or to raise them to new levels".[52]

Neil, while dumping permanent revolution, remains enthusiastic about its "theoretical underpinning...the 'law' of uneven and combined development", which he describes as "perhaps the most important [discovery] in 20th-century Marxism".[53] He is indeed a prominent contributor to the explosion in discussion of the concept of uneven and combined

---

50: Callinicos, 2011.

51: Davidson, 2012, pp609-610, 616-618; compare Gilly, 1983.

52: Draper, 1978, p20.

53: Davidson, 2012, p224. Early in his lengthy discussion of uneven and combined development, Neil says that Trotsky discovered the concept "between Chiang Kai-shek's coup in Shanghai in April 1927 and the completion of the first volume of *The History of the Russian Revolution*, the preface to which is dated 14 November 1930, where the term appears for the first time"—Davidson, 2012, p286. But, even though the expression "uneven and combined development" occurs relatively late, the *concept* is present in what Louis Althusser would call a "practical state" much earlier. I think Neil is partly led to this very restrictive interpretation because, in the debates on uneven and combined development, he has argued that "it takes account of the internal *effects* of uneven development." (Davidson, 2010b, p184; interestingly this sentence doesn't reappear in Neil's book.) This means that, perversely, he tends to subsume the combined development of capitalism at the global level under uneven development, even though Trotsky, during his polemics against the doctrine of socialism in one country in 1928, talks about "two fundamental tendencies" of capitalist development, uneven and (what he does not yet call) combined development—Trotsky, 1970, p20. But in any case, Trotsky already gives a brilliant account of the "internal effects" of uneven and combined development in Tsarist Russia in the opening chapters of *1905*, written in 1908-9 and revised for the 1922 Russian edition, foreshadowing the more developed analysis in *The History of the Russian Revolution*.

development among Marxists in recent years, and has kept his head, when some have seemed to lose theirs, on this subject at least. Uneven and combined development is undeniably a crucial concept in Marxist theory, and one that can be legitimately detached from its original context in the theory of permanent revolution (I've done this myself). [54] But there is an undoubted danger that the concept can be transformed into an ahistorical abstraction that is dogmatically invoked to explain everything. This is not how Neil uses it in his own historical work, but, by removing its political moorings in the theory of permanent revolution, he can unintentionally reinforce this unwelcome tendency. In his concluding remarks to Part Four he underlines the destabilising potential of uneven and combined development, but fails to notice that this makes it hard to counterpose social and political revolutions as starkly as he does.

I have spent quite a large part of this review criticising what Neil says about permanent revolution. But—although this doesn't necessarily misrepresent the substance of his book (a large part is devoted to the development and difficulties of the theory of permanent revolution)—this shouldn't be allowed to obscure my admiration for the grandeur of his achievement. *How Revolutionary Were the Bourgeois Revolutions?* has altered the landscape of historical materialism, and, even if some of us find parts of the terrain Neil explores a little boggy, this doesn't diminish our enjoyment as we wander around it.

54: Callinicos, 2009, chapter 2. See also Callinicos and Rosenberg, 2008, and, for some of the wider literature, Dunn and Radice, 2006, and Anievas, 2010.

References

Anderson, Perry, 1984, "Modernity and Revolution", *New Left Review*, I/114.

Anderson, Perry, 1992, "The Notion of Bourgeois Revolutions", in *English Questions* (Verso).

Anderson, Perry, 2005, *Spectrum* (Verso).

Anievas, Alex (ed) 2010, *Marxism and World Politics* (Routledge).

Aston, T H, and C H E Philpin (eds), 1985, *The Brenner Debate: Agrarian Class Structure and Economic Development in Pre-Industrial Europe* (Cambridge University Press).

Banaji, Jairus, 2010, *Theory as History: Essays on Modes of Production and Exploitation* (Brill).

Brandon, Pepijn, 2007, "The Dutch Revolt: A Social Analysis", *International Socialism 116* (autumn) www.isj.org.uk/?id=370

Brenner, Robert, 1989, "Bourgeois Revolutions and the Transition to Capitalism", in A L Beier (ed), *The First Modern Society* (Cambridge University Press).

Brenner, Robert, 1993, *Merchants and Revolution: Commercial Change, Political Conflict, and London's Overseas Traders, 1550–1653* (Princeton University Press).

Callinicos, Alex, 1982, "Trotsky's Theory of Permanent Revolution and Its Relevance to the Third World Today", *International Socialism 16* (spring), www.marxists.org/history/etol/writers/callinicos/1982/xx/tprtoday.html

Callinicos, Alex, 1989, "Bourgeois Revolutions and Historical Materialism", *International Socialism 43* (summer), www.marxists.org/history/etol/writers/callinicos/1989/xx/bourrev.html

Callinicos, Alex, 1990, *Trotskyism* (Open University Press), www.marxists.de/trotism/callinicos/index.htm

Callinicos, Alex, 1994, "England's Transition to Capitalism", *New Left Review*, I/207.

Callinicos, Alex, 2009, *Imperialism and Global Political Economy* (Polity).

Callinicos, Alex, 2010, "The Limits of Passive Revolution", *Capital & Class*, 34:3.

Callinicos, Alex, 2011, "The Return of the Arab Revolution", *International Socialism 130* (spring), www.isj.org.uk/?id=717

Callinicos, Alex, and Justin Rosenberg, 2008, "Uneven and Combined Development: The Social-Relational Substratum of 'the International'? An Exchange of Letters", *Cambridge Review of International Affairs*, 21.

Choonara, Joseph, 2011, "The Relevance of Permanent Revolution: A Reply to Neil Davidson", *International Socialism 131* (summer), www.isj.org.uk/?id=745

Cliff, Tony, 1963, "Permanent Revolution", *International Socialism 12* (first series) www.anu.edu.au/polsci/marx/contemp/pamsetc/permrev/permrev.html

Cominel, George, 1987, *Rethinking the French Revolution* (Verso).

Davidson, Neil, 2005, "How Revolutionary Were the Bourgeois Revolutions?", *Historical Materialism*, 13.3.

Davidson, Neil, 2010a, "Scotland: Birthplace of Passive Revolution?", *Capital & Class*, 34:3, http://cnc.sagepub.com/content/34/3/343.full.pdf+html

Davidson, Neil, 2010b, "From Deflected Permanent Revolution to the Law of Uneven and Combined Development", *International Socialism 128* (winter), www.isj.org.uk/?id=686

Davidson, Neil, 2012, *How Revolutionary Were the Bourgeois Revolutions?* (Haymarket).

Draper, Hal, 1978, *Karl Marx's Theory of Revolution*, II (Monthly Review).

Dunn, Bill, and Hugo Radice (eds), 2006, *100 Years of Permanent Revolution: Results and Prospects* (Pluto).

Geras, Norman, 1975, "Rosa Luxemburg after 1905", *New Left Review*, I/89, http://newleftreview.org/I/89/norman-geras-rosa-luxemburg-after

Gilly, Adolfo, 1983, *The Mexican Revolution* (Verso).

Hallas, Duncan, 1988, "The Bourgeois Revolution", *Socialist Worker Review*, 105 (January), www.marxists.org/archive/hallas/works/1988/01/bourgrev.htm

Harman, Chris, 1989, "From Feudalism to Capitalism", *International Socialism* 45 (winter).

Harman, Chris, 2004, "The Rise of Capitalism", *International Socialism 102* (spring), www.isj.org.uk/?id=21

Keegan, Timothy, 1986, *Rural Transformations in Industrialising South Africa: The Southern Highveld to 1914* (Ravan Press)

Krikler, Jeremy, 1993, *Revolution from Above, Rebellion from Below: The Agrarian Transvaal at the Turn of the Century* (Clarendon).

Lakatos, Imre, 1976, *Proofs and Refutations: The Logic of Mathematical Discovery* (Cambridge University Press).

Löwy, Michael, 1981, *The Politics of Uneven and Combined Development* (NLB).

Lukács, Georg, 1970 [1924], *Lenin: A Study in the Unity of His Thought* (NLB), www.marxists.org/archive/lukacs/works/1924/lenin/index.htm

Luxemburg, Rosa, 1971 [1913], *The Accumulation of Capital* (Routledge), www.marxists.org/archive/luxemburg/1913/accumulation-capital/index.htm

Marx, Karl, 1977 [1848], "The Bourgeoisie and the Counter-Revolution", in Karl Marx and Friedrich Engels, *Collected Works*, VIII (Progress), www.marxists.org/archive/marx/works/1848/12/15.htm

Marx, Karl, 1981 [1894], *Capital*, III (Penguin), www.marxists.org/archive/marx/works/1894-c3/

Marx, Karl, 1994, *Economic Manuscript of 1861-63* (Conclusion), in Karl Marx and Friedrich Engels, *Collected Works*, volume 34 (Progress).

Post, Charles, 2011, *The American Road to Capitalism: Studies in Class Structure, Economic Development and Political Conflict, 1620-1877* (Brill).

Teschke, Benno, 2005, "Bourgeois Revolution, State Formation and the Absence of the International", *Historical Materialism*, 13.2

Trotsky, Leon, 1970 [1928], *The Third International after Lenin* (Pathfinder).

Trotsky, Leon, 1972 [1936], *The Revolution Betrayed* (Pathfinder).

Van der Linden, Marcel, 2008, *Workers of the World: Essays Toward a Global Labour History* (Brill).

Wickham, Chris, 2005, *Framing the Early Middle Ages: Europe and the Mediterranean, 400 to 800* (Oxford University Press).

Wood, Ellen Meiksins, 2002, *The Origin of Capitalism: A Longer View* (Verso).

Yudelman, David, 1984, *The Emergence of Modern South Africa: State, Capital and the Incorporation of Organised Labour on the South African Gold Fields, 1902-1939* (David Philip).

The enemy's enemy: Disraeli and working class leadership

Ian Birchall

At this year's Labour Party conference party leader Ed Miliband caused a certain amount of consternation by praising Benjamin Disraeli (Tory prime minister 1868 and 1874–80), and repeatedly using Disraeli's most famous phrase "One Nation".[1] Just to make sure nobody had missed the point, he repeated the words 46 times.[2]

In invoking the Disraeli tradition Miliband was seeking to occupy territory that recent Tories have apparently abandoned. Margaret Thatcher preferred Friedrich Hayek and scorned "one nation" conservatism;[3] John Major preferred Anthony Trollope.

In his early years David Cameron was widely compared to Disraeli[4] and firmly identified himself with the Disraelian tradition of conservatism.[5] But Disraeli was most relevant to Cameron in his early years as leader, when he was creating a new image and promoting vacuous rhetoric about the "Big Society". The Disraeli tradition may seem less

---

1: Version of a paper given to the London Socialist Historians Group conference, "Making the Tories History", on 26 February 2011.

2: For the full text of the speech see Miliband, 2012.

3: "I am not sure what is meant by those who say that the party should return to something called '*One Nation* Conservatism'. As far as I can tell by their views on European federalism, such people's creed would be better described as '*No Nation* Conservatism'"—Thatcher, 1996.

4: Oborne, 2010.

5: Cook, 2009.

important now he faces a profound crisis and is under pressure from his party's right.

But Tories in trouble tend to go back to Disraeli.[6] This is not too surprising. Conservative theoreticians are quite thin on the ground, and there is not a wealth of choice of intellectual forbears. Perhaps Miliband hopes to forestall any such move by claiming "One Nation" for himself. Whatever his motives, it is testimony to the enduring memory of Disraeli— as well as to the poverty of thinking in today's Labour Party.

But what exactly is Disraeli's contribution to conservatism? Clearly he is a role model for ambitious young politicians. A second-generation immigrant, who attended neither a public school nor a university, he became a highly successful politician, twice prime minister. He was a master of parliamentary manoeuvre and manipulation. His biographer Robert Blake described him as "a politician of genius, a superb improviser, a parlia-mentarian of unrivalled skill"[7]—all qualities designed to make him a hero to Tories on the make. He wrote and spoke copiously, and left quotations to serve all purposes; even Thatcher quoted him on occasion.

But in the end the essence of Disraeli is summed up in a single phrase, the sound bite "one nation conservatism". As is the case with so many famous "quotations" Disraeli did not in fact use the term—it is extrapolated from a famous passage in his 1845 novel *Sybil*.[8]

Here Stephen Morley encounters Egremont, the novel's aristocratic hero, and declares that Queen Victoria reigns over two nations:

"Two nations; between whom there is no intercourse and no sympathy; who are as ignorant of each other's habits, thoughts, and feelings, as if they were dwellers in different zones, or inhabitants of different planets; who are formed by a different breeding, are fed by a different food, are ordered by different manners, and are not governed by the same laws."

"You speak of—" said Egremont, hesitatingly.

"THE RICH AND THE POOR."

6:   A point I recall Nigel Harris making to the Executive of the International Socialists many years ago.
7:   Blake, 1969, p477.
8:   Disraeli, 1980. All page references to this edition given in the text. One may, of course, wonder how many present-day Tories have actually read *Sybil*, just as one may wonder how many of those who applauded Michael Gove's speech at the 2010 Tory conference on reforming the English literature syllabus had actually read Dryden.

There follows a bit of cheap melodrama, featuring sunset and the evening hymn to the Virgin, designed to impress on the reader the importance of this passage, in case she had missed the fact that the novel had the alternative title of "The Two Nations".[9] Even this was not original; ten years earlier Alexis Tocqueville, whom Disraeli knew, had written of "two rival nations", the rich and the poor.[10] In fact this passage is much more problematic than is often assumed. But there is no doubt that it is widely known and represents a current of conservative thinking.

Sybil sold around 3,000 copies at a guinea and a half;[11] since this would be several weeks' wages for most working people, we can assume it was addressed exclusively to a readership of the rich and not the poor. But despite some tedious stretches and a number of obvious absurdities, it remains worth reading as a founding text of British conservatism for those who want to know the enemy better.[12]

Miliband is not the first on the left to have tried to appropriate Disraeli. Former Labour leader Michael Foot greatly admired Disraeli and wrote an essay on him entitled "The Good Tory"[13]—something of a provocation to those of us who think that the only good Tory is a dead Tory—in which he stressed Disraeli's sympathies with the Chartists. This was wishful thinking of the worst order. Veteran Stalinist critic Arnold Kettle likewise commended Disraeli as "extraordinarily intelligent", arguing that he supplied what Thomas Carlyle had called for, "articulate inquiry into the Condition of England Question".[14] Kettle clearly thought such "articulate inquiry" must come from outside, and, like Carlyle,[15] seemed to have had no confidence in the ability of the working class to articulate its own problems.

Frederick Engels was a rather more astute judge. Writing to August Bebel in 1892, he observed: "The Tories, because they are asses, can be induced by some outstanding personality, like Disraeli, to strike out boldly from time to time, which the Liberals are incapable of doing. But when no outstanding personality is available they fall under the sway of asses, as is the

---

9:   Disraeli, 1980, p96.
10: From Tocqueville's *Memoir on Pauperism* (1835), cited in Himmelfarb, 2006, p80.
11: Blake, 1969, p192.
12: For comrades who don't have the time there is quite a useful abbreviated version at www.btinternet.com/~glynhughes/squashed/sybil.htm
13: Foot, 1980, pp42-76.
14: Kettle, 1982, p172.
15: For Carlyle the working class were "these wild, inarticulate souls, struggling there, with inarticulate uproar, like dumb creatures in pain, unable to speak what is in them!"—Carlyle, 1840, p6. Given the flood of oratory and journalism produced by the Chartist movement, one can only conclude that Carlyle was very stupid and very ignorant.

case just now".[16] Engels recognised Disraeli's ability and intelligence, but had no illusions as to which side he was on.

Disraeli was a highly class conscious Tory. Despite—or more likely because of—his origins he identified with the class interests of the aristocracy, and it was fitting that in his last years he was incorporated into this class that he admired so much. But Disraeli also believed that the British ruling class in general, and the Tory party in particular, was failing to face up to the realities of 19th century society, and by so doing was not only neglecting its social and moral obligations, but, more seriously, was putting its own continuing hegemony at risk.[17]

Thus he could be devastating about the role of the Tory party. As a character in *Coningsby* put it:

> I observe indeed a party in the state whose role it is to consent to no change, until it is clamorously called for, and then instantly to yield; but those are concessionary, not Conservative principles. This party treats institutions as we do our pheasants, they preserve only to destroy them. But is there a statesman among these Conservatives who offers us a dogma for a guide, or defines any great political truth which we should aspire to establish? It seems to me a barren thing, this Conservatism, an unhappy cross-breed: the mule of politics that engenders nothing.[18]

And he recognised with an acuteness that retains all its relevance today that the Chartists were right to see no real difference between the main parties:

> They had long ceased to distinguish between the two parties who then and now contend for power. And they were right. Between the noble lord who goes out and the right honourable gentleman who comes in, where is the distinctive principle? A shadowy difference may be simulated in opposition, to serve a cry and stimulate the hustings; but the mask is not even worn in Downing Street; and the conscientious conservative seeks in the pigeon-holes of a whig bureau for the measures against which for ten years he has

---

16:   Engels, letter of 5 July 1892, in Marx and Engels, 1975-2005, volume 49, p459.
17:   Disraeli recognised a wide gap between the frivolity, self-indulgence and ignorance of the actual 19th century British aristocracy, and the historical role he envisaged for that class. There is perhaps a parallel with the way that Georg Lukács distinguished between the empirical consciousness of particular workers and the potential consciousness which can be historically imputed to the proletariat. See Lukács, 1971, p51.
18:   Disraeli, 1844, volume I, pp309-310.

been sanctioning by the speaking silence of an approving nod, a general wail of frenzied alarm.[19]

In particular Disraeli was concerned at the ignorance of the ruling class about the condition of the working class in Britain. As he put it in some unpublished notes:

Imperfect education of the "English Gentleman"—ignorance of the economical sciences—and their power of useful activity circumscribed by their obvious unacquaintance with the wants, feelings and difficulties of the working classes—an ignorance arising out of the exclusive habits of the upper classes. The whole moral and intellectual development of the upper classes must be advanced before the condition of the working classes can be essentially improved.[20]

He satirises the appalling smug ignorance of Lord Marney, who boasts that he has never seen a factory and does not want to see one.[21] Egremont, the novel's hero, adopts a false name in order to frequent working class circles and find out more about the conditions of the poor.

Disraeli claimed of *Sybil* that "there is not a trait in this work for which [the author] has not the authority of his own observation, or the authentic evidence which has been received by Royal Commissions and Parliamentary Committees".[22] In fact, there was nothing particularly new as far as factual material was concerned. Like Karl Marx, Disraeli spent a great deal of time studying the Blue Books (reports of parliamentary commissions set up to examine social conditions), and according to one scholar it was his "frequent practice to transcribe phrases, sentences and even short passages, with very little alteration from his sources". (A less kind critic might have used the word plagiarism.) Some of his sources were rather dubious; thus he drew on the writings of William Dodd who had been hired by Lord Ashley to investigate industrial conditions; in fact it had been revealed that Dodd "had threatened to report adversely…on certain industrialists unless they paid him blackmail".[23] The description of Wodgate is based on Willenhall, but Disraeli deliberately exaggerated the filth and irreligion.[24]

19: Disraeli, 1980, p331.
20: Cited Braun, 1981, p86.
21: Disraeli, 1980, p161.
22: Disraeli, 1980, p24.
23: Fido, 1977, p270.
24: Disraeli, 1980, p202ff; Flint, 1987, pp98-99.

Hence *Sybil* is not particularly valuable as a source of information about the working class; if we want that it would be better to go direct to the *Blue Books*. What is interesting in Disraeli's novel is what he tells us about the attitude of an intelligent Tory to the working class.

Disraeli's argument was that the aristocracy was the natural ally of the working class. As one of the young working class women in *Sybil* puts it: "If we can't have our own man, I am all for the nobs against the middle class".[25] He saw it as the duty of the Conservative Party to espouse the cause of the common people and to seek to remedy the ills it suffered from.

As a result Disraeli is quite radical in his account of working class oppression. He tells us a good deal about wages and working conditions, about female and child labour, about the squalor and misery of working class housing. He clearly believes that change is necessary, although his solution—of levelling up—lacks plausibility; in Egremont's words: "The future principle of English politics will not be a levelling principle; not a principle adverse to privileges, but favourable to their extension. It will seek to ensure equality, not by levelling the few but by elevating the many".[26] Any expropriation of the rich was thus ruled out.

Disraeli also recognises quite clearly that the oppression of the working class can lead to violence. Early in the book there are references to rick-burning, and later there is widespread rioting. Disraeli seems to have recognised well before Quintin Hogg that "if you do not give the people reform, they are going to give you revolution".[27] As he put it in a speech in 1848: "The palace is not safe when the cottage is not happy".[28] Disraeli was honest and intelligent enough to know that a ruling class must be able to understand the various forms of rebellion issuing from the oppressed classes. If it cannot understand how they occur, it will be impotent to deal with them. Unlike more timid politicians he was not afraid that explanation might be misinterpreted as justification.[29]

But that was as far as it went. What Disraeli could not admit into his picture was that the working class was capable of self-activity and self-organisation, that it could produce its own leaders. For to admit that would be to recognise that the working class was capable of developing into an alternative ruling class, thus making the aristocracy and its hangers-on

25: Disraeli, 1980, p452.
26: Disraeli, 1980, p354.
27: Hogg, 1943.
28: Blake, 1969, p556.
29: Compare the rather less intelligent and more vote-oriented John Major: "Society needs to condemn a little more and understand a little less"—Major, 1993.

quite unnecessary. As Carlyle summed it up: "If something be not done, something will *do* itself one day, and in a fashion that will please nobody".[30]

As early as 1834 Disraeli wrote: "I deny that a people can govern itself. Self-government is a contradiction in terms. Whatever form a government assumes, power must be exercised by a minority of numbers".[31] Hence Egremont's insistence to Sybil that the working class are incapable of developing their own leaders: "The people are not strong: the people never can be strong. Their attempts at self-vindication will end only in their suffering and confusion." Hence their only hope is with the aristocracy: "They are the natural leaders of the people, Sybil; believe me they are the only ones".[32] True, Sybil responds by insisting, with some plausibility, that "the conquerors will never rescue the conquered". But this is merely to reinforce her previous statement that she is without hope; there is no suggestion that the conquered might rescue themselves.[33]

Indeed, when she becomes involved in the Chartist agitation, Sybil is fairly rapidly disillusioned. She comes to suspect that "the world was a more complicated system than she had preconceived" (a classic conservative argument—the world is complex, so any attempt to change things will make them worse), and she is particularly shocked by the fact that there are disagreements among her own side: "The People she found was not that pure embodiment of unity of feeling, of interest, and of purpose, which she had pictured in her abstractions. The people had enemies among the people".[34] That such disagreements might be an inevitable consequence of working people thinking for themselves and trying to plan their own future does not seem to have crossed her innocent mind. All she can do is wait for salvation from an implausible dénouement.

Disraeli in some ways admired the Chartists. In a speech of 1839 he declared that "although we do not approve of the remedy suggested by the Chartists, it does not follow we should not attempt to cure the disease complained of". He recognised that Chartism had a real social base and was not simply whipped up by the seditious, as some of his fellow MPs believed:

30: Carlyle, 1840, p1. P J Keating argues that this is a common feature of all the novelists of working class life in this period: "It was his [the industrial worker's] suffering to which novelists drew attention, but his potential power that was their true concern. The possibility that the workers might have ideas of their own about the uses to which this power could be put was discountenanced by the novelists"—Keating, 1971, pp223-224.

31: *The Spirit of Whiggism*, cited Edwards, 1937, p115.

32: Disraeli, 1980, p334.

33: Disraeli, 1980, p354.

34: Disraeli, 1980, p349.

I cannot believe that a petition signed by considerably upwards of 1,000,000 of our fellow-citizens can have been brought about by those ordinary means which are always in existence, and which five, ten or 15 years ago were equally powerful in themselves without producing any equal results.

Yet while believing that the roots of the movement were in "an apprehension on the part of the public that their civil rights are invaded", he remained quite unable to believe that the working class was capable of elaborating its own political programme:

I admit also on the other hand that this movement is not occasioned by any desire of political rights. Political rights have so much of an abstract character, their consequences act so slightly on the multitude, that I do not believe they could ever be the origin of any great popular movement.[35]

Disraeli did make a certain effort to understand Chartist ideas. While researching *Sybil* he obtained through his friend the Radical MP Thomas Duncombe the correspondence of Chartist leader Feargus O'Connor, which he perused.[36] Just after completing *Sybil* he met, and tried to find a publisher for, Thomas Cooper, the Chartist poet who had just been released from jail. Disraeli was impressed by him as "a man of great talents, and extensive knowledge", adding rather ambiguously: "In appearance, Morley to the life!"[37]

Unlike Carlyle, Disraeli was well aware that Chartism was an expression of powerful proletarian articulacy, with its orators, mass meetings and numerous publications. The description of the torch-lit meeting is quite sympathetic.[38] Trade unionism is a rather different matter. The account of Dandy Mick's initiation into a trade union is presented in terms of heavy parody and would not be out of place in the *Daily Mail*. It was true enough that trade union organisation in the early 19th century involved a certain amount of clandestinity and oath-swearing. But Disraeli omits to tell his readers the basic reason for this—that trade unions had been illegal organisations. In the absence of this information the rituals can only seem to be a mixture of the sinister and the ridiculous.[39]

Disraeli takes a relatively relaxed view of working class violence. He sees it as an inevitable product of poverty and oppression, and mocks

---

35: Speech in Parliament, 12 July 1839; cited in Edwards, 1937, pp189-190.
36: Disraeli, 1877, pxiii.
37: Disraeli, 1989, pp168, 170.
38: Disraeli, 1980, p265.
39: Disraeli, 1980, pp267-271.

the aristocratic landlord who insists that rick-burning "originated in purely accidental circumstances; at least nothing to do with wages".[40] Certainly he shows working class violence as alarming, but at the same time it is clear that the state has ample means to control the violence. Disraeli claims a familiarity with mass violence not based on any extensive experience. Thus he writes of "one of those violent undulations usual in mobs",[41] which seems to mean very little but presents Disraeli as a connoisseur of such scenes, which he undoubtedly was not.[42]

Of the individuals involved in the Chartist movement, the one most sympathetically presented is Walter Gerard, father of the saintly and virginal Sybil. (Sybil herself, though she describes herself as "one of the lower order",[43] is not employed, and aspires to be a nun.) He is shown as a cultured and thoughtful man, sincerely committed to the interests of working people, and as a popular and effective orator. The paradox is that he is not really a worker at all, but an overlooker and hence part of the management structure, in what is rather implausibly presented as a humane and well-managed factory.[44]

He earns two pounds a week—five times as much as we are told an agricultural labourer receives,[45] and nearly seven times as much as my own mother's starting wage almost 100 years later. As the dénouement shows, he is actually of aristocratic descent—he is a member of the labour aristocracy in more than one sense. He disagrees with Stephen Morley about physical force—Morley is shown as a advocate of moral force. We get the impression that while Disraeli deplores working class violence, he also feels there is something a bit unmanly about moral force Chartism.[46] Gerard is provoked into violent resistance at the end of the novel and

---

40: Disraeli, 1980, p143.

41: Disraeli, 1980, p485.

42: Orwell pulls a similar trick in *Burmese Days*: "Next day the town was quieter than a cathedral city on Monday morning. It is usually the case after a riot"—Orwell, 1935, p283. On exactly how many riots was Orwell's assertion based?

43: Disraeli, 1980, p234.

44: In many factories it was common practice for overlookers to use gross brutality in disciplining child labour. See the testimonies at www.spartacus.schoolnet.co.uk/IRpunishments.htm There is, of course, no suggestion that anything of the sort occurred at the mill where Gerard worked, but presumably if he was employed as an overlooker, it was in order to discipline labour.

45: Disraeli, 1980, pp153, 143.

46: I would therefore not go along with Paul Foot's view that: "The central theme of the novel is the distinction between 'moral force' Chartism, espoused by the unblemished heroine, Sybil, and 'physical force' Chartism, described with obvious distaste"—Foot, 2005, p103. A similar position is argued by Basketter, 2012.

is promptly killed; his action reflects his courage and spirit of rebellion rather than his good sense.

Bishop Hatton, leader of the riotous Hell-cats in the final section of the novel, is presented as the exact opposite, as the worst type of working class leadership. Yet he too is not a worker at all, having been described by one of the workers of Wodgate as "the governor here over all of us".[47] He is shown as being totally ignorant of the movement he is taking advantage of, not knowing even the five points of the Charter. He degenerates into crude parody when he declares himself an opponent of washing—"I was always against washing: it takes the marrow out of a man".[48]

The problem is to explain how he wins support, how indeed he becomes followed more eagerly than the most intelligent and serious leaders. Again Disraeli is underlining his point that the working class is unable to select and recognise its own leaders, and thus constantly falls prey to agitators of the worst type. This is a frequent theme in the novels of the period. In Dickens's nasty little anti trade union tract *Hard Times*, he presents the "agitator" Slackbridge:

> Strange as it always is to consider any assembly in the act of submissively resigning itself to the dreariness of some complacent person, lord or commoner, whom three fourths of it could, by no human means, raise out of the slough of inanity to their own intellectual level, it was particularly strange, and it was even particularly affecting, to see this crowd of earnest faces, whose honesty in the main no competent observer free from bias could doubt, so agitated by such a leader.[49]

In other words, Dickens is telling us that he does not believe his own narrative, that the workers in the crowd were too intelligent to be taken in by such an agitator. Something similar is happening with Hatton. The decent and intelligent workers whom Disraeli has introduced us to are scarcely likely to be taken in by such an obvious charlatan.

But the depiction of violence has a clear ideological role. To show the working class as subject to excesses of irrational rage and violence is a very convenient myth. On the one hand it alarms the reader, convincing her of the gravity of the problem. Yet at the same time it confirms that the working class is not fit to rule; it does not have the intellectual or

---

47: Disraeli, 1980, p207.
48: Disraeli, 1980, p467.
49: Dickens, 1987, pp141-142.

emotional capacity to do so. For Disraeli's readers that was a profoundly consoling conclusion.

The most complex character is Stephen Morley. He is presented as a man of considerable culture, surrounded by books and immersed in political ideas. He too is not a worker, but a full-time journalist. He is also, it appears, some sort of socialist, although Disraeli does not use the word. In the run-up to the Two Nations speech, Morley tells us: "There is no community in England; there is aggregation, but aggregation under circumstances which make it rather a dissociating than an uniting principle".[50]

"Community" is one of those words that mean so many things that they scarcely have any precise meaning at all. It is as difficult to be against community as it is to be for sin. But it seems clear that Morley is in fact some sort of Utopian socialist, probably a follower of Robert Owen.[51] This is shown in the passage where he advocates the abolition of the family:

> The domestic principle has fulfilled its purpose. The irresistible law of progress demands that another should be developed... Home is a barbarous idea; the method of a rude age; home is isolation; therefore anti-social. What we want is community.

To this the more common-sense Walter Gerard simply responds: "I like stretching my feet on my own hearth".[52] But it would doubtless surprise many "one nation" Tories to know that the roots of their philosophy are in a character who advocated abolition of the family.

As the novel develops we become more and more aware that Morley is a nasty piece of work. He is in love with Sybil, who rejects him. First, despite his attachment to moral force, he physically assaults Egremont; later he tries to seduce Sybil by threatening not to enable her father to escape arrest and imprisonment unless she will submit to him. In short, the "two nations" theme has a very tainted source, reflecting Disraeli's own ambiguities about the possibility of social reconciliation.

It is always dangerous to attribute the views expressed by a character in a work of fiction to the author himself; Shakespeare would find himself lumbered with a very odd collection of opinions. But it is interesting to ask why Disraeli has made Morley the bearer of the idea of the Two Nations. In her conversations with Egremont, Sybil Gerard several times insists that

50: Disraeli, 1980, p194.
51: For Owenite advocacy of the abolition of the family, see Taylor, 1983, pp32-48.
52: Disraeli, 1980, p238.

the gulf between the two nations is "impassable".[53] A "one nation" Tory would have to reject this position. But the only character Disraeli can find to argue the possibility of overcoming the gulf is a social revolutionary who believes in a total transformation of the social order, thus leaving an unresolved paradox at the heart of the novel.[54]

Like any political novelist Disraeli had the problem of inserting what Irving Howe called "the hard and perhaps insoluble pellets of modern ideology"[55] into the course of his story-telling, of achieving a balance between narrative and political advocacy. Disraeli had no compunction about using his narrative voice, and *Sybil* contains a number of long—and sometimes virtually unreadable—passages where Disraeli sets out his own view of English history. But the absolutely crucial Two Nations speech is put into the very ambiguous mouth of Stephen Morley.

The only reason can be that Disraeli is much more concerned to point to the dangers implicit in the Two Nations than to offer any possible "one nation" solution. So Disraeli can wholeheartedly endorse the socialist critique of society—and Morley (as yet unnamed—perhaps because Disraeli sees there was a problem in reconciling the Two Nations speech with Morley's later development) is allowed to chill his readers' blood with the threats inherent in a class-divided society. But Disraeli cannot begin to attribute any legitimacy to Morley's socialist solution, and so Morley is transformed from hero to villain.

The only working class characters who survive and come out of the story reasonably well are Dandy Mick Radley and Devilsdust. They enter enthusiastically into the rioting, but then abandon their ideals in order to become capitalists, and Disraeli predicts that their descendants will eventually be incorporated into the aristocracy. This, of course, reflects a typical meritocratic myth—that the most talented members of the working class can rise out of it. Of course, Disraeli's belief in the hereditary principle is compatible with this. Devilsdust is the child of a single mother; his father is unknown. So it is always possible that he originated from a drop of aristocratic sperm.

53: Disraeli, 1980, p337.
54: Several critics have noted that there is a problem with Morley. Gertrude Himmelfarb reminds us that "it is Stephen Morley, the Chartist radical, speaking, not Disraeli, the Tory radical" (Himmelfarb, 2006, p81), and Thom Braun considers that "Morley is generally portrayed by Disraeli with a certain amount of irony, if not sarcasm", which might mean that the whole question of the two nations is a "mere point of rhetoric in terms of the world of the novel" (Braun 1981, pp107, 110). But they do not explore the political implications of this.
55: Howe, 1992, p20.

Disraeli is less sure of himself when dealing with the women characters. Apart from Sybil herself, who is implausibly pure and profoundly serious in her ideas, the other female characters are shown as rather frivolous and light-minded. Barbara Taylor's *Eve and the New Jerusalem* shows that there were some very articulate working class feminist socialists around in this period.[56] Disraeli in fact met one of these women, Anna Wheeler, but his recorded comments show that he failed to take her seriously: "not so pleasant, something between Jeremy Bentham and Meg Merrilies, very clever, but awfully revolutionary".[57]

The dénouement is one of the least satisfactory parts of the novel. (For those who have not yet read the book I should add "spoiler alert" at this point.) It seems Disraeli has grown tired of his political purpose and has decided to resolve the novel in purely personal terms. As the lefty lecturer in David Lodge's *Nice Work* points out: "All the Victorian novelist could offer as a solution to the problems of industrial capitalism were: a legacy, a marriage, emigration or death".[58]

All four solutions, in one form or another, are used in *Sybil*. Egremont, elevated to the House of Lords by his elder brother's death, seems to feel that his parliamentary duties are no longer necessary. Sybil discovers her noble ancestry, enabling her to bridge the impassable gulf and marry Egremont, forsaking the poor who had depended on her charitable gifts. Egremont and his bride go for a year-long honeymoon in Italy.[59]

For Disraeli it is ignorance and misunderstanding which lie at the root of social conflict.[60] Sybil herself, becoming disillusioned with the factionalism of the Chartist leaders, inclines to this view:

She would ascribe rather the want of sympathy that unquestionably exists between wealth and work in England, to mutual ignorance between the classes which possess these two great elements of national prosperity; and though the source of that ignorance was to be sought in antecedent

---

56: Taylor, 1983, pp57-82.
57: Taylor, 1983, p61. Meg Merrilies was a gypsy described in a poem by Keats.
58: Lodge, 1988, p52.
59: A couple of years later revolution would spread across northern Italy; a republic was declared in Venice in 1848 and an emergent working class began to make its presence felt. See Ginsborg, 1979.
60: Compare Marx's mockery of Lamartine, who in 1848 argued that the Second Republic would get rid of the "terrible misunderstanding" between classes—Marx, *The Class Struggles in France*, in Marx & Engels 1975-2005, volume 10, p58.

circumstances of violence and oppression, the consequences perhaps had outlived the causes, as customs survive opinions.[61]

Here Disraeli was undoubtedly wrong. A century and a half on, the ruling class employs thousands of sociologists to poll the opinions of the working class and examine their lifestyles and consumption patterns; while the poor have television screens on which they can inspect the most intimate details of the lives of the rich and celebrated. Yet class struggle continues.

Disraeli took Chartism and the rise of the working class very seriously. But because of his belief that the working class could not produce its own leadership, he seems to have been largely indifferent to the development of socialism on an international scale. The Young England group, in which Disraeli was a leading figure, did have some links with continental socialists; Disraeli's associate George Smythe was a friend of the French socialist Louis Blanc.[62]

Disraeli himself dined with Louis Blanc in Paris in 1846, but his recorded comments merely noted that Blanc was small in stature with a "boyish face" and was "agreeable and unaffected"; he seems to have been utterly uninterested in Blanc's ideas.[63] When the 1848 Revolution took place in France, Blanc was one of the two first socialists ever to enter a national government. Disraeli merely noted that "Smythe has gone off to Paris to see his friend Louis Blanc, and some other successful blackguards".[64]

Disraeli was initially deeply alarmed by events in France, though he seems to have had little idea about the causes and motivations of the events. On 29 February 1848 he wrote: "The catastrophe of Paris is so vast, so sudden, so *inexplicable*, so astounding, that I have not yet recovered from the intelligence of yesterday afternoon".[65]

But by 13 March he was reassured:

Lionel Rothschild has just returned from Paris, and in much better spirits. He says the Communists have no power whatr [sic], and the only real trouble are the unemployed workmen, but that there are remarkable opportunities at present to occupy them.[66]

61: Disraeli, 1980, p350.
62: Millar, 2006, pp231, 234.
63: Disraeli, 1989, p212.
64: Disraeli 1993, p18.
65: Disraeli 1993, p13. Emphasis added.
66: Disraeli 1993, p19.

He was particularly concerned, however, with the threat of nationalisation, writing on 10 May:

> They will also confiscate the Great Northern Railroad for certain, the workmen having announced yesterday that they will have 1 france [sic] a day increase of wages and *half* the profit of the line—and if they don't give up to the workmen, the state will seize all.[67]

On the advice of the Rothschilds, Disraeli had invested heavily in the French railways, and this clearly preoccupied him more than the ferment of ideas issuing from the Parisian workers.

Disraeli went on writing novels, on and off, for the rest of his life. But he never returned to any extensive treatment of the working class, preferring to portray social groups he was more familiar with. In *Lothair* (1870) there are references to Fenians and French republican secret societies, but nothing specifically proletarian.[68] In his last completed novel, *Endymion* (1880), there is an intriguing glimpse of a character called Enoch Craggs (once again an overlooker!) who advocates "CO-OPERATION", and insists that workmen "make the capital ... and if they make the capital, is it not strange that they should not be able to contrive some means to keep the capital?"[69] But Craggs does not reappear and the theme is not followed up. It is as though Disraeli is aware that the working class is posing some unanswered questions.

That there were such questions is confirmed by a rather strange three-hour meeting that Disraeli had just a few weeks before his death with the eccentric "Marxist" Henry Hyndman. Hyndman bizarrely announced that he was considering doing entry work in the Conservative Party. Disraeli said he did not wish to discourage him, but very realistically reminded Hyndman that if he attempted to advocate "collective control and ownership" in the Conservative Party, he would come up against "a phalanx of the great families who would thwart you at every turn: they and their women". We have only Hyndman's account of the meeting, and it is impossible to say whether Disraeli's remarks reflected mere politeness, or whether he was genuinely interested in the emergent socialist movement.[70]

Hence the Tory appropriation of Disraeli, inasmuch as it is anything more than superficial rhetoric, is not as simple as it seems. *Sybil* is a

---

67: Disraeli, 1993, p26.
68: Disraeli, 1877.
69: Disraeli, 1881.
70: Hyndman, 1911, pp237-245.

complex and contradictory text; its great merit is that it shows a powerful and class-conscious awareness of the fact that society is profoundly and dangerously divided—that there are indeed two nations. From there to one-nation conservatism is quite a jump—Disraeli had a shrewd grasp of the problem, but little idea of the solution. As a review in the *Spectator* noted, "philosophical young England can only *imagine* two models of amalgamating the two nations—killing off the poor, or making them rich".[71]

The Young England group was scorned by Marx as embodying "feudal socialism".[72] Robert Blake, from a very different standpoint, came to a similar judgment, seeing it as "the reaction of a defeated class to a sense of its own defeat—a sort of nostalgic escape from the disagreeable present to the agreeable but imaginary past".[73] John Manners, one of Disraeli's close associates, summed up the group's vision of an organic utopia in the lines:

Each knew his place—king, peasant, peer, or priest—
The greater owned connexion with the least;
From rank to rank the generous feeling ran
And linked society as man to man.[74]

This appalling doggerel carried the equally appalling message: "We're all in it together."

Disraeli was not a Tory Utopian but a practical politician—and a careerist, if the two are not the same thing. He had no idea how to reconcile the two nations, so he moved on to other things. As Nigel Harris has pointed out, he redefined the argument so that it became a question of uniting two wings of the ruling class, the landowners and the industrialists: "The two nations became one by characteristic verbal sleight of hand, for the two nations had been rich and poor, but they became land and the millocracy".[75]

It would be unnecessarily harsh to argue that Disraeli's sympathy with working class suffering was entirely insincere. But he did not let it get out of hand. Thus in 1850 he spoke and voted against a bill proposing inspection of coal mines because of his connections with the mine owner Lord Londonderry.[76]

71: *Spectator*, 17 May 1845, cited Braun, 1981, p89.
72: Marx and Engels, *Manifesto of the Communist Party*, in Marx and Engels, 1975-2005, volume 6, pp507-508.
73: Blake, 1969, p171.
74: Schwarz, 1979, p82.
75: Harris, 1968, p113.
76: Blake, 1969, p296.

Disraeli played a key role in the passing of the 1867 Reform Bill, which substantially extended the franchise, and went much further than Disraeli's own original intentions, because of the need to respond to extra-parliamentary agitation.[77] Though he may have deplored it,[78] Disraeli could doubtless see that further expansion of the franchise was now inevitable. If he maintained an interest in the working class, it was certainly not because he thought it should play an active role in shaping society, but because he realised that the Tory party would need working class supporters. As he wrote to the members of a workingmen's club: "None are so interested in maintaining the institutions of the country as the working classes. The rich and powerful will not find much difficulty under any circumstances in maintaining their rights, but the privileges of the people can only be defended and secured by popular institutions".[79] If his government introduced legislation that gave certain rights to trade unions, it was doubtless because he recognised that any government would have to come to some sort of accommodation with the emerging labour movement; as he boasted, the new laws would "gain and retain for the Conservatives the lasting affection of the working classes".[80]

There was a strong element of pragmatism in Disraeli's politics; his attitude to public ownership was far removed from that of modern Tories. If Thatcher privatised British Telecom, it was Disraeli who nationalised it in the first place.[81]

But for the theorist of the Two Nations the question of the nation was ever more important; it was the nation that could reconcile opposing interests.[82] Hence in his later years Disraeli's continuing insistence on the importance of the nation and in particular on the role of the Empire. In a celebrated speech at Crystal Palace in 1872 he insisted that the working

77: For a detailed account of Disraeli's role in this period, see Foot, 2005, pp151-158; also Blake, 1969, pp456-67.
78: As he said on 18 March 1867: "We do not live—and I trust it will never be the fate of this country to live—under a democracy"—cited in Foot 2005, p152.
79: Cited in Briggs, 1970, p294.
80: Blake, 1969, p555.
81: Under Disraeli's government in 1868 "the first measure of nationalisation was carried when the government passed a bill empowering the Post Office to buy up all the telegraph companies"—Blake, 1969, p495.
82: Robert Blake rather bizarrely claims that Disraeli "simply did not understand nationalism". As he makes clear, Disraeli understood the nationalism of oppressor nations only too well; it was the nationalism of the oppressed for which he had no sympathy. He even caused great offence to what he referred to as "the Scotch" by refusing to use the term "British" and always preferring "English"—Blake, 1969, pp405, 481.

classes are "proud of belonging to an imperial country, and are resolved to maintain, if they can, their empire".[83]

This preoccupation with nation drew Disraeli towards a fascination with race.[84] Heredity and breeding are central themes in *Sybil*. As one of my students pointed out, even Sybil's dog Harold is described as having an "air of proud high-bred gentleness".[85] And despite his stress on Englishness, Disraeli never quite forgot his Jewish roots, so that he also stressed the historical role of Judaism, notably in that strange and semi-mystical novel *Tancred*. It is as though he thought he could belong to two master races at the same time.[86]

Disraeli was an acute social observer—far more acute in his day than any of our contemporary Tories. But because he denied the working class's capacity to organise itself and to develop its own leadership, he ended up with a range of contradictory and often reactionary positions. The rhetoric of "one nation" does not lead to any coherent practical policies. Whether deployed by Tories or by Labour, it offers no solutions for our present ills.

83: Blake, 1969, p. 523.

84: As Nigel Harris points out, for some conservatives leadership is linked directly to blood and biology since the "magical powers of leaders" are "transmitted through the blood"—Harris 1972, p8.

85: Disraeli, 1980, p244.

86: See, for example, the claim by Sidonia in *Coningsby*: "The fact is you cannot destroy a pure race of the Caucasian organisation... No penal laws, no physical tortures, can effect that a superior race should be absorbed in an inferior, or be destroyed by it. The mixed persecuting races disappear; the pure persecuted race remains. And at this moment, in spite of centuries, of tens of centuries, of degradation, the Jewish mind exercises a vast influence on the affairs of Europe"—Disraeli, 1844, volume 2, pp200-201.

References

Basketter, Simon, 2012, "Disraeli: the 'One Nation' Tory that Ed Miliband learned to love", *Socialist Worker* (13 October), www.socialistworker.co.uk/art.php?id=29739

Blake, Robert, 1969, *Disraeli* (Methuen).

Braun, Thom, 1981, *Disraeli the Novelist* (George Allen & Unwin).

Briggs, Asa, 1970, *Victorian People* (University of Chicago).

Carlyle, Thomas, 1840, *Chartism* (James Fraser).

Cook, Sheila, 2009, "What is Conservatism?" (21 October), http://news.bbc.co.uk/1/hi/uk_politics/8317013.stm

Dickens, Charles, 1987 [1854], *Hard Times* (Methuen).

Disraeli, Benjamin, 1844, *Coningsby* (Henry Colburn) (three volumes).

Disraeli, Benjamin, 1980 [1845], *Sybil* (Penguin).

Disraeli, Benjamin, 1877, *Lothair* (Longmans, Green and Co).

Disraeli, Benjamin, 1881, *Endymion* (Longmans, Green and Co).

Disraeli, Benjamin, 1989, *Letters Volume IV, 1842-1847* (University of Toronto).

Disraeli, Benjamin, 1993, *Letters Volume V, 1848-1851* (University of Toronto).

Edwards, HWJ (ed), 1937, *The Radical Tory* (Jonathan Cape).

Fido, Martin, 1977, "'From his own Observation'; Sources of Working Class Passages in Disraeli's 'Sybil'", *The Modern Language Review*, volume 72, number 2.

Flint, Kate (ed), 1987, *The Victorian Novelist* (Croom Helm).

Foot, Michael, 1980, *Debts of Honour* (Davis Poynter).

Foot, Paul, 2005, *The Vote* (Viking).

Ginsborg, Paul, 1979, *Daniele Manin and the Venetian Revolution of 1848-49* (Cambridge UP).

Harris, Nigel, 1968, *Beliefs in Society* (CA Watts).

Harris, Nigel, 1972, *Competition and the Corporate Society* (Methuen).

Himmelfarb, Gertrude, 2006, *The Moral Imagination* (Ivan R Dee).

Hogg, Quintin, 1943, speech in the House of Commons, 17 February.

Howe, Irving, 1992, *Politics and the Novel* (Columbia UP).

Hyndman, Henry, 1911, *The Record of an Adventurous Life* (Macmillan & Co).

Keating, P J, 1971, *The Working Classes in Victorian Fiction* (Routledge & Kegan Paul).

Kettle, Arnold, 1982, "The Early Victorian Social-Problem Novel", in Boris Ford (ed), *From Dickens to Hardy* (Penguin).

Lodge, David, 1988, *Nice Work* (Secker & Warburg).

Lukács, Georg, 1971, *History and Class Consciousness* (Merlin).

Major, John, 1993, interview in *Mail on Sunday* (21 February).

Marx, Karl, and Frederick Engels, 1975-2005, *Collected Works* (Lawrence & Wishart).

Miliband, Ed 2012, "Conference Speech", http://labourlist.org/2012/10/ed-milibands-conference-speech-the-transcript/

Millar, Mary S, 2006, *Disraeli's Disciple: The Scandalous Life of George Smythe* (University of Toronto Press).

Oborne, Peter, 2010, "Cameron is our Disraeli", *Spectator*, 6 January.

Orwell, George, 1935, *Burmese Days* (Victor Gollancz).

Schwarz, Daniel R, 1979, *Disraeli's Fiction* (Macmillan).

Taylor, Barbara, 1983, *Eve and the New Jerusalem* (Virago).

Thatcher, Margaret, 1996, "Keith Joseph Memorial Lecture", in Robin Harris (ed), *The Collected Speeches of Margaret Thatcher* (Harper Collins).

Hegemony and mass critical intellectuality

Panagiotis Sotiris

During the past years there has been an impressive wave of student movements.[1] What has been distinctive about them is their tendency to be more radical politically in comparison to most forms of student protest in the 1980s and 1990s. They did not limit themselves to protesting against the various student grievances (higher tuition fees, diminished value of degrees, etc), but also have presented themselves as part of a broader movement against neoliberalism and the current form of capitalist politics. This was facilitated by student participation in the various forms of the movement against globalisation, from the first campaigns against sweatshops to the big international demonstrations. This renewed politicisation of student protest has been even more evident in most post-2005 movements (the 2006-2007 Greek student movement, the 2005-2006 French mobilisation, the December 2008 explosion of the Greek youth, the 2009 wave of occupations in California, the 2010 student demonstrations in Britain and the 2012 student movement in Quebec).[2]

What has also been distinctive has been the emergence along this

---

1: The first version of this text was presented at the Second International Conference on Critical Education, Athens, 10-14 July 2012, and has benefited by the comments made in its presentation. The writer also wants to thank Alex Callinicos for his comments and suggestions.
2: On the recent wave of student movements, see Solomon and Palmieri, 2011.

movement of a new wave of critical theorising. This has been facilitated by the fact that many faculty or junior faculty members and postgraduate students have supported and taken part in the movement (exemplified in the presence of radical academics in the movement in both Britain and the United States). This has also led to a new flourishing of theoretical debate and production by students and academics, that tend to combine political activism and theoretical work.

This is a very important development. On the one hand, we should stress the renewed interest in the political importance of theory. This has not only the sense of an apprehension of the politics of the theory, something evident in the 1980s and 1990s in disciplines such as poststructuralist literary and cultural studies, radical feminism and gender studies and postcolonial studies, but also in the importance of theory for radical politics today. On the other hand, we can see the emergence of new militant forms of theoretical production on the margins (or even outside of) academia. It is obvious that the divorce between theory and practice that Perry Anderson presented in the 1970s as the distinctive feature of "Western Marxism",[3] and as the condensation of the crisis of the Communist movement, for the first time shows some signs that it can be overcome.

That is why we need to think of new forms of militant collective intellectuality, new ways to articulate militant practice and theoretical work, new synergies between theory and the movement. However, in order to do that we need to go back to the traditions of the revolutionary movement and radical theory and revisit their attempts to come to terms with these major theoretical and political questions. That is why in this paper we will try to discuss attempts at presenting a theory of critical intellectuality.

The Workers' Inquiry: from Marx to the workerists.

The first has to do with the concept of workers' inquiry. Karl Marx first thought about a novel way to inquire about the actual condition of the working classes. The result was a big questionnaire written by Marx and circulated through *La Revue Socialiste*, a French socialist journal.[4] The aim was to gather as many completed questionnaires by workers, and then use them to study their condition. The use of a militant journal, the attempt to get the help of the workers themselves, making them active subjects and not simply "objects under observation", the form of the questionnaire that

---

3:   Anderson, 1976.
4:   Marx, 1997.

was designed to help the researcher and at the same time to help the worker gradually come by himself to the realisation of the conditions of exploitation, mark the distinctive characteristics of Marx's *Enquête Ouvrière*.

In the 1960s this theme of the "workers' inquiry" was taken up by the workerist tendency of Italian Marxism.[5] The first forms of expression of the workerist tendency, organised through the reviews *Quaderni Rossi* and *La Classe Operaia*, were based on the combined work of academics and political and trade union activists. They were oriented mainly to an audience of union activists and not necessarily academics, despite the theoretical richness and profundity of the texts appearing there, especially by Raniero Panzieri and Mario Tronti. It is here that the very concept of workers' inquiry became a central tenet of workerists, both as a theoretical concept but also as a particular practice.

In the case of the workerists, the workers' inquiry served a double purpose. On the one hand, it served the attempt actually to study the condition of the working classes, the forms of neo-capitalism, the operations of capitalist power within the workplace and especially the modern factory, and the forms of resistance. This created the conditions for a militant sociology of advanced capitalism. At the same time, it stressed the importance of workers' resistance as the driving force of capitalist rationalisation and modernisation. On the other hand, it served the attempt actually to relate to the workers, to create a form of a common practice that would be not only theoretical or research oriented but also deeply political, a new way to help the formation of political vanguards deeply rooted in the workplace and to overcome the exteriority of politicised students and researchers to workers. As Stephen Wright has shown, taking the work of sociologists oriented toward field researches, interviews and life stories, such as Danilo Dolci and Danilo Montaldi,[6] the workerists thought of the workers' enquiry as both an analytical and a political tool. In the case of Panzieri this was linked to his conception of Marxism as a sociology conceived "as a political science, the science of revolution".[7] The aim of the inquiry must be to investigate the balance of forces but also to track the changes and the new tendencies. The same conception is obvious in Dario Lanzardo's long excursus on Marx's "Enquête Ouvrière" in *Quaderni Rossi*, still one of the most interesting readings of workers'

5: For an overview of Italian workerism see Wright, 2002.
6: Wright, 2002, pp22-23.
7: Panzieri, 1965, p110.

inquiry.[8] For Lanzardo the object of workers' inquiry is exactly to help the workers understand that the capitalist reality is historical and not natural.[9] This was exemplified by the pioneering research by Romano Alquati in workplace conditions and struggles in companies such as Fiat and Olivetti.[10] The long cooperation of students, academics and workers around the big chemical complex in Porto Maghera in the Veneto area and other sites of struggle exemplified this tendency.[11] It was also expressed in the richness of reviews such as *Primo Maggio* that combined militant engagement and political oriented interventions with highly sophisticated inquiries into questions of theory of value, history of the labour movement, analyses of the changes and restructurings of capitalism.[12]

Foucault and "specific intellectuals"

Another example, contemporaneous to the long experience of the workerist tendency, was Michel Foucault's insistence on the need for a new form of *specific intellectuals*. Foucault in his long interview "Truth and Power" made a distinction between the figures of the traditional intellectual as "the bearer of the universal",[13] as a "universal consciousness",[14] with writing as the principal form of expression, and the new emerging figure of the specific intellectual. Although he admits the radicalisation of traditional intellectuals expressed in the "relentless theorisation of writing we saw in the sixties",[15] he points to a new figure of politicised intellectual emerging after the Second World War. He calls this figure the "specific intellectual", and thinks that it was the nuclear physicist that offered the first such example of an intellectual that constituted a threat to political power "no longer on account of a general discourse he conducted but because of the knowledge at his disposal".[16] He also attributes this to the rising importance of the "technico-scientific structure" in modern life. Foucault is aware of the dangers specific intellectuals can face in their political

---

8: Lanzardo, 1965.
9: The openly political character of the *workers' inquiry* is exemplified in the following passage from a text by Antonio Negri in the 1970s: "Workers' inquiry is a political battle right from the start: it is a political battle on the side of theory as well as praxis"—Negri, 2005, p72.
10: Alquati, 1985; Armano and Sciortino, 2010; Wright, 2002, pp42-58.
11: Wright, 2002, pp110-114.
12: A full series of *Primo Maggio* in pdf format can be found at www.autistici.org/operaismo/PrimoMaggio/La%20rivista/
13: Foucault, 2002, p126.
14: Foucault, 2002, p127.
15: Foucault, 2002, p127.
16: Foucault, 2002, p128.

intervention: the risk of engaging in partial struggles, the risk of manipulation, the risk of isolation for lack of a global strategy or outside support.[17] At the same time, he insists that we cannot go back to the nostalgia for a universal intellectual, nor can we attack specific intellectuals as serving the interests of capital. On the contrary, we must see how intellectuals can intervene in the specific "politics of truth"[18] in modern capitalist societies, which for Foucault is a battle "about the status of truth and the political and economic role it plays".[19] Although Foucault insists—as in many other instances—on opposing any global and all-encompassing project of emancipation, he nevertheless stresses the need for radical intervention:

> It's not a matter of emancipating truth from every system of power (which would be a chimera, for truth is already power) but of detaching the power of truth from the forms of hegemony, social, economic and cultural, within which it operates at the present time.[20]

It is obvious that what Foucault had in mind is a whole wave of militant scientists and researchers connected to radical social movements, especially in relation to struggles around nuclear energy, pollution, the state-prison complex, psychiatric power, feminism. Contrary to the traditional left's conception of science as being inherently progressive (as opposed to the supposed tendency of capital to fetter the development of science, an assumption that ran contrary to the very development of science under capitalism) Foucault offers a much more complex conception of the politics of science. It is important that in this conception we treat militant scientists and researchers as active subjects engaged in struggles and not as passive *savants* simply waiting for the labour movement to liberate them and their respective role.

It is also important to note that part of the impetus for this conceptualisation of the specific intellectual came not only from the experiences of critical sciences and movements challenging the neutrality of science, but also from Foucault's own engagement in militant scientific practice around the *Groupe d'Informations sur les Prisons*, part of which was also the drafting of a questionnaire for prisoners.[21]

17: Foucault, 2002, p130.
18: Foucault, 2002, p132.
19: Foucault, 2002, p132.
20: Foucault, 2002, p133.
21: Brich, 2008. The *Groupe d'Informations sur les Prisons* (Group for Information on Prisons) in the early 1970s tried to bring attention the horrible conditions in the French penal system and to defend the rights of prisoners and was based on the work of both intellectuals and activists.

Bourdieu and the need for a scholarship with commitment

In the 1990s Pierre Bourdieu emerged as one of the vocal proponents of the need for socially and politically engaged public intellectuals. In a series of interventions,[22] exemplified in his support of the 1995 French strike movement—a rare exception in the French theoretical landscape, he opposed all forms of current neoliberal ideology and particularly the accommodating positions adopted by most prominent French intellectuals. For Bourdieu, in a period of neoliberal attack on social rights intellectuals have an obligation to support social movements, instead of being ideologues of the capitalist politics.

What is particularly interesting in the interventions by Bourdieu is that he did not limit himself simply to calls for a return to the figure of the public intellectual as bearer of social and political virtue, in the classical sense of the term, what Foucault would have called a universal intellectual. Bourdieu also insisted on the need for a new engaged, collective intellectual effort, the creation of a collective intellectual in collaboration with the movement, including new forms of collaboration between activists and intellectuals. The following passage summarises the exigencies especially for social scientists:

> Social scientists are not fellow-travellers, in other words hostages and guarantors, figureheads and alibis who sign petitions and who are disposed of as soon as they have been used; nor are they Zhdanovian apparatchiks who come in to exercise apparently intellectual powers within the social movements which they cannot exercise in intellectual life; nor are they experts coming in to give lessons—not even anti-expert experts; nor are they prophets who will provide answers to all questions about the social movement and its future. They are people...who can point out that the people here are not present as spokespersons, but as citizens who come into a place of discussion and research, with ideas, with arguments, leaving their slogans, platforms and party habits in the cloakroom.[23]

Gramsci, hegemony and intellectuality

Finally, I come to a theorist who preceded the interventions discussed so far: Antonio Gramsci. I believe that in Gramsci's work one can find the most advanced confrontation with the question of a new militant intellectuality able to serve the purpose of social emancipation. Gramsci in such

---

22: Bourdieu, 1998, 2001, 2002.
23: Bourdieu, 1998, p56.

a reading was not simply a theoretician of the role of intellectuals. He was a theoretician of the articulation of politics, culture and knowledge, exemplified in the richness and complexity of the theory of hegemony as a theory of social and political power in modern capitalist societies. Moreover, the question of mass militant intellectuality was for Gramsci one of the main challenges for emancipatory politics:

> For a mass of people to be led to think coherently and in the same coherent fashion about the real present world is a "philosophical" event, far more important and "original" than the discovery by some philosophical "genius" of a truth which remains the property of small groups of intellectuals.[24]

For Gramsci the question of proletarian hegemony also entailed the emergence of new forms of mass intellectuality, a transformed common sense, and new strata of intellectuals. Gramsci was led to this position by his study of the emergence of bourgeois hegemony, the importance of mass cultural forms, the role of intellectuals and the institutions responsible for their reproduction but also for the dissemination of their work and ideas. However, he insisted that these new intellectuals could not be in simple continuity to traditional intellectuals: "If the 'new' intellectuals put themselves forward as the direct continuation of the previous 'intelligentsia' they are not new at all".[25] Moreover, for Gramsci the emergence of new types of intellectuals was the manifestation of the ripeness of the new historical situation. This demand for new intellectuals formed within the workers' struggle for hegemony, but also within the practical effort for new forms of social organisation and production, is exemplified in the complexity of extracts such as the following:

> The mode of being of the new intellectual can no longer consist in eloquence, which is an exterior and momentary mover of feelings and passions, but in active participation in practical life, as constructor, organiser, "permanent persuader" and not a simple orator (but superior at the same time to the abstract mathematical spirit); from technique-as-work one proceeds to technique-as-science and to the humanistic conception of history, without which one remains "specialised" and does not become "directive" (specialised and political).[26]

24: Gramsci, 1971, p325.
25: Gramsci, 1971, p453.
26: Gramsci, 1971, p10. We should note that for Gramsci directive refers to the essence of revolutionary politics, the ability to lead a social class in the struggle for self-emancipation.

What is interesting about this conception of the militant intellectual is that Gramsci seems to overcome the universal-specific dichotomy evident in Foucault's theorisation of the specific intellectual. For Gramsci the new intellectuals must be at the same time specific, linked to particular practical questions, immersed in practical questions of politics, science, economy (hence the acceptance that they should be "specialised"), and have a broad and critical ideological and cultural orientation, able to facilitate the struggle for hegemony.

For Gramsci this process of the forming of new intellectuals is a collective process. The political party is responsible for the formation of new intellectuals. Moreover, Gramsci insists that all members of a political party should be treated as intellectuals. In the words of Gramsci: "That all members of a political party should be regarded as intellectuals is an affirmation that can easily lend itself to mockery and caricature. But if one thinks about it nothing can be more exact".[27] This collective conception of the emergence of mass forms of militant intellectuality is made evident in Gramsci's conception of the political party as laboratory.

> One should stress the importance and significance, which, in the modern world, political parties have in the elaboration and diffusion of conceptions of the world, because essentially what they do is to work out the ethics and the politics corresponding to these conceptions and act as it were their historical "laboratory"... The relation between theory and practice becomes even closer the more the conception is vitally and radically innovatory and opposed to old ways of thinking. For this reason one can say that the parties are the elaborators of new integral and all-encompassing intellectualities and the crucibles where the unification of theory and practice understood as real historical process takes place.[28]

This is also evident in Gramsci's reference to the figure of the _democratic philosopher_. Gramsci suggested that the need for a different practice of philosophy would lead to the need for a new type of philosopher, the

---

27: Gramsci, 1971, pp5-6.
28: Gramsci, 1971, p335. I have slightly altered the translation. Hoare and Nowell Smith translate as "elaborators of new integral and totalitarian intelligentsias". However, in the Italian original Gramsci refers to political parties as "_elaboratori delle nuove intelletualita integrali e totalitarie_" (Gramsci, 1977, p1387), so I choose to translate _intelletualita_ as intellectualities, following here the French translation of the _Prison Notebooks_ (Gramsci, 1978). Moreover, since totalitarian had a different meaning in the early 1930s than its post Second World War meaning, I translate _totalitarie_ as all-encompassing.

"democratic" philosopher who "is a philosopher convinced that his personality is not limited to himself as a physical individual but is an active relationship of modification of the cultural environment".[29] The figure of the democratic philosopher suggests the need for a new form of intellectuals where the important distinction has exactly to do with their awareness of the limits of their subjectivity and the need for them to engage in collective political and knowledge practices that are the necessary conditions for their critical intellectual activity. This is a highly original conception of a non-subjective or post-subjective condition of intellectuality

The notion of the democratic philosopher is one of Gramsci's most insightful moments, because it grasps not only the relation between philosophy, history and politics, but also the need for a relational and transformative conception of philosophy as social practice and not only as subjective thinking, a conception also evident in Gramsci's treatment of man as "historical bloc".[30]

It is obvious that with Gramsci we have a much more elaborated conception of the need for new militant forms of mass intellectuality. His conception encompasses both the need to work side by side with the movement in practical relations of knowledge, collective self-awareness and common struggle that was evident in the practice of workers' inquiry, and also the need to combine militancy with knowledge, including technical knowledge, as envisaged by Foucault in his conception of the specific intellectual. Moreover, Gramsci's conception also includes the need for profound changes and a radicalisation of the institutions producing intellectualities along with the need for new institutions. At the same time, he avoids certain dangers: the danger of particularism, the identification of specificity with the academic division of labour (something evident especially in the way Bourdieu treats intellectuals as specialists in their field), the refusal to engage in collective forms of militancy.

Militant intellectuality today

All these examples show us that there can be militant forms of intellectuality, both in the sense of critical and politically engaged theoretical production oriented towards projects for emancipation and in the sense of mass intellectuality and a change in common sense and mass ideological practices. At the same time, we have to confront the whole process through which 1960s

---

29: Gramsci, 1971, p350. For a reading of the importance of the concept of the democratic philosopher, see Thomas, 2009, pp429-436.
30: Gramsci, 1971, p360.

and 1970s theoretical radicalism lost both its momentum and its political engagement. The well-known story about radical academics becoming self-entrenched within the confines of academia and all the rituals of formal academic research, losing touch with urgent social and political exigencies, although in most aspects a distortion of reality, did indeed capture some of the problems of post-1970s radical theorising. Even today, with an impressive wave of young Marxist or more generally radical academics (mainly in junior positions) in place, one can still sense the gap separating theoretical and political activity or participation in movements. The standardisation of academic research, the quantification of research assessment, both individually and institutionally, the pressure for immediate results, papers and quantifiable research outcomes surely contributes to this.

However, there have also been other forms. To give one example: The edu-factory network has been more than instrumental in promoting both a radical anti-capitalist agenda regarding the entrepreneurialisation of higher education and forms of coordination between activists and activist networks.[31] To give another example: all the international networks of economists helping movements against globalisation, against Third World Debt, in favour of debt-auditing processes.[32]

Recently the notion of mass intellectuality has gained new interest, especially in the work of writers working in a post-workerist direction such as M Lazzarato and Paolo Virno.[33] According to this theme, the importance of intellectual "immaterial" labour in post-Fordist capitalism makes mass intellectuality even more important, as is evident in the intellectual (in the sense of non-manual) character of many work processes and in the need for capital to exploit not just labour time but also collective knowledge, skills, representations. This follows the workerists' emphasis on the "Fragment on Machines" from the *Grundrisse* where Marx refers to the *General Intellect*.[34] For this tradition mass intellectuality is an analytical concept, a description of the objective and subjective conditions for post-Fordism, and follows the

---

31: See Edu-factory Collective, 2009.
32: See, for example, the work done by the Committee to Abolish Third World Debt (www.cadtm.org) or the work of the Initiative for the Greek Audit Commission (www.elegr.gr).
33: Lazzarato, 1996 and Virno, 2004.
34: For the "Fragment on Machines", see Marx, 1973, pp690-712. Marx refers to the general intellect in the following phrase: "The development of fixed capital indicates to what degree general social knowledge has become *a direct force of production*, and to what degree, hence, the conditions of the process of social life itself have come under the control of the general intellect and been transformed in accordance with it"—p706. On the concept of the general intellect in the *Grundrisse* and its subsequent use by post-workerists see Haug, 2010.

workerist tendency to ground insurrectionary tendencies in the ontology of labour. However, it is not a concept that can account for the complexity of the division between intellectual and manual labour in capitalist production, of the recurring tendency both of the incorporation of scientific knowledge and technique in the production process and of the trivialisation of tasks, and of the forms of the transformation of science into a productive force. It is also a one-sided reading of Marx that stresses the importance of the *Grundrisse* but tends to leave aside Marx's more elaborate confrontation with questions of science and technology, especially in the *Economic Manuscript of 1861-63*.[35] In those notes a more complex conception emerges of the relation of science to capitalist production, one that, instead of a simple image of a collective intellectual capacity being put under the command of capital, stresses the importance of technology and machinery on the transformation of science into a production force and the processes of skilling and deskilling associated with this process. Moreover, the post-workerist emphasis on immaterial intellectual labour as the "hegemonic form",[36] can easily lead to an underestimation of all other forms of labour and misrepresent capitalist exploitation as mainly some form of blocking the creative capability of the multitude.

By contrast, I am using intellectuality here much more in the sense that Gramsci uses it, as a strategic concept describing a condition to be attained, the result of (counter)hegemonic apparatuses and projects, the outcome of struggles and new forms of collective organisation. We have to see how this increased importance of intellectual labour in modern capitalism (something that Gramsci also stressed) creates conditions for collective practices and networks of militant intellectuality. In this sense mass intellectuality is not something given in advance; it is a political stake of social and political antagonism and of the collective practices of social movements.

In the light of the above, we can discuss some of the tasks facing us today. We need more examples of critical intellectuality and of politically engaged theoretical production. We need radical academics and researchers providing theoretical material to activists. We want activists and militants to have a much more theoretical background acquired not only through formal academic channels. We want radical social movements to become also theoretical sites, to develop their own knowledge institutions, both in the sense of producing and of disseminating knowledge and critical theory. The current protest cycle can only help this process. Social movements,

35: Especially in Marx's extended notes on machinery and the utilization of the forces of nature and society (Marx, 1989, pp318-346; Marx, 1991, pp372-501; Marx, 1996, pp8-61).
36: On this see Hardt and Negri, 2005, pp103-115.

especially when they are politicised in a collective and non-hierarchical manner, are also knowledge processes. People engaging in them have to know things, have to form arguments, and at the same time they learn from the very collective experience of struggle. The presence of radical theorists and researchers alongside militants surely helps, but this is not enough. We need to go beyond this relation of externality between the movement and critical theory and build new institutions of knowledge within the movement itself, new knowledge practices, and new forms of militant research. Only in this way will it be possible to actually not only produce new readings of the conjuncture but also discuss new projects and alternative social forms and arrangements, exactly what is more needed in order to galvanise support for radical politics and social change. We also need a new ethics of research and scientific engagement, stressing the importance of independence from corporate interests, the work alongside the movement, the timely publication of results, especially regarding dangers for society, the need for a critical popularisation of scientific findings, the acceptance of the questions and needs of people from the movement as legitimate concerns.

Such a conception also offers a way out for that growing segment of highly trained scientific and technical workforce, employed in corporations or the state, that in a period of radicalisation wants to find an outlet not only for political activism, but also for its knowledge and expertise (a small example being all those corporate economists who used intensive blogging in the period after the eruption of the current economic crisis as a means to offer to the general public a critical perspective on economic developments, based on their knowledge and expertise). The same goes for teachers in both primary and secondary education, whose scientific training is usually used only for the reproduction of the curriculum, whereas they could be at the forefront of community based and localised collective forms of mass intellectuality.

Such a collective work will help us change the way people think and consequently act. The emergence on a mass scale of new collective representations, mentalities, worldviews and discursive practices, of new ways for working people to understand social reality and their place within it and realise the collective potential to transform it, can never be simply a question of effective propaganda. It must also be a collective effort to change "common sense", putting into practice the necessary dialectic of revolutionary theory on the one hand and the knowledge and collective experience that working people get from their participation in struggle, in order to achieve new forms of hegemony in the fight for radical social change. This is an indispensable aspect of revolutionary politics today.

Above all we must think of radical left parties, political fronts and organisations as knowledge practices and laboratories of new forms of mass critical intellectuality. In a period of economic and political crisis but also of new possibilities to challenge capitalist rule, questions of political organisation gain new relevance. Thinking of organisation simply in terms of practical or communicative skills for mobilisation, or of electoral fronts and tactics is not enough. It would be better, in order to build today's parties and united fronts, to revisit Gramsci's (and Lenin's) conception of the party as a democratic political and theoretical process that produces knowledge of the conjuncture, organic intellectuals, new worldviews, social and political alternatives, as a potential (counter)hegemonic apparatus. We need forms of organisation that not only enable coordination and networking, democratic discussion and effective campaigning, but also bring together different experiences, combine critical theory with the knowledge coming from the different sites of struggle, and produce both concrete analyses but also mass ideological practices and new forms of radical "common sense".

Mass radical intellectuality is at the same time a prerequisite and an expression of a new hegemony emerging. Contrary to the tendency of many people on the left to think simply in terms of electoral dynamics, we need to start thinking in terms of hegemony and the construction of an alternative.

References

Alquati, Romano, 1985 (1962-3), "Organische Zusammensetzung des Kapitals und Arbeitskraft bei OLIVETTI", *Quaderni Rossi*, www.wildcat-www.de/thekla/05/t05_oliv.pdf

Anderson, Perry, 1976, *Considerations on Western Marxism* (New Left Books).

Armano, Emiliana, and Raffaele Sciortino, 2010, "In Memory of Romano Alquati", www.generation-online.org/p/p_alquati.htm

Bourdieu, Pierre, 1998, *Acts of Resistance: Against the new Myths of Our Time* (Polity).

Bourdieu, Pierre, 2001, *Contre-feux 2. Pour un Movement Social Européenne* (Raisons d'agir).

Bourdieu, Pierre, 2002, "The Role of Intellectuals Today", *Theoria* volume 49, number 99.

Brich, Cecile, 2008, "The Groupe d'Information sur les Prisons: The Voice of Prisoners? Or Foucault's?", *Foucault Studies*, 5.

Edu-factory collective (ed), 2009, *Towards a Global Autonomous University* (Autonomedia).

Foucault, Michel, 2002, *Power: Essential Works of Foucault 1954-1984*, volume 3 (Penguin).

Gramsci, Antonio, 1971, *Selections from the Prison Notebooks* (Lawrence and Wishart).

Gramsci, Antonio, 1977, *Quaderni del Carcere*, 4 volumes (Einauidi).

Gramsci, Antonio, 1978, *Cahiers de Prison*, 4 volumes (Gallimard).

Hardt, Michael, and Antonio Negri, 2005, *Multitude: War and Democracy in the Age of Empire* (Hamish Hamilton).

Haug, Wolfgang Fritz, 2010, "General Intellect" (from the Historical-Critical Dictionary of Marxism), *Historical Materialism* 18:2.

Lanzardo, Dario, 1965, "Marx et l'Enquête Ouvrière", in *Quaderni Rossi*, 1968, *Luttes Ouvrières et Capitalisme d'Aujourd'hui* (Maspero).

Lazzarato, Mauricio, 1996, "Immaterial Labor", in Paolo Virno and Michael Hardt (eds), *Radical Thought in Italy. A Potential Politics* (University of Minessota Press).

Marx, Karl, 1973, *Grundrisse* (Penguin), www.marxists.org/archive/marx/works/1857/grundrisse/

Marx, Karl, 1989, 1991, 1996 [1861-63], *Economic Manuscript of 1861-63*, in *Marx—Engels Collected Works*, volume 30, 33, 34 (Progress/Lawrence and Wishart).

Marx, Karl, 1997 [1880], "A Workers Inquiry", www.marxists.org/archive/marx/works/1880/04/20.htm

Negri, Antonio, 2005, *Books for Burning. Between Civil War and Democracy in 1970s Italy* (Verso).

Panzieri, Raniero, 1965, "Conception Socialiste de l'Enquête Ouvrière" in *Quaderni Rossi*, 1968, *Luttes Ouvrières et Capitalisme d'Aujourd'hui* (Maspero).

Solomon, Clare and Tania Palmieri (eds), 2011, *Springtime. The New Student Rebellions* (Verso).

Thomas, Peter 2009, *The Gramscian Moment: Philosophy, Hegemony and Marxism* (Brill).

Virno, Paolo, 2004, *A Grammar of the Multitude* (Semiotext(e)).

Wright, Steve, 2002, *Storming Heaven. Class Composition and Struggle in Italian Autonomist Marxism* (Pluto).

Divided they fell: the German left and the rise of Hitler

Florian Wilde

Eighty years ago, on 30 January 1933, President of Germany Paul von Hindenburg appointed Adolf Hitler to the position of Chancellor of the Reich.[1] In the years preceding Hitler's appointment the Nazis and their paramilitary units, the SA and SS, had already been engaging in a steady campaign of terror against the labour movement while the state looked the other way. On 30 January 1933 this terror was made legal. By February SA and SS units were being deployed as auxiliary police officers and given official powers. Their fight against the labour movement had become an officially sanctioned state policy.

Brutal attacks and murders of well-known anti-fascist activists followed immediately after Hitler's ascension to power. Hit most quickly and most heavily by Nazi repression was the Communist Party (KPD). Nazi thugs stormed and closed the KPD headquarters, the Karl Liebknecht House, on 23 February 1933 and banned their newspaper, *Die Rote Fahne*, a few days later. The burning of parliament on 27 February was used to justify yet another wave of terror against the left. Over 1,500 Communists were arrested that night in Berlin alone. Unable to fit so many political prisoners into the

---

1:     Originally published in German as "Gespalten in den Untergang. Die Linke und der Aufstieg Hitlers", in *Block Fascism! Geschichte, Analysen und Strategien für Eine antifaschistische Praxis* (Linksjugend/Die Linke.SDS). Translation by Loren Balhorn with financial assistance from the Rosa Luxemburg Foundation.

existing prison system, the Nazis erected the first concentration camps during this wave of repression. The last federal elections were held on 6 March: despite the Nazi repression, the KPD still received 12.3 percent (4.8 million votes) and the Social Democratic Party (SPD) 18.3 percent (7.3 million votes). The Nazis had not received an absolute majority, but were able to form a cabinet together with a right wing party. Hitler forced through the so-called "Enabling Act" in the same month, giving the government the right to pass laws contrary to the constitution. The Communists were not able to participate in parliament by that time, as most deputies had either gone underground or had already been arrested by the Nazis. As it was, the SPD was the only party in parliament to vote against the Enabling Act—every bourgeois party voted in favour. Germany's march towards a fascist dictatorship could no longer be halted.

The trade unions were expropriated and disbanded on 2 May and in July the SPD was banned as well. The Nazis had reached their first goal: the destruction of Germany's Marxist labour movement. Breaking the back of labour was the first necessary step towards the Nazis' other goals: the re-arming of Germany in preparation for the most destructive war in history, the construction of a classless *Volksgemeinschaft* (national community) and the destruction of all "enemies of the people"—a campaign that would end in the industrial murder of millions of European Jews.

The German left was largely powerless to act against the Nazi assumption of power. This was a cause for great concern and international debate at the time: how could fascism take power in Germany, the birth-place of Marxism and a country endowed with powerful trade unions, a strong Social Democratic Party and the largest Communist Party outside of the Soviet Union? How was Hitler able to take power without causing a civil war, or even a general strike? How could both the SPD and KPD be destroyed without massive resistance?

Swastikas flew in front of the Brandenburg Gate for the first time in 1920, when reactionary military officers attempted a coup against the young post-war republic: the so-called "Kapp Putsch". The SPD-led gov-ernment at the time retreated to Stuttgart without a fight, as the army was unwilling to defend the government from a right wing attack. The German workers, however, were willing. A spontaneous uprising erupted against the coup, climaxing in a nationwide general strike encompassing 12 million workers—the largest in German history. The leaders of the putsch had lost control of the telegraphs as well as the railways. In many cities workers formed militias to attack brigades of monarchist soldiers. Faced with nation-wide popular resistance, the Kapp Putsch collapsed after a matter of days.

This article seeks to explain why 1933 did not witness similar levels of resistance from the German labour movement. It will address the dynamics of socialist and fascist organisation in the context of global economic crisis, and what lessons the German experience can offer anti-fascists today while developing strategy in the midst of the deepest economic crisis since 1929.

Global crisis and the rise of the Nazi Party

The rise of the Nazi Party cannot be understood outside the context of the world economic crisis that broke out in 1929. Prior to the crisis, Weimar Germany's fascist movement was a marginal phenomenon consisting of various competing factions. They were prone to street violence against leftists and Jews but remained by and large politically irrelevant. Electoral success also proved elusive for the fascists before the economic crisis began. The Nazi Party received only 2.8 percent (810,000 votes) in the 1928 federal elections. This would only change as the economic crisis and the German government's harsh austerity measures brought unbelievable suffering to the population. Unemployment skyrocketed from 1.2 million in June 1929 to 6 million in January 1932. In addition to this were 2 million unregistered unemployed and 6 million short-time workers. Production dropped 41.4 percent from 1929 to the end of 1931, resulting in greatly increased poverty, suffering and desperation for the masses. Virtually the entire youth population was unemployed. Spending hours in soup kitchen lines became a daily reality for millions of Germans.

The German population quickly lost hope in bourgeois democracy and the capitalist system's ability to improve their situation. The Nazis were able to profit from this disillusionment by deploying propaganda against "money-grubbing financial capital" and the parliamentary system, in addition to Jews and Marxists. By September 1930 they had won 18.3 percent (6.4 million votes) and in July 1932 37.4 percent (13.8 million votes)—in only four years the Nazis had increased their support by 13 million votes. Their membership rose from under 100,000 in 1928 to 850,000 by 1933. The Nazi paramilitary wing, the SA, grew from 60,000 to 400,000 members.

The depth of the crisis and the rapid growth of the Nazis caused more and more German capitalists to take notice of them. The captains of German industry and finance feared a social revolution in the country, and hoped to use the Nazis to smash the labour movement. They were also interested in starting a war to avenge the dishonour of Versailles—and to increase their profits. Here their interests converged with those of the Nazis, who already enjoyed the support of Prussian landowners, military officers and other sections of the German elite. While currying the favour of the

German ruling class behind closed doors, the Nazis employed an economic populist and ultra-nationalist rhetoric to build their mass base. They were able to take advantage of and build upon the nationalism proffered by conservative politicians. Many Germans perceived their country to have been the victim of the First World War, and the Nazis together with the bourgeois parties used this issue to deflect class anger away from German capital and towards perceived foreign enemies. The Social Democrats (SPD) contributed to this nationalist fervour by refusing to discuss Germany's own role in causing the war to break out. Having supported the war themselves, the SPD could not afford to condemn it retrospectively.

With the state until the bitter end—the role of the SPD

The SPD were the political party that identified most with the Weimar Republic. They committed themselves to defending the republic "from attacks by both left and right". The party had already shown its readiness to crack down brutally on the radical left after the November revolution in 1918 and the ensuing civil-war-like battles around local revolutionary councils. At that time the SPD had allied with the old economic and military elites of imperial Germany to defeat the revolutionary upsurge and establish a democratic republic with some social reforms, but also ensured that capitalist property relations remained untouched. Because of this historic compromise, the Weimar Republic found itself burdened with a broad layer of military officials, judges and government clerks opposed to the republican reforms. It was precisely this layer that was open to fascist politics and moved closer and closer to the Nazis after 1929.

The SPD's identification with the Weimar Republic became increasingly problematic for the party as the crisis deepened. As the majority of the population increasingly lost hope in capitalism and the republic, millions searched for a political alternative. Because the population identified the SPD with the republic it proved impossible for it to capitalise on this widespread radicalisation, let alone channel it in a socialist direction. The Social Democrats became victims of the economic, social and political crisis that racked the Weimar establishment and were dragged down with it.

The SPD participated in a governing coalition with bourgeois and conservative parties from 1928 to 1930. From 1930 to 1932 they tolerated the authoritarian, right wing government by decree of Heinrich Brüning as a sort of lesser evil opposed to the Nazis. Brüning's solution to the economic crisis was austerity and deflation. He savaged the welfare state, raised indirect taxes and pushed down wages. These measures spelled untold suffering for the millions of workers who supported the SPD. Government employees found their wages cut by 25 percent, unmarried adults were forced to pay an additional tax of 10 percent and workers' pension contributions quadrupled; simultaneously, social spending was reduced by two thirds. Illness increased as more and more people could no longer afford to see a doctor. The SPD, having campaigned on the left but governed on the right, were punished at the polls. Their lack of credibility led them to go from 30 percent of the vote in 1930 to only 18 percent in 1933. The party leadership steadfastly refused to engage in extra-parliamentary mobilisations or workplace struggles to defend workers' standards of living.

The party's self-identification with the Weimar Republic also led it to the mechanical conclusion that all opponents of the republic, ie the Communists and the Nazis, were to be treated the same. Socialist historian Wolfgang Abendroth described the situation as such: "'No difference between Thälmann [the KP leader] and Hitler, between Nazis and Communists'—these were the wretched slogans of the SPD leadership with which they deepened the split in the labour movement".[2] The strategy that was needed—a united front with the Communists against capitalist austerity and fascist terror—was considered unthinkable. The split in the labour movement between the SPD and the KPD and the lack of a united response to the capitalist crisis drove more and more of its victims into the arms of the Nazis. In 1931 the SPD formed the "Iron Front" together with trade unions and athletic clubs numbering 3.5 million members. At its core were a quarter of a million fighters active in the brigades of the *Reichsbanner Schwarz-Rot-Gold*, a paramilitary organisation designed to protect the republic against subversion. However, its fixation on parliamentarism and legality hindered an effective struggle against the Nazis, who did not respect the trappings of bourgeois democracy in their own quest for power.

Militant but sectarian: the KPD

The Communist Party emerged out of the radical left wing of the SPD in response to the said party's support for German involvement in the First World War. By the early 1920s the KPD had become a mass party characterised by a high degree of internal democracy and freedom of discussion; different currents competed for influence within the party. One of the central controversies between these currents was how to relate to the Social Democrats, the party responsible for the deaths of Rosa Luxemburg, Karl Liebknecht and hundreds of revolutionary workers: should they struggle

---

2:   Abendroth, 1997, p253.

head-on against them, as the "left" Communists demanded? Or should the party initiate united fronts with them against the capitalists? The united front was predicated upon the idea that the mass of Social Democrats' interests diverged from those of their leadership. Even if one detested the SPD, they were still the largest political party of the working class and it was vital to prove to the membership that their leadership was not prepared to fight for them. The initiation of united fronts would bring SPD and KPD members together in common struggle, allowing the radicalising dynamic of mass movements to push Social Democrats to the left and into the arms of the Communists. This strategy was designed to win a majority of the working class over to the Communist Party—a necessary prerequisite for a successful workers' revolution.

The Communist Party organisation began to change fundamentally in the mid-1920s. Concomitant with the degeneration of the Russian Revolution, Stalinisation of the KPD began under the leadership of Ernst Thälmann. Freedom of discussion and internal democracy were replaced piece by piece by a mood of unquestioning discipline and authoritarian leadership. Oppositional currents were discouraged from speaking openly and eventually forced out of the party. No longer held politically accountable to the membership, in 1929 Thälmann and Stalin agreed upon an ultra-left course against the SPD, concluding that the Social Democrats represented a form of "social fascism". This disastrous line would eventually prove fatal for both the Social Democrats and the Communists.

The theory of social fascism dictated that Nazis and Social Democrats were essentially two sides of the same coin. The primary enemy of the Communists was supposedly the Social Democrats, who protected capitalism from a workers' revolution by deceiving the class with pseudo-socialist rhetoric. The worst of them all were the left wing Social Democrats, whose rhetoric was particularly deceptive. According to the theory, it was impossible to fight side by side with the SPD against the Nazis under such conditions. Indeed, the KPD declared that defeating the social fascists was the "prerequisite to smashing fascism". By 1932 the KPD began engaging in isolated attempts to initiate broader anti-fascist fronts, most importantly the *Antifascischistsche Aktion*, but these were formulated as "united fronts from below"—ie without the leadership of the SPD. Turning the logic of the united front on its head, SPD supporters were expected to give up their party allegiance *before* joining, as opposed to the united front being a *first practical step* towards the Communist Party. Throughout this period the leaderships of both the SPD and the KPD never came to a formal agreement regarding the fight against Nazism.

Another fatal consequence of the KPD's ultra-leftism was that the term "fascism" was used irresponsibly to describe any and all opponents to the right of the party. The SPD-led government that ruled Germany until 1930 was considered "social fascist". When Brüning formed a new right-wing government by decree without a parliamentary majority in 1930, the KPD declared that fascism had taken power. This went hand in hand with a deadly underestimation of the Nazi danger. Thus Thälmann could declare in 1932: "Nothing could be more fatal for us than to opportunistically overestimate the danger posed by Hitler-fascism".[3] The KPD's seeming inability to distinguish between democratic, authoritarian and fascist expressions of capitalist rule proved to be its undoing. An organisation that continually vilified bourgeois democratic governments as fascist was unable to understand the true meaning of Hitler's ascension to power on 30 January 1933, the day the KPD infamously (and ominously) declared: "After Hitler, we will take over!"

The KPD was able to grow tremendously during the economic crisis. Its radical anti-capitalist rhetoric proved attractive to a large minority of the working class. In elections the KPD went from 10.6 percent (3.2 million votes) in 1928 to 16.9 percent (6 million votes) in November 1932. Its membership doubled in the same time, from 130,000 to almost 300,000. Most of this growth came from the ranks of the unemployed. But despite its phenomenal growth, the KPD was never able to unleash the German proletariat's revolutionary potential or fundamentally challenge the capitalist system. Its confrontational stance towards the SPD prevented a united struggle against the Nazis as well as the austerity imposed by the capitalist parties. The KPD's strategy also prevented the development of a realistic socialist perspective that could have pulled many of the Nazis' unemployed and petty bourgeois supporters back towards the labour movement.

It should be noted that despite employing a strategy that prevented an effective, united struggle, the Communists were at the same time those who fought the Nazis the hardest: hundreds of Communists fought in the civil-war-like street battles that became a common sight in Germany from 1929 to 1933, costing the lives of a hundred Nazis and even more KPD members. After Hitler's ascension to power no group resisted harder or paid as high a price in blood as the KPD. Nearly every third KPD member went to prison under Nazi rule and thousands were murdered.

3:   Meyer-Leviné, 1977, p177.

A fruitless struggle for unity: the independent left

The smaller, independent radical left groups between the SPD and KPD saw the danger posed by the Nazis much more clearly than either of the large parties did. They tried desperately to convince the leaderships of both to join in a united anti-fascist front. The most important of these groups was the Socialist Workers' Party of Germany (SAP), counting roughly 25,000 members. The SAP had been founded by left wing SPD members who rejected their party's compromises with the right wing government in 1931.[4] The SAP saw the struggle against fascism and the struggle against capitalism as interrelated, arguing that it was the crises of capitalism that allowed the Nazis to gain support in the first place. They put forward the argument for a united front of the entire left against the Nazis and against austerity. In 1932 they issued a public appeal to the KPD, the SPD and the trade unions in which they stated: "The divisions in the labour movement run deep, but not as deep as the desire, in this hour of imminent danger, to temporarily overcome these divisions in order to prevent the labour movement, regardless of our strategic and tactical differences, from being defeated entirely. There is unity in the desire to push back fascism, to push back wage decreases, to defend the welfare state and to prevent war. Therefore we suggest to you [leadership of KPD, SPD and trade unions] to take these four points as the basis for a common struggle involving all of the organisations of the working class".[5] The SAP saw the fight against the Nazis as an opportunity to bring the deeply divided labour movement back together and give workers a feeling of strength again. Thus it was stated in their action programme: "The most important task is, through united action, to bring the working class back to its senses and make it conscious of its own power once again".[6] Successful fightbacks against fascism were a necessary prerequisite to developing the self-confidence necessary to defeat capitalism and thereby removing the social basis upon which fascism could grow.

Precise analyses of fascism and wise strategic proposals for the German left were also to be found from the KPD (Opposition), the expelled oppositional group around August Thalheimer and Heinrich Brandler; as well as from Leon Trotsky's followers in Germany. They both encouraged the leaders of Germany's major workers' parties to begin a common and decisive struggle against Hitler's victory, which by now was fast approaching.

4: A core of the SPD left and later the SAP was the current around Paul Levi, former KPD chairperson who rejoined the SPD together with his supporters in 1922 and died in 1930.
5: Winkler, 1987, p617.
6: Niemann, 1991, p267.

Trotsky issued desperate warnings from his exile in Turkey about the fatal danger the Nazis posed for the labour movement. Against this danger, only a united struggle of all workers could succeed: "'The policies of our parties are irreconcilably opposed; but if the fascists come tonight to wreck your organisation's hall, we will come running, arms in hand, to help you. Will you promise us that if our organisation is threatened you will rush to our aid?' This is the quintessence of our policy in the present period".[7]

The concept of the united front that the SAP and other independent left groups presented was based upon two assumptions: firstly, that a direct confrontation with the Nazis demanded complete unity of the working class in order to be successful; secondly, that the Nazis could only be defeated if the left provided the victims of the economic crisis with a positive and realistic socialist alternative to both capitalism and Nazism—otherwise the Nazis would continue to grow, regardless of how strong the united front was. A socialist alternative only seems plausible if it is accompanied by mass struggle. The main workers' organisations have to be engaged in a united fight to defend and improve workers' standards of living. Thus the united front against the fascists and the fight for socialism had to go together.

The potential for the united front to unleash far greater political forces had been seen in 1926, when the KPD initiated a referendum calling for the expropriation without compensation of the German princes, who had already been removed from power in the aftermath of the First World War. Unity committees were founded and led campaigns all across Germany. The pressure exerted on the SPD was so strong that the party was ultimately forced to support the referendum. 14.5 million voters supported the referendum as well—more votes than both parties combined had ever received in an election. Even after 1929 many rank and file members of both parties ignored the confrontational policies of their leaderships and formed neighbourhood and shop floor anti-fascist defence squads.

The independent left proposed the only strategy with any chance of defeating the Nazis: the united front. In the last free federal elections in November 1932 the KPD and SPD together still received 1.5 million votes more than the Nazis. Because these other groups remained relatively small throughout the period, they have been reduced to a footnote in the history books. They were never large enough nor was their influence strong enough to turn the SPD and KPD away from their disastrous policies, and thus were condemned to understand and anticipate the coming victory of fascism without being able to prevent it.

7:    Trotsky, 1930.

Relevance for today

The German experience of fascism is not only interesting from a historian's perspective, but is also an important reference while developing socialist strategy in Europe today. The continent is undergoing an economic crisis similar in intensity to that of 1929. Greece, Europe's neoliberal laboratory, shows particular parallels to Germany after 1929. Similar to the Germany at the time, Greece's economy has shrunk by over 20 percent. The austerity measures imposed by the Troika also resemble those pursued by the Brüning government in Germany: drastic curtailments in government spending, cuts in pensions and increases in indirect taxation. These policies have already affected Greece now as badly as they did Germany then: unemployment stands at 25 percent—for young people it even reaches 50 percent; the suicide rate is exploding; many Greeks can no longer afford to visit a doctor; poverty and homelessness are becoming widespread phenomena. More and more Greeks are losing their faith in capitalism as a result. Political polarisation has also increased exponentially and Pasok, the social democratic formation similar to the German SPD, has already seen its support collapse to under 10 percent. This polarisation brings encouraging developments on the left, such as the massive growth of the left-wing coalition Syriza. Simultaneously Golden Dawn, an openly fascist party that spent years as an obscure sect (as did the Nazis before 1929), received 7 percent in the June elections and is already reaching over 10 percent in the polls now. Fascist thugs are beginning to patrol the streets of Greece in a way eerily reminiscent of the Nazi brownshirts.

Given this context it is vital to learn from the German left's failure to stop the rise of the Nazis between 1929 and 1933, as it continues to offer critical lessons for today. For example, it is crucial to realise that fascism poses a potentially deadly threat to the entire labour movement, as well as to all other social movements and minorities (religious, ethnic, etc). The grim lesson offered by the German experience is that once fascism takes power there is no turning back. Fascism destroys any and all opposition and thus is life-threatening for all organisations of the left. Under no conditions may the rivalries and differences among left organisations be allowed to block the united struggle against the Nazis. Building broad and united anti-fascist fronts has to be the priority of every socialist organisation. To trust the police and the state to stop the fascists is as foolish today as it was then. Time and time again we have seen how the state and the police protect fascist demonstrations, undermine anti-fascist activities and sometimes even support fascists outright—Greek readers know this all too well. The task of an anti-fascist movement is to encourage self-activity and self-organisation against the

Nazis, to allow them no space in society and to combat them on all levels and with all necessary means whenever and wherever they show their faces.

The task of socialists within the movement, however, has to go beyond simply defending the status quo against fascist encroachment. The repeated crises of capitalism are what drive people to such desperation that they will even listen to racists and fascists in the first place; thus socialists have the responsibility to develop and present a realistic alternative: namely a socialist alternative. This alternative must be positive and appear convincing; it must be grounded in solidarity, cooperation and class struggle and emphasise a democratic, socialist response to capitalist crisis.

We should take the experience of the SPD before 1933 as a warning: a workers' party that allows itself to become an administrator of the capitalist system by joining or supporting bourgeois governments—and thereby providing left wing cover to austerity—runs the danger of becoming identified with the system itself. It risks discrediting any claim to be an alternative to the status quo. In times of economic crisis like 1929 in Germany or today in Greece, however, millions begin to turn their backs on a status quo that no longer offers them a future. It is precisely then that a credible socialist alternative is needed to channel the anger of the masses in an emancipatory direction. The building of such an alternative is a task the importance of which must not be understated, particularly in the midst of the deepest economic crisis since 1929.

References

Abendroth, Wolfgang, 1997, *Einführung in die Geschichte der Arbeiterbewegung: Von den Anfängen bis 1933* (Distel).

Drechsler, Hanno, 1983, *Die Sozialistische Arbeiterpartei Deutschlands: Ein Beitrag zur Geschichte der deutschen Arbeiterbewegung am Ende der Weimarer Republik* (SOAK-Verlag).

Meyer-Leviné, Rosa, 1977, *Inside German Communism: Memoirs of Party Life in the Weimar Republic* (Pluto).

Niemann, Heinz, 1991, *Auf verlorenem Posten? Linkssozialismus in Deutschland. Zur Geschichte der Sozialistischen Arbeiterpartei* (Dietz).

Seydewitz, Max; Adler, Max, 1931, *Die Krise des Kapitalismus und die Aufgaben der Arbeiterklasse* (Verlag der Marxistischen Büchergemeinde).

Trotsky, Leon, 1930, *The Turn in the Communist International and the Situation in Germany*, www.marxists.org/archive/trotsky/germany/1930/300926.htm

Wilde, Florian, 2010, "'Den nach Hoffnung hungernden Massen den Sozialismus als einzig mögliche Rettung aus der Krise zeigen.' Die Entwicklung der SPD-Linken von der Klassenkampf-Gruppe zur Sozialistischen Arbeiterpartei (SAP)", in Marcel Bois and Bernd Hüttner, *Beiträge zur Geschichte einer Pluralen Linken, Heft 1: Theorien und Bewegungen vor 1968* (Rosa-Luxemburg-Stiftung).

Winkler, Heinrich August, 1987, *Der Weg in die Katastrophe. Arbeiter und Arbeiterbewegung in der Weimarer Republik 1930-33* (J H W Dietz).

Climate change: it's even worse than we thought

Martin Empson

Whatever else it is remembered for, 2012 is likely to go down in history as the year when climate change began noticeably to change the face of the planet. The trends we are beginning to see mean that global warming is going to get far worse, far quicker than anyone expected.

Most obviously this was seen in the polar north. The summer of 2012 saw a record low in Arctic ice levels which fell to a fifth of what they were 30 years ago. The Arctic Ocean is likely to be ice free in the summer within the next decade, 80 years earlier than expected.[1] Because there is less ice and snow, less solar energy is reflected back into space. This accelerates the warming and the Arctic is now warming twice as fast as any other region of the planet.[2]

Such effects, when global warming leads to accelerated warming, are known as feedback mechanisms and they are one of the reasons that older models of climate change are proving inadequate to explain the rate at which changes are taking place on the planet.

The melting of the Arctic is a symbol of a rapidly warming world. But it also has far reaching consequences. One of these is more extreme weather in the northern hemisphere as ocean currents, wind patterns and temperatures change. As the Arctic warms it encourages melting elsewhere. The frozen

---

1:    Kerr, 2012.
2:    Le Page, 2012, pp34-35.

permafrost around the Arctic Circle has begun to warm, releasing greenhouse gases that have been trapped there for thousands of years. Greenland's ice cap is also melting at an increased rate. Unlike Arctic ice that floats on water, melt water from Greenland causes sea levels to rise. This rise is now taking place at an accelerating rate. "Most glaciologists now think that sea levels will rise by at least a metre by 2100, and possibly by as much as two metres", though some scientists think the situation might be far worse. Studies show that the rate of melting is currently doubling every decade.[3]

Weather and climate

As the world warms extreme weather events will become more common. The world's weather will also become even more unpredictable. Hurricane Sandy is a poignant reminder of what this might mean in the future. It is very difficult, though not always impossible, to link a particular weather event to global warming. So we cannot say with any certainty that Sandy was directly linked to climate change. But again trends are that extreme weather is getting more common:

> Work by researchers from Taiwan and China found that the increase in rainfall intensity over the past three decades has been an entire order of magnitude greater than global climate models predict. As for extraordinary heatwaves such as those in Europe in 2003 and 2010, events so far from the norm were only projected to occur towards the end of this century.[4]

In 2012 the US saw its worst and most widespread drought since the mid-1950s. In July around 80 percent of the country was considered "abnormally dry".[5] The US National Oceanic and Atmosphere Administration reported that "June 2012 also marks the 36th consecutive June and 328th consecutive month with a global temperature above the 20th century average".[6]

The US drought destroyed crops across extensive areas of the US. This has helped to increase prices of food, though climate change is only exacerbating a problem caused by banks and multinationals speculating in food prices. But as climate change causes crops to fail possible price rises make price speculation even more attractive to companies and banks.

3: Le Page, 2012, p37.
4: Le Page, 2012, p36.
5: BBC, 16 July 2012, www.bbc.co.uk/news/world-us-canada-18864753
6: NOAA, 2012

Early climate models, including those used by the United Nations' Intergovernmental Panel on Climate Change (IPCC) discussed below, tended to predict that some global warming would be good for crop yields. Higher levels of carbon dioxide can act as a fertiliser for plants in some conditions. In 2007 the IPCC predicted that yields of crops would increase unless warming exceeded 3.5°C, when they would drop. While scientists are still debating the exact impact of global warming on agriculture, some studies show that the IPCC were over-optimistic in their predictions.

A 2011 study from Stanford University "looked at global production of wheat, maize, rice and soybeans—crops that provide three quarters of humanity's calories—from 1980 to 2008. Based on what we know about how temperature, rainfall and CO_2 levels affect growth, the analysis suggests that average yields are now more than 1 percent lower than they would have been with no warming. Without the fertilising effect of increased CO_2, they would have been 3 percent lower".[7]

As the world warms, dry regions are likely to become drier, making it harder to irrigate crops. Extreme and unpredictable weather will cause more and more failures. The future for the world's farmers is likely to be much harder. In particular, those working family farms or smallholdings are less likely to be able to survive the financial crises caused by failed crops.

Emissions and global response

We have seen that many of the predictions made in the recent past about the effects of global warming are inadequate. There are a number of reasons for this. The IPCC, for instance, produces reports based on the collaboration of hundreds of scientists from many different disciplines. Out of necessity the reports are based on consensus which tends to discourage more extreme predictions.

Another problem is that, as one climate scientist has put it, "most scientists have underplayed the significance of the emissions story to make their message politically more acceptable".[8] Unfortunately, despite overwhelming evidence that global warming is far worse than expected, the emissions of greenhouse gases that are the root cause of the problem are rising rapidly.

The amount of greenhouse gases in the atmosphere reached a new record high in 2011. Figures for 2012 are not yet available, but are likely to be higher still. The UN World Meteorological Organisation points out that between 1990 and 2011 there was a 30 percent increase in the warming

---

7:   Le Page, 2012, pp36-37.
8:   Le Page, 2012, pp38-39.

effect on our climate because of emissions of carbon dioxide and other greenhouse gases.[9] Despite the economic recession which caused a slight dip in emissions after 2008, global emissions are rising faster than ever. In fact they are close to the IPCC's worst case scenario.

The last IPCC report was published in 2007. Then the IPCC concluded that with current emissions levels we would see a 4°C rise in average global temperatures by 2100. But more recent computer modelling has demonstrated that the IPCC predictions were too low. Now "best estimates" are that there will be a 5°C or 6°C rise by 2100 and approximately a 10 percent chance that the rise will be 7°C by the end of this century. This means that many of the readers of this journal will live to see "severe" climate change.[10]

In his 2007 book *Six Degrees* Mark Lynas painted an apocalyptic picture of a world four degrees hotter than the pre-industrial era. Heat waves ravage Europe, even in winter months killing thousands. Sudden temperature fluctuations cause enormous floods as mountain snows melt. In the summer rivers dry up completely limiting agriculture still further and rendering hydro-electric power a thing of the past. Millions of people become refugees from flooding and rising sea levels and cities like New York and London require billions of pounds to be spent on flood defences.[11]

A November 2012 report by the World Bank concludes that:

> A 4°C world will pose unprecedented challenges to humanity…the picture that emerges challenges an often-implicit assumption that climate change will not significantly undermine economic growth. It seems clear that climate change in a 4°C world could seriously undermine poverty alleviation in many regions. This is supported by past observations of the negative effects of climate change on economic growth in developing countries. While developed countries have been and are projected to be adversely affected by impacts resulting from climate change, adaptive capacities in developing regions are weaker. The burden of climate change in the future will very likely be borne differentially by those in regions already highly vulnerable to climate change and variability. Given that it remains uncertain whether adaptation and further progress toward development goals will be possible at this level of climate change, the projected 4°C warming simply must not be allowed to occur.[12]

9: WMO, 2012.
10: Le Page, 2012, pp38-39.
11: Lynas, 2007, pp173-204.
12: World Bank, 2012, p64.

Yet despite these warnings politicians fail to agree to action on climate change. In June 2012 Rio de Janeiro hosted the UN conference on Sustainable Development. Marking 20 years since the very first "Earth Summit" the Rio event was designed to showcase global action on environmental questions. Prior to Rio recent UN conferences on climate change had ended in failure. Most importantly, in 2009 the Copenhagen conference had ended in chaos as President Obama led the leaders of China, Brazil, India and South Africa in passing a White House written accord that offered no action.

Desperate to avoid a similar debacle in Rio, the Brazilian hosts worked hard to produce a document that would be acceptable to all parties. As a result it contained nothing of substance other than committing governments to action at some indeterminate point in the future.[13] In a post-conference statement Oxfam described the event as a "hoax" and declared that participants were "paralysed by inertia and in hock to vested interests; too many are unable to join up the dots and solve the connected crises of environment, equity and economy... The poorest people on earth are paying the highest price".[14]

This year the UN climate conference takes place far from any criticism in the oil-rich state of Qatar. Ahead of the conference there is little expectation of an outcome that will lead to serious action being taken on climate change.

The British coalition government, despite promises to be the "greenest ever", is increasingly split over its environmental policies. The Tory energy minister John Hayes described wind farms as "a bourgeois left article of faith" and committed himself to making sure that only a minority of onshore wind farms that are currently at the planning stage get built. While attitudes towards renewable energy are creating tensions with their coalition partners, there is wider agreement between David Cameron and Nick Clegg that the free market can solve the environmental crisis.

At the Rio conference Nick Clegg spoke at the "Natural Capital Conference" and made clear the British government's commitment to an environmental strategy that is based on putting a price on nature in order to give business an incentive to protect it. Such ideas are rooted in a belief that capitalism can save the planet. Yet market solutions have simply failed to reduce emissions. The environmental problems we face are caused by an

---

13: I have written more about the failure of the Rio Summit in Empson, 2012.
14: www.oxfam.org/en/grow/pressroom/reactions/oxfam-final-statement-rio20-rio-will-go-down-hoax-summit

economic system where the blind accumulation of wealth for the sake of accumulation is the driving force of production. One example of this is the World Bank itself. On the one hand it produces a report on the threat from climate change and on the other it continues to invest in fossil fuel intensive plants around the globe. In 2010 World Bank funding for coal plants hit a record $4.4 billion, according to Christian Aid.

The current economic crisis offers opportunities for socialists to link the question of climate change to the wider struggle against austerity. We can argue that, rather than relying on the free market, there should be investment in jobs and industry that can reduce emissions and help mitigate the effects of global warming. But such arguments are also a stepping stone towards a radically different way of organising society. Capitalism will always cause environmental destruction. At a time when the system is failing to deal with one of the greatest threats humanity has ever faced, the argument for an alternative socialist society can make sense to millions of people.

References

Empson, 2012, "Fiddling while Rome Burns: A Report from Rio", *Irish Marxist Review*, volume 1, number 3, www.irishmarxistreview.net/index.php/imr/article/view/32

Kerr, Richard, 2012, "Ice-Free Arctic Sea May Be Years, Not Decades, Away", *Science* (28 September).

Le Page, Michel, 2012, "Climate Change: It's even worse than we thought", *New Scientist* (4 November), www.newscientist.com/special/worse-climate

Lynas, Mark, 2007, "*Six Degrees: Our Future on a Hotter Planet*" (Fourth Estate)

National Oceanic and Atmospheric Administration (NOAA), 2012, "State of the Climate: Global Analysis" (June), www.ncdc.noaa.gov/sotc/global/2012/6

World Bank, 2012, "Turn Down the Heat: Why a 4°C Warmer World Must be Avoided", http://climatechange.worldbank.org/sites/default/files/Turn_Down_the_heat_Why_a_4_degree_centrigrade_warmer_world_must_be_avoided.pdf

World Meteorological Organisation (WMO), "Greenhouse Gas Concentrations Reach New Record" (20 November), www.wmo.int/pages/mediacentre/press_releases/pr_965_en.html

The NPA in crisis: We have to explain because we have to start again

Denis Godard

We will not dwell here on signs that the New Anti-capitalist Party (NPA) is in crisis or on comparisons between the dynamics at its foundation with the current situation. The failure is so severe as to be undeniable. We failed. But the reasons that led us to create the NPA are still there. We have to understand why we failed, especially as we have to start again.

One of the hypotheses developed in this article is that the NPA is not born yet. But this does not mean that nothing has been done. Our experience has put us in a better position to understand the challenges we haven't been able to meet. And this experience has also helped to change the situation in which we must now operate. To paraphrase Daniel Bensaïd: because we have tried, we have earned the right to start again.

We are the failure

The temptation is always great to make our responsibilities seem less important because of external reasons, be they the period we're in, or the creation of the Front de Gauche (FdG),[1] which has occupied part of our "space".

1:    The Front de Gauche is the coalition formed in 2009 between the French Communist Party and the newly-formed Parti de Gauche, the latter being in the main a left split from the social democratic Parti Socialiste. Other smaller groups have also joined the Front de Gauche. This article was translated by Sylvestre Jaffard. It originally appeared in French in *Que Faire?* number 10, August–October 2012, http://quefaire.lautre.net/spip.php?article309

These bad explanations must be cast aside.

The times we live in have seen no less than the start of a systemic crisis of capitalism, quantitatively the largest social revolt in France since 1968 (the movement for pensions), the Arab revolutions, the Indignados movement in Spain and Greece, the Occupy movement in the United States. How can you make such a period the reason for the failure[2] of an anti-capitalist party? The opposite is true: the inability of the NPA to show its usefulness in this period of crisis of the system and of mass revolts was the reason for its internal crisis. Movement setbacks and the progress of reactionary forces—first and foremost the fascists—do not invalidate this analysis, even though they can help change the situation in which we operate. In times of deep crisis for the system, the subjective element is crucial. The same conditions can benefit one side or the other, depending on their ability to take the initiative, to build appropriate responses...or depending on the paralysis of the opposite forces.

The months and years ahead will be explosive. This makes it all the more important to draw correct balance sheets.

Another "bad" explanation: the Parti de Gauche (PG) and the Front de Gauche. Was the space for the NPA suddenly occupied by these new political realities? It would probably be useful to clarify what is meant by space.[3] In any case, it is not an inert substance to be manipulated. We're talking about conscious individuals who we believe will be the actors of their collective emancipation. The birth of the Parti de Gauche, followed by that of the FdG came slightly after that of the NPA. Here again the truth is the reverse: these forces benefited—at least in part—from the weakness of the NPA. The inability to build a "useful" force for tens of thousands of trade unionists, activists associations, neighbourhood youth, etc led some of them to cast their hopes on the FdG, at least for a time.[4]

2:    True, events of such magnitude can unleash internal crises. Their novelty and their importance should, in any organisation worthy of the name, spark many discussions in order to analyse them and to develop responses. It is indeed through this kind of debate and through attempts to intervene effectively that a new party can be forged. Alas, everyone will agree that this hasn't been the NPA's problem. We are therefore talking here about a failure.

3:    For further developments on this question of the "space to be occupied", see my answer to a debate between Alex Callinicos and François Sabado at the foundation of the NPA— Godard, 2009. But the answer itself is dated and shows what the experience of the NPA has brought along, despite its failure: it remains well below a proper awareness. of the changes to be made in our approach. See the following theses.

4:    To put it clearly, the FdG has seized the zeitgeist better than the NPA, at least when it comes to elections. Mélenchon's radical speeches call for a "participatory" campaign, the use of such modes of mobilisation as the occupation of public squares. Yet, and this will be a problem for comrades who join the FdG, its ability to "capitalise" on its voting base is

Electoral crystallisations, just like organisational crystallisations are the non-mechanical product of processes of political polarisation, radicalisation and experimentation. These are still in progress. The current failure of the NPA is not the end of the story. *Syriza* *Law of successive approximations*

The "new" is not born yet

Be it limitation or opportunity, the merit of the initiative to found the NPA is that of the Ligue Communiste Révolutionnaire (LCR), which remained the only organisation of significant size during the founding process and has played the role of propulsive force. This wasn't necessarily an obstacle to the construction of a new party.[5] But it gave a central responsibility to activists from the LCR to "let go".

Any structure, any organisation creates its own conservatism in ideas as well as in practice. This is what gives an organisation the stability needed to hold out in difficult times and to withstand the pressures of the dominant ideology. But this conservatism, which always involves dangers, becomes a real obstacle when the situation changes.

The decision by a majority of the LCR to initiate the creation of a new party was not necessarily a turn away from its struggles or from its ideas. But it meant that the LCR as a tool, as it had existed, was no longer adequate to the tasks of the period.

Unlike the old, the new is, by definition, not written. It develops, experiments, adapts, builds itself. To be new, to learn to be useful in a new period, the NPA could only be built through a continuous process, with initially limited structures, as flexible as possible, leaving plenty of room for new and emerging debates and all kinds of experiments.

However, the shape and the disagreements at the root of the current crisis of the NPA are clear: the crisis of the NPA looks just like a crisis of the LCR. Disagreements bear on issues that had been raging within the

---

still largely unproven. I tend to think there are too many obstacles for this: the strength of the Communist Party, which will oppose a "common house", the focus on institutions, the tensions between the forces.

5:    See Sitel, 2008. For Francis Sitel, who knew the organisation well, creating a new party with just the LCR as an organised force was dangerous. Many of his arguments are interesting. The problem is that we do not start from what we wish we had, but from what exists. On this basis, we must find solutions. Otherwise we look for shortcuts. Francis Sitel left the NPA at its very beginning, with the Gauche Unitaire, LCR activists who instead rallied to the Front de Gauche. This grouping probably earned more positions by joining the FdG early on. But its political evolution is such that the Gauche Anticapitaliste often forgets to mention it among the currents that could form an anti-capitalist pole within the FdG. Should this be a warning for the GA, which broke away in June 2012?

LCR for over a decade (alliances with other left forces and intervention in elections). All the tendencies which were formed and then separated come from the LCR: Gauche Unitaire, followed by Convergences et Alternatives and now Gauche Anticapitaliste (GA). All the tendencies since the birth of the NPA, built in ways that are inherited from the LCR, were led by former leaders of the LCR (with one small exception).

not simply temporary fashions.

This simple observation shows us that the "old" has dominated the "new" party. The LCR only opened the doors to its house. Generously, no doubt. We turned the light on, we offered coffee. We even sometimes moved some furniture around. But it was the LCR's house, the one the members of the LCR knew, and they knew how it worked. Others could only be guests. It turned out that that house was actually not suited to the tasks of the new period.

Underestimating the novelty of the period

1) Just a space to occupy… But why was there resistance to change on the part of a majority of the LCR? It was not a case of bad faith. A large majority had voted for the creation of a new party. Many were excited by the beginning of the process. Why then? Mainly because the reasons given—within the LCR—for the need to build the NPA did not take into account the radically new character of the period. As a result, the awareness of the need to let the new express itself remained superficial. Looking in two directions is not an effective way of orienting oneself.

In the prevalent analysis of the LCR, the start of the new era was basically "the collapse of the USSR and of Eastern bloc countries combined with neoliberal capitalist globalisation",[6] the end of a cycle started in 1917. The analysis was that the crisis of the Communist parties and the neoliberal evolution of the social democratic left opened up a space that had to be "occupied". But through all this we stayed within the paradigm, frequently expressed in LCR, of "revolutionaries without a revolution", that is to say "without immediate revolutionary perspectives",[7] a strange though catchy phrase, by the bye.

What mattered mainly in the founding of the new party were therefore somewhat wider programmatic boundaries designed to attract some of the orphans of the traditional parties while remaining radical enough to maintain,

---

6:     Adam and others, 2009.

7:     Johsua, 2006. Johsua notably concludes: "Outside a revolutionary period, it is impossible to have a mass popular party (or something approaching) without an institutional basis."

for the future, revolutionary perspectives. The idea of programmatically opening up the LCR a little could only lead, for the majority of the members of the LCR, to opening up the LCR a little organisationally.

2) ...or a more radical change? In this analysis of the novelty of the period two elements remained marginal: the systemic crisis of capitalism and above all the return of mass struggles and of an anti-capitalist consciousness. The systemic crisis of capitalism means we are talking of a long-term new period of development of all the contradictions within the system. These can only be solved through a succession of political crises and large-scale confrontations.

Why is this important? It is through concrete experiences in the process of crisis and confrontation that our class (broadly defined) may, on a mass scale, acquire levels of consciousness and organisation making it suitable for a revolutionary transformation. And it is in the context of these experiences that various party political strategies will be tested. To take but one current example.[8] During the first few months after the fall of Mubarak in Egypt, the few who dared to criticise the army were completely marginalised on this issue. A year later their position on this point is more widely adopted and their audience has grown, especially among the youth.

The other factor is the return of mass struggles: the strikes of the winter of 1995 in France, the mass uprisings in Indonesia and South Korea, Seattle in 1999 and the emergence of a global movement, counter-summits and social forums, the global movement against the war in Iraq (to take examples preceding the launch of the NPA). In this dynamic process a global critique of the system has resurfaced—the consciousness, at least at an embryonic stage, that all struggles are linked by an overall logic, that the fight must be against a whole system. This is expressed in a stronger form still since the ideological hegemony of the neoliberal model has collapsed with the crisis. A generation of tens of thousands of activists has been in formation for the past 15 years or so on the basis of these experiments.

From propaganda to strategy as the heart of the new party
There is therefore not a fixed space needing to be filled. Rather, radically

---

8:    All the revolutionary processes of history are fascinating to study from this point of view, from 1848 France to the 1974 revolution in Portugal, the Russian Revolution of 1917 or the Iranian Revolution of 1979. Failures are more linked to the inability of the revolutionary process to have parties up to the task than to lack of determination and radicality of the movements. It is true that in the historical analysis it is easier to deduce that the "masses" are lacking in this or that. This is a prime trick for evading responsibilities. The other is to blame the "treacherous" leaders of the class. Comfortable, certainly...but not very useful in strategic terms.

different possibilities open up in the struggle for another society. What makes a new party both necessary and possible is the conjunction of a period which can set in motion millions of people with the emergence of tens of thousands of activists within various fronts of the movement, who are their practical leaders on a day to day basis.

Without them the hundreds of workplace confrontations each year would be impossible, as would be the more generalised movements, strikes and mass demonstrations (for pensions, against Jacques Chirac's attempt to take back the rights of young workers, against the war...). Without them the heroic struggle of the undocumented, the mobilisation around Palestine, the struggle against nuclear power or local struggles such as those conducted against the airport at Notre Dame des Landes, the struggles in poor neighbourhoods, etc could not be maintained. This is the basis for the aim of a force that brings together and coordinates them, making it possible to develop a global strategy for the movement to victories and to give a perspective of collective liberation.

Revolutionary activists should, of course, play a role in this process. But this requires, on their part, a "cultural" revolution in order to be up to the task. They must break with ways of thinking and operating cultivated over decades of marginalisation of the extreme left, of being "revolutionaries without a revolution". We must move from "the weapon of criticism" to the "criticism of weapons" and not underestimate the radical change this leads to, in practice as in theory.[9] We must stop confining ourselves to propagandism, to the cult of the "correct" programme, to the "general strike" mantra and to criticising traditional leaderships of the working class movement as the only possible orientation.

We have failed to make this cultural revolution: moving from propaganda from outside the movement to elaborating a strategy from within the movement. This requires not only an awareness of the issues but also leaning on the thousands of activists in the movement in order to begin to create a new revolutionary culture, gradually developing on the basis of our shared experiences and on the achievements of the revolutionary tradition. It requires a strategy capable of bringing along the whole movement, which would pose anew the major debates and reformulate the project for emancipation.

The party remained external to the concerns of activists

1) A party for struggles...or for elections? Despite what was announced, the NPA was never conceived as a party for struggle, a party of the movement.

9:     See Marx, 1975, p251.

Following on from Olivier Besancenot's performance at the polls, it has worked primarily as an electoral outlet. Let us remember that the foundation of the NPA was rushed in order to present candidates for the European elections, as the first nationwide public action for the new party.

There followed many debates and incessant (and unresolved!) strife on electoral tactics while resources were invested primarily in national election campaigns, but few discussions on union work, building an anti-racist movement, a movement against debt, the defence of public services, concrete solidarity with the Arab revolutions. How many debates and exchanges of experiences on the development of struggles in local areas? How much was put into the building, by the whole party, of the Copenhagen, Strasbourg or Frankfurt counter-summits, the march of the undocumented, the collectives against debt, etc? Not to mention topics such as police brutality or the Front National, or new ways of mobilising and organising.

2) Politics outside the movement: This orientation is rooted in a theory of the autonomy of social movements not challenged and not discussed at the foundation of the NPA. In the new period this theory has become the theory of the depoliticisation of the movement.

With the downturn in the 1980s, and the predominance of defensive struggles against neoliberal capitalist restructuring, it was much more difficult concretely to experience the emancipatory potentialities of the movement. This opened the way for a division between the field of "social" struggles and the field of the "political" fight. This separation was sanctioned by the appearance of the phrase "social movement", as an umbrella term for struggles and groupings, as opposed to the political field defined narrowly as the confrontation between parties, mainly on the electoral terrain.

This affected the LCR, which defended "the autonomy of social movements". To understand how such a conception could develop, it should be added that it was nurtured and encouraged by a fundamentally sound critique of the tradition developed by the traditional parties (first and foremost the Communist Party) of using the trade union movement or other groupings for their own benefit—meaning that these organisations instead of being actors of emancipation became tools for party strategies.

In the name of this conception, LCR activists increasingly intervened in movements as individuals. Sometimes they played a key role and brought with them their general conceptions. But there was less discussion of strategy within the party, and less collective testing. Gradually the consequences became profound for the functioning of the party itself: a separation arose between those most involved in the movement and those working within the party. The leadership became less subject to the pressure of the movement, the questions it raises and the need for strategic development it imposes. Conversely it reinforced the "pragmatic" bent for activists becoming heavily involved in specific, mainly defensive movements.

Last but not least: with the decrease in discussions on the issues raised by the movement, the party's intervention became dominated by programmatic delimitations with other parties. This led to an increasingly central place being given to elections.

3) Politics in the movement: The NPA was born out of the development of mass movements, yet this conception has in fact continued to dominate its orientation and its practice. It does not meet the needs of movements constantly confronted with the question of the overall logic of the system, nor does it convince activists, who are brought outside of their place of intervention.

The autonomy of the movement is a fine thing, but it needs to be thought through: the movement transforms society, not elected individuals or political parties. In other words: the revolutionary transformation of society can only be the work of the majority of the movement of the oppressed and exploited.

This does not mean autonomy of the movement vis-à-vis politics but that the movement itself evolves and becomes political. Political in the sense that it becomes the alternative,[10] that it struggles for power, not aiming to replace those who are at the head of existing institutions with its own representatives, but in order to replace existing institutions with its own collective forms of power—and that it starts to build them in today's struggles.

This does not mean that the movement must stay away from political parties but it means they must prove the validity of what they stand for within the movement itself—it also means they can only prove this through understanding and respecting the rhythms of the movement and through developing a useful strategy for the movement.

It follows that a revolutionary strategy is a strategy that shows how the movement can become political, through all the experiences of the class struggle on all fronts (including elections)—rather than one which theorises the separation between the social movement and the political movement.

It follows that the party cannot invent this strategy from outside. It should first aim to promote the generalisation of experiences and dynamics from the movement itself: just look how examples as diverse as the *Indignados*, Occupy, the Arab revolutions, workplace occupations, "Can't

---

10: About what is meant by political movement see Godard, 2011.

pay, won't pay" movements pose—at least in embryonic form—the question of another power, of a real democracy. They also are—more positively—the expression of the distrust that exists toward institutions as expressed also by low voter turnout, the rejection of the mainstream media or riots where what is identified with the "institutions of society" gets broken.

Unmoving conceptions externally imposed

1) "Our response to the crisis": a strategic discussion aborted: The dominant conception in the NPA is that the "correct" programme (and the correct demands) can be brought to the movement from without by the party. Hence the emphasis on elections as a way to address a mass audience. Hence the emphasis on programmatic delimitations in order to differentiate between true anti-capitalists and "treacherous" leaders.

If a programme is necessary it should be a programme that combines goals and the means of achieving them, a guide to action. It cannot be a "perfect", fixed programme, born in the mind of a few revolutionaries; it must be modified by experiences and developments. The elaboration of such a programme is therefore inseparable from the development of the movement itself and of debates on the experiences and issues raised. From this point of view, probably nothing is more indicative of the failure of the NPA than the text "Our response to the crisis", adopted at the first congress in 2009.[11]

This text could have opened up a debate on what an anti-capitalist strategy in a period of deep crisis and mass struggles would look like. Yet the discussion was confined to the contents of a programme, a list of demands, which some found not radical enough and others too radical, everyone being obsessed with what boundaries to establish or not to establish with the Front de Gauche.

Let's be clear, the more or less implicit reference for many comrades in this debate was the *transitional programme* advocated by Trotsky in 1938.[12] We will not discuss here the validity of the reference. What is striking, however, when we take the transitional programme as it was defended by Trotsky is that it has an element of an action programme, each demand being combined with a suitable organisational form: strengthening trade unions and struggling within them and factory committees for the opening of account ledgers and workers' control, pickets and workers' militia for the arming of the proletariat, councils grouping factory committees and

---

11:   NPA, 2011.
12:   Trotsky, 1938.

neighbourhood organisations on a geographical basis for the workers' and peasants' government.

Separation of thought + action.

This articulation of demands with specific forms of organisation of the movement is exactly what is missing in "Our response to the crisis". We discussed demands, but it proved impossible to move on to a discussion on the ways in which these demands could be carried out by the movement.

2) No need for concrete analysis? The lack of strategic concern leads to a lack of concern in the analysis of concrete reality. This has led to the lack of analysis of a long cycle of evolution (and recomposition) of the capitalist organisation of production, the destructuration of the traditional working class and the reconstruction of a new class composition. Yet it is also the reconfiguration of the reality of our class which has put in crisis the traditional organisations of the labour movement. Is there a specific revolutionary subject? Should we still think in terms of strategic productive sectors?

Assuming that we should, are they the same as 20 or 30 years ago? Should we think in terms of organising struggling workers by occupation, by trade or by location? Don't the development of migration and the feminisation of labour alter the relationship between struggles against discrimination and struggles in workplaces? Don't the fragmentation of production units and contracts, the development of precariousness and the growth in service jobs lead to a change in the role and in the methods of struggle in inner-city areas? These discussions—but we could cite others—were absent in the construction of the NPA, not to mention the changing face of the state or of imperialism, the role of the media, of social networks.

A new workers' movement capable of developing strategies and organisational forms that correspond to the new realities of class composition must be rebuilt. This should be combined with resistance to restructuring in the old sectors where the old organisations remain the best established. The articulation should be put in these terms rather than in the choice between reconstruction and recomposition.

Is one born a revolutionary, or does one become one?

A party cannot develop a strategy if its members are not involved in the movement in different ways. This also works in reverse: it is through discussions necessary for elaboration and through tests made within the movement that a "new" revolutionary consciousness may be forged among the collective members of the party, and that previous ideas may be modified, enriched and criticised.

This requires a break with the idea of a ready-made revolutionary theory created by the leaders of party tendencies, and with its mirror image: a misconception of reformism as a simple "mind manipulation". The influence of reformism cannot be reduced to the "treacherous" leaders betraying addled masses to whom the truth must be revealed.

Reformism is the product of a contradictory consciousness reflecting a contradictory experience. On the one hand the experience of domination (exploitation and oppression) and competition that promotes feelings of powerlessness and makes the idea that only elected officials can improve things seem sensible. On the other hand, the experience of resistance to this domination, which not only tears individualism apart, and recreates solidarity, but which also puts in question the power of the boss and the neutrality of the state.

This means that reformism cannot be fought only in terms of ideology (with propaganda). The return of mass struggles and the experiences and failures of those involved in them are the basis for changes in mass consciousness. But we need to understand this change as a process. There is no binary switch at an individual or collective level in the evolution of consciousness from reformism to revolutionary politics.

Fighting against the influence of reformism and developing a revolutionary consciousness are tied together. They cannot be advanced through proclamations but through practical demonstrations to promote all experiences demonstrating practically the collective strength we have and the superiority of a strategy based on it compared with institutional strategies.

Tinkering is not enough; we must rebuild

1) *Still possible…and still necessary:* The task of building is still before us. The audience won by the Front de Gauche has shown the availability of hundreds of thousands of young people and workers for a political and radical perspective. The Front de Gauche is caught as in the straitjacket of a cartel of organisations whose main objective is not self-organisation and the development of counter-powers—but an institutional perspective. It therefore cannot be the basis for the force we need to build. Struggles go on outside these organisations in the youth, in the *banlieues*, often in a fragmented manner.

The nature of the times makes the construction of an anti-capitalist force not just possible; it makes it more necessary than ever. Without the coordination of movement activists and the progressive development of an anti-capitalist strategy, victories become increasingly difficult to gain for specific struggles, as demonstrated by the movement on pensions, the anti-racist struggle or the anti-war movement.

During the movement over pensions the strategy of union leaders imposed itself by default. This is because there was not a force bringing together tens of thousands of radical unionists with the respect of their workmates in all sectors and regions, arising from the development of combative local unions or rank and file committees, linked to the majority of young people in high schools and colleges, able to organise local support. Such a force could have proposed an alternative strategy to that of the union leaders through generalising from the best experiences.

In other words, victories, even partial victories, require that strategies of confrontation with the logic of the system be proposed widely to the movement and that forms of grassroots organisation and counter-powers be developed. Such a force is also made necessary by the general tendency of the capitalist system. Without a perspective of global transformation and emancipation, reactionary "solutions" will have the upper hand. Therefore, we must try again.

2) *Rebuilding, saying it and doing it:* We should not be ashamed of our failure. We all have the merit of having tried. But failure it is that has demoralised thousands of activists and developed scepticism more widely still. We must therefore say publicly that we have failed; it is a necessary condition if we want to be trusted in our desire to try again. We also need to say that we do not want to patch up what didn't work, but that we are calling for a radical overhaul of the NPA. These conditions are necessary but not sufficient. We are not asking to be believed on trust. We'll be judged by our actions. And this cannot be postponed.

3) *Where to start?* Proclaiming a different mode of operation or a different programme will not create a new party. Departures have left the structures of the party in a fragile state, from local committees to national structures (commissions, press, national leadership bodies...). We should "take advantage" of the situation to restart a process of foundation on the basis of the local committees—national structures can simply, at least for the time being, "manage" current affairs.

Committees for a real refoundation should be autonomous—regarding their local involvement, mode of operation, the organisation of their debates—and coordinated for national campaigns on which they agree and for debates relating to the rebuilding of the party. These committees should be completely open to the outside, encouraging the participation of movement activists, even if they do not join the party. At all levels we should encourage discussions between activists of other parties of the radical left.

At least during a transition period, the newspaper could serve primarily as a liaison organ between the committees: reports of experiences made by the committees, announcements of protests, meetings, events, contributions to the debate, etc.

The cornerstone of this process should be involvement in the movement and the development of our strategy as a basis for an exchange of experiences and as a basis for discussions, including theoretical debates. From this point of view, the development of campaigns against austerity and public debt—related to the refusal of redundancy plans and to international solidarity—and the fight against the development of racism and the extreme right should be dominant axes for our activities.

Conclusion

Nothing would be worse than making the forthcoming NPA congress a sham. The process leading to this congress must be a part of the wider process of rebuilding: not limited to internal debate but encouraging open discussion with the outside on all subjects and at all levels, starting work on our strategy and our functioning without excluding more theoretical debates (the dynamics of capital/labour, movement/institutions, oppression/exploitation).

This process will be a live one if it takes as a basis action within the movements, experiments made by the various committees, and if it does not claim to solve in advance discussions that must remain open.

In this sense the preparation for this congress should be seen as a refounding process on the basis of contributions going back and forth between committees rather than platforms made "at the top", on which party members should position themselves. The congress itself should be thought of not as an end (of the process) but as a step on the way: the party itself should be conceived of as a process–party, an experimental party.

Finally, at this conference the youth must be put back at the heart of the party, of its committees, of its experiences, of its debates, and not as something separate, but as central to its activity, and even as a driving force. This is also a prerequisite for building a party for the future, a movement party, a new anti-capitalist party.

References

Adam, Hélène, Daniel Bensaïd, François Coustal, Léon Crémieux, Jacqueline Guillotin, Samuel Johsua, Alain Krivine, Olivier Martin, Christine Poupin, Pierre Rousset, François Sabado, Roseline Vachetta, 2009, "De la LCR au NPA", www.preavis.org/breche-numerique/article1155.html

Godard, Denis, 2009, "The NPA: a Space for Rebuilding", *International Socialism* 123 (Summer 2009), www.isj.org.uk/?id=561

Godard, Denis, 2011 "Qu'est-ce qu'on veut : Tout!" *Que faire?* 8 (second series).

Johsua, Samy, 2006, "Mélanges Stratégiques", *Que faire?* 5 (1st series), http://quefaire.lautre.net/spip.php?article86

Marx, Karl, 1975, *Early Writings* (Penguin), www.marxists.org/archive/marx/works/1843/critique-hpr/intro.htm

NPA, 2011, "Nos Réponses à la Crise", http://tinyurl.com/cl3wgeb

Sitel, Francis, 2008, "Nouveau Parti Anticapitaliste, Espoirs et Pièges" in *Critique Communiste*, 187 (June), http://orta.dynalias.org/critiqueco/pdfs/187-sitel.pdf

Trotsky, Leon, 1938, *The Death Agony of Capitalism and the Tasks of the Fourth International*, www.marxists.org/archive/trotsky/1938/tp/index.htm

Book reviews

The age of Hobsbawm

Siobhan Brown

Gregory Elliott, **Hobsbawm: History and Politics** (Pluto, 2010), £12.99

For many, Eric Hobsbawm represented the archetypal Marxist historian. His many works on empire, class, nations and states are for many new to Marxism the first way in to understanding a history that he described as "the sweat, blood, tears and triumphs of the common people, our people". In particular, his vast series *The Age of Revolution*, *The Age of Capital*, *The Age of Empire* and then *Age of Extremes* are some of the most comprehensive contributions to Marxist historiography.

Hobsbawm received admiration from beyond the left. An obituary printed in *New Left Review* following his death in October 2012 said: "Even the mainstream media agreed that Hobsbawm was a great historian——some even said 'the greatest living historian'."* As well as achieving a vast scale of work, Hobsbawm was key in fighting for a space for the working class in the study of history, while not limiting himself to academia.

Published before Hobsbawm's last publication *How to Change the World: Reflections on Marx and Marxism*, Gregory Elliott draws on Hobsbawm's own work

yet also situates his life within a wider perspective of debates on the British and international left, with much success.

In the first section Elliott details Hobsbawm's early life, in order to explain the basis of his politics throughout the rest of it. Hobsbawm joined the Communist Party in 1936, becoming active while a student at Cambridge. Hobsbawm's political life was framed, therefore, by the central political questions for the CPGB at the time: anti-fascism and the civil war in Spain in particular.

It is perhaps unsurprising then that Hobsbawm's commitment to popular frontism is the most striking theme of the work. Hobsbawm describes the strategy as "concentric circles of unity—united front between communists and socialists, popular front between labour movements and bourgeois liberals, national front of all anti-fascist forces, international front of all anti-fascist powers". Elliott is not without criticism here, and addresses squarely the failure of the policy: arguing that "concentric circles either failed to materialise…or predictably struggled to survive their internal stresses". This seems like an underestimation: the example of the Spanish Civil War (1936-9), which Hobsbawm was so shaped by, means that it can be asserted more concretely that the policy was inherently flawed.

It is here too where Hobsbawm's position on nationalism crosses over: although the author omits much analysis of Hobsbawm's work on nations and nationalism, it is fairly clear that his

* Donald Sassoon, 2012, "Eric Hobsbawm, 1917-2012", *New Left Review* II/77.

interest would have come from this early point of political importance.

Hobsbawm became a founding member of the Communist Party Historians Group following the Second World War. For him and his contemporaries, among them Christopher Hill and E P Thompson, the popular front idea was essential to its outlook: they cultivated relationships with others within academia, but also recognised the inseparability of theory and practice, continuing as party activists.

The events of 1956 illustrate firstly Hobsbawm's shift to the right, but also the state of the CPGB at the time. The party's crisis rested largely on debates around the Hungarian Revolution. Hobsbawm, along with numerous others, expressed concern. They wrote in a letter to the *Daily Worker* "that the uncritical support given by the Executive Committee (to the suppression of the Hungarian revolution)... is the undesirable culmination of years of distortion of fact". The CPGB lost a quarter of its membership and the Historians Group was shaken, with many leading and talented members leaving. Although the group continued to exist—and work with those who had left the party—their productivity and clarity dipped noticeably.

Hobsbawm remained a party member. He later wrote that the reason he retained his membership was largely due to his formative years, with the Russian Revolution in mind and the centrality of the CPGB to the anti-fascism of the day. Elliott correctly asserts that this could not be reason enough, recognising a noticeable rightward shift in Hobsbawm's perspective. Despite the strength of the memory of the 1930s, Hobsbawm now argued that a non-revolutionary "Eurocommunist" approach to socialism was the way to overthrow capitalism. He described himself as a spiritual member of the PCI, the Italian Communist Party, and Elliott asserts Hobsbawm's new direction as "a reorientation towards the position of Western Marxism". In the second half of the 70s the PCI supported in government the Christian Democrat Tory party, an illustration of the failure of such positions in maintaining any revolutionary credentials.

Due prominence is placed on Hobsbawm's attachment to Western Marxism, as well as his appropriation of Antonio Gramsci in particular. It is noted that "Gramsci formed a striking contrast to the other main communist theorists in the Western Marxist tradition, Lukács and Althusser, both of them marginal figures in the parties", the latter of whom Elliott also profiled in a major study first published in the 1980s.

Hobsbawm's rightward drift continued into the 1980s and 90s and towards the end of his life. He played an important role in shifting Labour to the right during the 80s. His Marx Memorial Lecture in 1978, "The Forward March of Labour Halted?" provoked much debate among the left and within the Labour Party. Lauded as "Kinnock's favourite Marxist" Hobsbawm's perspective that the working class was in decline fitted with a Labour Party continuing to move away from its base. Although Elliott locates accurately how Hobsbawm contributed to Labour's rightward shift, he fails to assess the impact on the future of the Labour Party, and the parallels with Hobsbawm's relationship with the European left.

Following 1989, he argued that the collapse of the Soviet Bloc and what he considered the only alternative to capitalism—Stalinism—meant there was a crisis in the working class itself. His entanglement in the embracing of social democracy from a Eurocommunist position as well as his unwavering support for Stalinism and the CPGB meant that he was left with no confidence in the working class to change the world.

Elliott provides on the one hand a detailed account of this important historian's life and influences. On the other, by placing Hobsbawm's work within the context of the events of his "very much 20th century life", he gives an honest and nuanced analysis of his judgement, or lack thereof. Aside from Elliott's tendency to litter the work with unnecessary French phrases, the writing holds clarity, successfully and authoritatively placing Hobsbawm, especially in reference to Eurocommunist and Gramscian trends, within more general tendencies of the British and international left.

Sweet dreams aren't made of this
Jonny Jones

Slavoj Žižek, **The Year of Dreaming Dangerously** *(Verso, 2012), £7.99*

Slavoj Žižek has been an important point of reference for many activists and intellectuals who were caught up in the protests of recent years, from the student revolt to the Occupy movement. In this small book he offers his take on the emancipatory potential of the events of 2011.

Žižek begins by making three sweeping claims about contemporary capitalism. He asserts that capital accumulation increasingly relies upon rent rather than profit. This leads to a changing role of unemployment in which "the opportunity to be 'exploited' in a long term job is experienced as a privilege". Finally, he draws on the work of French linguist and psycho-analyst (and former Maoist) Jean-Claude Milner to suggest that these processes have given rise to a "salaried bourgeoisie" made up of, among others, "experts, administrators, public servants, doctors, lawyers, journalists, intellectuals and artists". The lower levels of this extraordinarily nebulous grouping make up, for Žižek, the people who are protesting "against the threat of being reduced to a proletarian status".

To my mind, this eclectic bricolage, masquerading as political economy and class analysis, is not only wholly unsubstantiated but also seriously weakens Žižek's entire analysis of the events of 2011.

So the English riots of August 2011 become an example of how our "post-ideological age" leads to angry inner city youth targeting "the hard won acquisitions of the very stratum that the protesters originated from...envy masked as a triumphant carnival". Žižek simply ignores the fact that the vast majority of looting was targeted at chain stores. Quite what is different from these riots to earlier riots that took place before the inauguration of this "post ideological age" he doesn't make clear. For all his criticism of liberal responses to the riots, he steps awfully close to the liberal conceit that "good riots" only happen elsewhere or in the past.

When it comes to the most important elsewhere—Egypt—Žižek once again slips up. Echoing those who saw the election of the Muslim Brotherhood in Egypt as the dawn of an "Islamist winter" after the Arab Spring, Žižek argues that "the summer of 2011 will likely be remembered as the end of the revolution, as the suffocating of its emancipatory potential. Its grave-diggers are the army and the Islamists." As I write this, the tens of thousands who are protesting against President Mursi's power grab indicate that there is life in the revolution yet.

As always, Žižek is at his best when discussing ideological, philosophical and cultural questions. The book contains interesting and engaging excursions into Lacanian discourse, and there is a whole chapter on the TV show *The Wire*. Even here, however, he is on shaky ground. The chapter aims to confront "the difficult question of how to fight the system without contributing to its enhanced functioning". Žižek is right to rail against social democratic notions of reforming capitalism, but he underestimates the way in which struggles to defend gains won under the system can grow over into the kinds of movements which point towards a new society, elements of which he says "are here in our space, but whose time is in the emancipated future".

He is right to say that "this future is not 'objective'; it will come to be only through the subjective engagement that sustains it." This conception could be a hostage to "prefigurative" autonomist readings. But such sustenance cannot come through indefinite occupations or creating islands of non-capitalism within the wider system. Žižek recognises this and argues that the movements of 2011 require "a new form of organisation, discipline and hard work". But beyond this, Žižek doesn't seem to have much insight into what such an organisation might look like or how it might be constructed.

We end the book rather ominously, "guiding ourselves on nothing more than ambiguous signs from the future". This smacks of a "wait and see" attitude devoid of any serious "subjective engagement", which surely requires an understanding of how an interventionist organisation can play an important role in transforming the balance of class forces.

Unfortunately, such lacunae abound in *The Year of Dreaming Dangerously*, rendering it a deeply disappointing and frustrating book.

Climate of conflict
Camilla Royle

Harald Welzer, **Climate Wars: What People Will be Killed for in the 21st Century** *(Polity, 2012), £20*

In this translation of a book originally published in German in 2007, Harald Welzer makes a gloomy argument: that climate change is already causing dramatic changes to people's lives and that violence is always an option as a response to these changes. Using examples from the Vietnam War, the Rwandan genocide, the collapse of the Easter Island civilisation, Darfur and, in particular, the Holocaust, he attempts to explain not just the causes of extreme violence but the way violence is sustained and becomes part of a "violence economy".

The book could be accused of being more about war than about climate change. It fails to mention the debates on the relationship between natural disasters and climate change or on the way climate change will affect specific populations. The section on climate change makes some misleading points, such as the suggestion that everything will be alright if we can limit temperature rises to two degrees above pre-industrial levels. There is no "safe" level of temperature rise. Welzer clearly sees himself as a social scientist, and he suggests that it is not his place to delve into scientific debates. However, by calling the book *Climate Wars*, he does acknowledge the social disaster that climate change seems certain to cause—disproportionately affecting the people least responsible for it and intensifying conflicts as refugees are held back by increasingly sophisticated border controls.

Welzer argues that the 21st century will

see a revival of old forms of conflict: "We have seen a revival of fault lines that one would have thought more typical of the 19th century than the 21st." These conflicts might look different from those of the past. New technologies will make violence possible on an ever greater scale, but conflict will nevertheless focus on the same issues. There will be wars over resources, class and faith, he claims.

Welzer's background is in social psychology. In an earlier work, *Grandpa Wasn't a Nazi,* he used interview data to record how the children and grandchildren of Germans who had been Nazi sympathisers reinterpreted their older relatives' stories, attempting to explain away the worst parts even when the older relatives had admitted being involved in Nazism. Here he uses various concepts from psychology to attempt to understand how people in supposedly enlightened, rational societies can commit terrible acts of violence, especially when faced with unforeseen changes in their personal circumstances.

In the case of the Holocaust, Welzer argues that one factor is the concept of "shifting baselines". He imagines a Holocaust with no start point; after the election of Hitler the Jewish population was excluded and oppressed gradually, using progressively harsher laws and propaganda. The concentration camps and mass murders, which would have been unthinkable in 1933, were acceptable (to some) eight years later as people had come to accept this way of relating to "non-Aryan" groups. Welzer also points out that the perpetrators of the Holocaust were able to distance themselves from their crimes. The job of designing more effective ways of killing people and disposing of the bodies was contracted out to the private sector. Some aspects of modern warfare are also carried out by private military companies and mercenaries. The US government signed 3,512 contracts with private companies for security functions in 2003 alone.

However, Marxists have attempted to find underlying explanations for the Holocaust that go beyond the ability of individuals to carry out violent acts. For instance, Leon Trotsky's account of fascism proposed that the petty bourgeoisie, who felt threatened by both big capital and the organised working class, formed the core base of support for such movements. Hitler was able to draw these elements together and, in a period of deep social and economic crisis, offer them to the ruling class as a force that could destroy working class organisation. In such an account, the Holocaust cannot be explained just by referring to class interests: ideology also played a role, with Hitler using pseudo-revolutionary rhetoric and, of course, pseudo-scientific racism to galvanise his supporters and hold them together. Welzer's attempt to explain the rise of Nazi ideology falls short. If it is all about psychology, why did the rise of the Nazis emerge in Germany and not elsewhere? Why at that particular time?

Welzer proposes that theory should be developed to explain instances of extreme and unexpected violence, as opposed to conventional social theories which, he argues, are concerned only with normality. He claims that it should be possible to apply social theory to identify some common factors and better predict where a *potential* for mass violence will result in an application of violence. This implies that there are common factors in every form of violence from cannibalism in the tribal society on Easter Island to immigration controls in 21st century Europe. The book misses out on a consideration of how capitalism in particular might perpetuate violence—and it draws no moral distinction between violence carried out by the most powerful in society and that carried out by desperate people trying to defend themselves. Welzer seems to find all violence equally regrettable. There is no explicit consideration of how private companies might profit from violence, how the powerful will use it to defend their property or how states operate to legitimise their own violent acts. The link between environmental change and conflict is doubtless an urgent topic for debate, but it is one that cannot be explained wholly by social psychology.

The Dice Man
Ross Speer

Mikko Lahtinen (Gareth Griffiths & Kristina Köhli, trans.), *Politics and Philosophy: Niccolò Machiavelli and Louis Althusser's Aleatory Materialism* (Haymarket, 2011)

There are two mainstream interpretations of the work of Niccolò Machiavelli: he is seen either as the "the father of immoral 'Realpolitik'" or as the "Renaissance era representative of the republican tradition" that sought to revive the political traditions of ancient Greece and Rome. In popular discourse it is the language of repression that passes for "Machiavellianism"; within the academy it is the republican Machiavelli, associated with the Cambridge scholar Quentin Skinner, that is dominant. In *Politics and Philosophy* Mikko Lahtinen seeks to uncover an alternative reading of Machiavelli's work—the "aleatory materialist" approach first set out by the French Marxist philosopher Louis Althusser.

Lahtinen describes how, for Althusser, Machiavelli was a part of a tradition running through the "underground" of materialist philosophy which he termed aleatory (dice-like) materialism, or "the materialism of the encounter". Starting with the ancient Greek philosopher Epicurus and moving through Machiavelli, Spinoza, Hobbes, Rousseau, Marx and Heidegger aleatory materialism represented a "dangerous" current that questioned the "philosophical-religious, judicial and moral doctrines in which... the existing social order is legitimised" through its presentation as "the natural or rational order". Throughout history this current was "underground", subversive and hidden, as it ran against the common sense idealism in which divine or natural laws were held to determine the rationality of *what is*. Aleatory materialism stresses the contingency of the social order: what exists did not, and does not, have to. To craft a new society the range of alternatives that may result from human action, the possibilities for self-determination, must be understood. There is an "ultimate lack of guarantees" as to the path history may take. History has no pre-ordained end. The trajectory of the historical process is, then, influenced by active individuals or groups, actors or agents, which must pay particular attention to the strategy and timing of interventions if they are to be effective in achieving their aims.

For Althusser, Machiavelli was first and foremost a theorist of the "conjuncture", a concrete moment of a complex whole determined by its specific characteristics. In each historical-political case the general and the specific are linked together to produce a unique combination. Lahtinen explains how, in Althusser's Marxism, the nature of this unique combination is determined by the process of over- and under-determination. While the fundamental contradiction of capitalist society, between labour and capital, may be determining "in the last instance", it manifests itself in different, more readily understood, ways. The contradictions in society are inter-dependent, and become *displaced* and *congealed* onto the overdetermined contradiction. The accumulation of these contradictions undermines the cohesiveness of the social formation, thereby presenting revolutionary opportunities, with the implication being that struggles erupt over issues that may not appear "fundamental" but nonetheless represent challenges to the system as it is. In deploying these concepts to analyse the conjuncture and understand the specific articulation of these antagonisms, a "concrete analysis of a concrete situation" could be produced and the revolutionary actor could derive the most appropriate course of action.

Lahtinen's purpose in *Politics and Philosophy* is not solely to contribute to scholarship of Machiavelli, nor to intervene in the controversy that continues to surround Althusser's Marxism, but to show what Machiavelli's perspectives may offer us today. Seen through the lens of Althusser's aleatory materialism Machiavelli becomes an "intellectual pointer, a revolutionary weapon, on the battlefield of global capitalism in our own 'conjuncture'".

In Machiavelli, Althusser found a Lenin of the Renaissance. If Lenin can be considered the paramount organic intellectual of the early 20th century proletariat, so Machiavelli was the organic intellectual of the "rising city-state bourgeoisie". Much of Althusser's earlier work (most famously *Reading Capital* and *For Marx* of the 1960s) was directed towards uncovering what he claimed was the "real" Marxist tradition. His study of Machiavelli (*Machiavelli and Us*) is part of his later, aleatory, work. But its purpose

is the same: to uncover the subversive elements of a well-known writer, the true revolutionary nature of which had been obscured in the prevailing interpretations. Like Lenin, Machiavelli was a *"theoretician of praxis"*, a "man of action" who teaches us how to answer the question, *"What is to be done?"*

Lahtinen describes how Althusser treads between the two dominant interpretations of Machiavelli. His most famous work, *The Prince,* was neither "a guidebook for tyrants" nor a "guidebook to democracy" for the people, as supposed in the republican reading. Instead Althusser argues that, while *The Prince* is indeed written from "the viewpoint of the people", the people did not constitute the primary agent in his political project—Machiavelli's call is for a "new prince". With this in mind it becomes a thoroughly bourgeois text, conditioned unapologetically by the conditions in which it was written. Althusser's aleatory interpretation stresses the "struggles and conflicts", the outcomes of which are not predetermined, that come before any "moment of passivity".

Machiavelli's *The Prince* was directed towards unification of the Italian Peninsula, a response to the declining power of the city-state form in view of the rise of the absolutist monarchies of France and Spain. The "organisation of a durable state" is his primary intention. For this, the aleatory must be tamed. Lahtinen only begins to unpack what the application of this concept to understanding modernity and state formation might mean: "Population censuses and statistics, timetables and calendars, the standardisation of measurements and monetary units, as well as nationalistic ideologies" are directed towards reducing unpredictability "by controlling the population with different methods." Aleatoriness is simultaneously "a threat that should be averted" and the "possibility for political interventions and mass movements".

Machiavelli articulated this within his own conjuncture. In order to construct a new type of polity, thus reducing the external threats that had plagued the city-states of the region, the class struggle between nobles and people must be displaced; the new prince must ally with the latter in order to form a mass movement that could take advantage of the concrete moment. Founding a new unified state is Machiavelli's solution to the problem of a high degree of unpredictability, but the possibility of doing so relies upon that same unpredictability. His radically new form of state was to be a "national-popular" one, complete with an army based on a popular constituency as an early form of ideological state apparatus. The masses must enter the stage of history in order for Machiavelli's project to become realised. But, in order to secure the new state, they must also be persuaded to exit it.

Despite successfully weaving together Althusserian Marxism with the political theory of Machiavalli, Lahtinen is sometimes at pains to explain the relevant elements of Althusser's Marxism to the reader, and here there are far better introductions. Althusser's particular, often elitist, conception of Marxism receives little critical analysis. *Politics and Philosophy* could have benefited from engaging with the debate that continues to surround Althusser—in particular, the potential problems of his aleatory materialism and a comparison with Antonio Gramsci's reading of Machiavelli. Furthermore, the text is often hampered by lengthy footnotes that, while interesting to the specialist, do not aid the development of the overall argument.

However, in attempting to reintroduce Machiavelli to Marxists, Lahtinen performs a valuable service. Ignored in mainstream interpretations is the common concern between Machiavelli and Marx for the *problem of power* for the respective social groups they sought to represent. It should come as no surprise that Machiavelli was of great interest first to Gramsci, and second to Althusser. Third, he should be of interest to us. Published in English over a decade after its initial appearance in Finnish, *Politics and Philosophy* makes a timely arrival at the conjuncture the English-speaking Marxist tradition faces today.

Pick of the quarter

International Socialism hosted a weekend school on the topic of Marxism and Revolution Today in late September. The school brought together over 100 people to discuss revolutionary transformations that have occured since 1989 and their implications for the future of revolutionary politics. Videos of all the sessions can be found online.* Thanks to Colin Barker for his work organising the event.

The latest issue of *New Left Review* (II/77) carries an interesting interview with the economist Richard Duncan.† He argues that breaking the link between the dollar and gold in 1971 created a new "dollar standard", which has "enabled worldwide credit bubbles to be created". The result is an economic system different from capitalism, which Duncan calls "creditism", in which the state subsidises the main industries, the central bank creates unlimited amounts of money, and growth is driven not by investment but by the credit that continually floods the economy. This is what lies behind the present economic crisis. Duncan believes, moreover, that the measures that the US and other leading states have taken to prop up the financial system have merely postponed economic collapse.

One of the strengths of Duncan's analysis is that he highlights the extent to which, despite the attempts to overcome the crisis with yet more neoliberalism, the state continues to play a central economic role. Its weakness is his failure to place these developments in the context of the global process of capital accumulation. The diagnosis, as Duncan acknowledges, is close to that of Friedrich von Hayek and other so-called Austrian economists, who argue that crises are caused by excessive credit creation, though he rejects their solution—a balanced budget—and argues for a global minimum wage and investment in new industries such as genetic engineering.

Nigel Harris offered a very different take on the role of the state in contemporary capitalism in *International Socialism 135*. The podcast of a debate on this subject between him and Alex Callinicos is available online.‡ It may also be worth taking a look at a splendid attack by Perry Anderson on Jürgen Habermas, court philosopher of the new German-dominated European Union. After the EU received "what might be termed the Nobel Prize for Narcissism", Anderson bitingly comments, "Oslo can be counted on to surpass itself: next year, we can only hope the Nobel Committee awards the prize to itself".§

The new issue of *Historical Materialism* (20.3) is dominated by a symposium on Ben Fine's and Dimitris Milonakis's

---

* www.isj.org.uk/?id=842
† http://newleftreview.org/II/77/richard-duncan-a-new-global-depression

‡ http://soundcloud.com/talking-shop/talkingshop-141112/s-Zlyue
§ www.zcommunications.org/europe-speaks-german-by-perry-anderson

important critique of mainstream economics, *From Economics Imperialism to Freakanomics*. Dick Bryan and Michael Rafferty defend their analysis of financial derivatives as a form of money from Tony Norfield's criticisms in the previous issue. And Joseph Choonara reviews two books that increase our understanding of labour and the left in Bolivia, and more particularly of Trotskyism, which had an important influence in the workers' movement at the time of the 1952 Revolution.

Issue 86 of *International Socialist Review* carries a number of fascinating articles. Jesse Hagopian's "A People's History of the Chicago Teachers' Union" examines over a century of the union which recently resisted Chicago mayor Rahm Emmanuel's attack on public education. Elsewhere, Joe Richard offers a critical appraisal of the legacy of the International Workers of the World, or the Wobblies, while Paul Le Blanc reviews no less than nine recent biographies of Lenin.*

Anybody who has been following the debate on permanent revolution that has appeared in this journal over the past few years may well be interested in Lars Lih's article on the topic in October's issue of *Science and Society*. Lih argues—contra the editors of a recent collection of the historical records regarding the theory—that Trotsky's conception of permanent revolution was quite different from those of his contemporaries.

International Socialism contributor Adrian Budd has an article in the *International Journal of Management Concepts and Philosophy*, volume 6, number 3, entitled "Can the BRICS Help Global Capitalism escape its Crisis?" Adrian argues for caution regarding the capacity of emerging economies to act as independent elements in global economic recovery and that "that there are plenty more shocks in line for both the global economy and the economies of the BRICS countries. Neither will be immune from the consequences."

Finally, *International Socialism* readers might be aware of the Historical Materialism Book Series published by Brill. The series offers a wide range of titles, from newly-translated Marxist classics to contemporary works by well-known authors. Haymarket Books reprints the series in affordable paperback editions, which are available from Bookmarks in Britain or from Haymarket directly.†

AC & JJ

---

* Available at their website: www.isreview.org

† See www.bookmarksbookshop.co.uk and www.haymarketbooks.org/